ABOUT PRICE WATERHOUSE

Price Waterhouse is committed to providing the ideas, information and advice that will help our clients make better business decisions. Through a global network of firms practicing in 115 countries and territories, Price Waterhouse professionals work together to provide accounting, auditing, tax planning and compliance, management and technology consulting, litigation support and business advisory services to corporations, individuals, nonprofit organizations, and government departments and agencies.

Price Waterhouse frequently consults with the Treasury Department and the Internal Revenue Service on behalf of clients on tax issues. The firm also offers seminars and publishes a variety of periodicals and booklets on tax and personal financial planning.

Through more than 100 U.S. offices and its legislative monitoring service in Washington, D.C., Price Waterhouse advises businesses and individuals nationwide on the planning and compliance implications of the tax law.

Price Waterhouse

The
Price Waterhouse
Investor's
Tax
Adviser

THE
Price Waterhouse
INVESTOR'S
TAX
ADVISER
THIRD EDITION

Prentice Hall
New York • London • Toronto • Sydney • Tokyo • Singapore

This publication is designed to provide accurate and authoritative information in regard to the subject matter covered. It is sold with the understanding that the author and publisher are not engaged in rendering legal, accounting, or other professional service. Laws vary from state to state, and if legal advice or other expert assistance is required, the services of a competent professional should be sought.

The author and publisher specifically disclaim any liability, loss, or risk, personal or otherwise, which is incurred as a consequence, directly or indirectly, of the use and application of any of the contents of this book.

Prentice Hall General Reference
15 Columbus Circle
New York, NY 10023

Library of Congress Cataloging-in-Publication Data

ISBN: 0-671-87525-6

Manufactured in the United States of America

1   2   3   4   5   6   7   8   9   10

CONTENTS

INTRODUCTION

If the gyrations of the financial markets in the past few years accomplish nothing else useful, they remind us that uncertainty is every investor's companion.

We ignore uncertainty at our peril. That's why smart investors seek ways to profit regardless of whether the markets go up or down. One of those ways is to keep more of the money you make from investing in your bank account — not the government's.

That's where *The Price Waterhouse Investor's Tax Adviser* comes in. The purpose of this book is to provide you with the information you need to keep more of what you make from your investments by minimizing your taxes.

Our book explains in plain English how you can legally and honestly reduce your federal tax liabilities as well as formulate strategies for paring down your tax bill.

What's more, it alerts you to little-known rules and regulations that may — if you're not careful — cost you hundreds or thousands of dollars or more in extra taxes.

Being aware of the tax implications of your investments is even more important than you might think. Why? Because cutting your tax bill to the legal minimum can dramatically affect your after-tax return, particularly over the long haul.

EXAMPLE

You're a taxpayer in the 28 percent tax bracket, married and file a joint return, and have $10,000 to invest. You want to know whether you'll earn more in a tax-free municipal bond fund that currently yields 5 percent or in a fully taxable mutual fund that yields 7 percent.

If you choose to invest in a municipal bond fund, the income from that fund (which you could choose to reinvest in the same fund) is exempt from federal income taxes.

During the first year, your investment will grow to $10,500. What about in subsequent years? If the yield remains the same — that is, 5 percent annually — your investment will multiply to $16,289 over 10 years and to $26,533 over 20 years.

Now, what if you choose to invest your $10,000 in a fully taxable mutual fund? Assuming that the yield holds at 7 percent, you remain in the 28 percent bracket, and you reinvest your earnings, your investment will grow to $10,504 by the end of year one, after you subtract $196 in taxes. Your after-tax return adds up to 5.04 percent — not the advertised pre-tax yield of 7 percent.

What if you hold the investment for ten years? It will grow to $16,351 — only $62 more than if you'd invested the same amount in the municipal bond fund. And if you hold the investment for 20 years, it will grow to $26,736 — only $203 more than if you'd invested your dollars in the municipal bond fund.

So, as a taxpayer in the 28 percent bracket, you're only slightly better off putting your money in the taxable mutual fund than the tax-free municipal bond fund.

But let's change the scenario just slightly and now you're a taxpayer in the 36 percent bracket, married, and file a joint return.

If you invest $10,000 in a mutual fund earning 7 percent, it will grow to $10,448 by the end of year one, after you subtract $252 in taxes.

By the end of ten years, your investment will grow to $15,500, and, by the end of 20 years, $24,025 — or $2,508 less than if you'd invested in the municipal bond fund. And, if you're subject to the new itemized deduction limitation and the phaseout of personal exemptions (see Chapter 1 for details) your effective marginal tax rate may be higher than 36 percent, thereby further reducing your after-tax return from a taxable mutual fund.

So, your pre-tax yield of 7 percent becomes an annual after-tax yield of only 4.48 percent — 0.52 percent less than the yield on the municipal bond fund. That means, as a taxpayer in the 36 percent bracket, you're a little better off putting your money in the municipal bond fund.

Tax Exempt Yield	3%	4%	5%	6%	7%
Equivalent taxable yield:					
28% bracket	4.17%	5.56%	6.94%	8.33%	9.73%
31% bracket	4.35%	5.80%	7.25%	8.70%	10.14%
36% bracket	4.69%	6.25%	7.81%	9.38%	10.94%
39.6% bracket	4.97	6.62	8.28	9.93	11.59%

This chart does not take state taxes, the phaseout of personal exemptions, or the itemized deduction limitation into consideration.

Although a discussion of the tax rules for the various states would fill an encyclopedia, one last example illustrates the dramatic difference between investing in a taxable versus tax-free fund if you live in a state, such as California or New York, which levies its own tax on individual income. Let's say you're in the 36 percent bracket for federal income tax and an 8 percent bracket for state income tax. Your net effective tax rate is 41 percent (we'll show you how we reached 41, not 44, percent in Chapter 2).

With a 7 percent taxable fund, your investment is worth $10,412 in year one. Your $700 pre-tax interest dwindles to $412 as a result of your federal and state tax burdens, effectively leaving you with an annual after-tax yield of 4.12 percent. Compare this yield to the 5 percent tax-free bond (make sure to check with your tax adviser to see if those bonds are also tax-free for state tax purposes). After 20 years, your initial $10,000 has grown to $22,429, compared to $26,533 or $4,104 less than if you invested the same $10,000 in the tax-exempt fund.

The moral of these simple examples is clear. You must take the impact of taxes into account when planning your investment strategies and assessing the return on your investments. There's really only one way to know the impact of taxes on return from your investments, and that is to know the tax rules (federal and state) and to run the numbers. Once you determine your return on investment, you can make informed investment choices based on the economics of the investment as well as other non-tax considerations (for example, your risk tolerance and your long- or short-range investment goals).

Obviously, taxes do make a difference — often a big difference — in the amount of money you'll realize from your investments.

So, we hope what you learn from this book will help you become a more astute — and, therefore, more successful — investor.

1

MASTERING THE FUNDAMENTALS

■ What is your tax rate?

■ How do the personal exemption and itemized deductions phaseouts impact your effective tax rate?

■ Which tax reporting requirements apply to you?

Income you earn from your investments is generally subject to taxation. Like almost everything in life there are always exceptions. One exception to this rule is income from a municipal bond or municipal bond fund that's specifically excluded from taxation by law.

In the following chapters we take a look at the entire menu of *taxable* and *nontaxable* income — from interest and dividends to gains from the sale of stocks and mutual fund shares. Specific tax-saving strategies are also provided.

Before beginning, though, we need to define a few terms used frequently in this chapter — and the ones that follow.

Taxable income is the amount on which your federal income tax is calculated. It is determined by subtracting your allowable deductions from your income — wages, dividends, interest, and so on — from all sources.

Your *marginal tax rate* is the rate you pay on your last dollar of taxable income. For example, if you're single and your taxable income was $52,000 in 1993, your last dollar was taxed at 28 percent. Accordingly, your marginal tax rate was 28 percent.

It's important to know your marginal rate if you're considering making an investment. That way, you can calculate the tax consequences of your decision, which in turn affects the after-tax rate of return on your investment.

Your *effective tax rate* is the overall rate at which your income is taxed. You calculate this rate by dividing your total tax paid by your taxable income. For example, if you're married, file jointly, and your taxable income in 1993 was $100,000 you paid 15 percent on your first $36,900 of income, or $5,535, 28 percent on the next $52,250 or $14,630, and 31 percent on the remaining $10,850 or $3,364, for a total tax of $23,529.

To determine your effective tax rate divide your total tax — $23,529 — by your taxable income — $100,000. The result — 23.53 percent — is your effective tax rate for 1993.

Tax Rates

In 1993 there were five regular tax brackets, 15 percent, 28 percent, 31 percent, 36 percent and 39.6 percent. Please refer to the current year's edition of the *Price Waterhouse Personal Tax Adviser* for the rates applicable to the current year.

The maximum tax rate on long term capital gains was 28 percent in 1993 for all individual filers. Again, refer to the current year's edition of the *Price Waterhouse Personal Tax Adviser* for the rate applicable to the current year. See Chapter 4 for a further discussion of the capital gains tax rate and how the rate may affect your tax liability.

Hidden Tax Increases

Although the maximum tax rate was 39.6 percent in 1993, your *effective marginal federal tax rate* may have actually been higher because of two wrinkles in the tax law — the phaseout of personal exemptions and the floor on certain itemized deductions.

Neither of these items **directly** increases the tax rate applied to your income. Rather, both decrease the amounts you may deduct in calculating your taxable income, thereby increasing your *effective* marginal federal tax rate.

Personal exemption phaseout

When your adjusted gross income (AGI) exceeds certain statutory threshold levels which are inflation adjusted each year, you must reduce the amount of the personal exemption deduction you can claim.

For example, the 1993 threshold levels were as follows:

- $162,700 for married couples filing jointly and surviving spouses;
- $135,600 for heads of household;
- $108,450 for single people; and
- $81,350 for married couples filing separately

The deduction for personal exemptions is phased out by 2 percent for each $2,500, or fraction of $2,500, that your AGI exceeds the threshold level applicable to the current year and to your filing status. The phaseout rate is 4 percent for married persons filing separately.

To calculate the phaseout amount, subtract the phaseout threshold level for your filing status from your AGI. Next, divide the remainder into increments of $2,500. The law provides a 2 percent phaseout for each increment of $2,500 or fraction of $2,500. Accordingly, you must always round the result of this calculation up to the next whole number. (For example, 10.1 is rounded up to 11.)

This number is then multiplied by 2 percent (4 percent if married filing separately). This is the percentage of the personal exemption deduction phaseout.

EXAMPLE

Your AGI for 1993 was $213,700. You are married, have 2 children and file a joint return. So you had 4 exemptions for 1993, which gave you a total personal exemption deduction before the phaseout of $9,400 (4 times $2,350).

Adjusted Gross Income—1993	$213,700
Less: Phaseout level income	(162,700)
Difference	$51,000
Divided by:	2,500
Equals	**20.4**

Now round the 20.4 up to 21 and multiply it by 2 percent, which gives you 42 percent. The result? Your deduction for personal exemptions is reduced by $3,948 ($9,400 times 42 percent). You get to deduct $5,452 ($9,400 minus $3,948).

As the result of this calculation there is a "phaseout range" in effect for a "range of income" (the benefit of your personal exemptions will be entirely phased out at the upper limit of this range). For example, in 1993, the "phaseout range" was as follows:

Filing Status	1993 AGI Levels at which your exemptions are phased out
Married filing jointly, and surviving spouses	$162,701 to 285,200
Heads of household	$135,601 to 258,100
Single	108,451 to 230,950
Married filing separately	$ 81,351 to 142,600

Note: These amounts are for 1993 and will be adjusted for inflation. Consult your current year copy of *The Price Waterhouse Personal Tax Adviser* for the proper levels.

The maximum tax savings of one personal exemption in 1993 was $846 — assuming you're in the 36-percent tax bracket ($2,350 times the maximum tax rate of 36 percent). In the example above, the phaseout of personal exemptions costs you approximately $1,421 in additional tax ($846 times 4 exemptions times 42 percent).

Thus, if your adjusted gross income falls within the exemption phaseout range, the phaseout has the effect of increasing your effective marginal tax rate by a little more than ⅔ of one percent (.68 percent for 1993) for each exemption you claim. So the effective marginal tax rate for the couple in our example increases from 36 percent to more than 38 percent.

Itemized deduction floor

The second wrinkle in the tax law that may increase your effective marginal tax rate is the "floor" on itemized deductions. If your AGI exceeds the designated threshold, a portion of your itemized deductions will not be deductible. Again, this threshold is inflation adjusted each year. For example, the threshold amount is $108,450 ($54,225 for married couples filing separately) for 1993. Please refer to the current year's edition of the *Personal Tax Adviser* for the threshold levels applicable to the current year.

The floor is imposed on all expenses that would otherwise be deductible — with the exception of medical expenses, casualty and theft losses, investment interest, and gambling losses to the extent of gambling winnings.

The rules require you to reduce these otherwise allowable deductions by an amount equal to three percent of the amount by which your AGI exceeds the threshold amount. Itemized deductions, however, will never be reduced by more than 80 percent of their total.

Therefore to calculate the proper reduction, you must make two calculations.

EXAMPLE

You're married, file jointly, and your AGI in 1993 adds up to $200,000. Itemized deductions are: $11,000 in state and local taxes, $7,000 in mortgage interest, $1,000 in investment interest, and $2,000 in charitable contributions for a total of $21,000.

Since your AGI of $200,000 tops the 1993 threshold amount of $108,450, the rules require you to reduce the amount of itemized deductions you claim on your return by either:

• Three percent of the excess of your AGI over the threshold, or

• 80 percent of the deductions, whichever is less.

The calculation is as follows:

Adjusted gross income	$200,000
Threshold amount	(108,450)
Difference	$91,550
Multiplied by	3%
Total	$2,747

Next, determine 80 percent of the sum of your state and local taxes, mortgage interest, and charitable contributions — 80 percent of $20,000. The result here is $16,000. (Keep in mind that you ignore the $1,000 investment interest expense — and any medical expenses, casualty and theft losses, or gambling losses, if you have deducted those items — when you calculate the 80 percent limitation.)

Since $2,747 is less than $16,000, your floor for deducting itemized deductions is $2,747. Accordingly, you may deduct a total of $18,253 in itemized deductions comprised of the $1,000 in investment interest, which is not subject to the floor, plus the $17,253 that remains once you subtract $2,747 from $20,000, the rest of your deductions.

If you are subject to the three percent floor, your marginal tax rate increases by approximately 1 percent. That means it jumps from a rate of 36 percent (if you are in the 36 percent bracket) to approximately 37 percent — or even higher if your personal exemptions are phased out! If you are in the 39.6-percent bracket the rate increase will be even greater — approximately 1.2 percent.

CAUTION

Before computing the reduction, you must first apply any other limitations on itemized deductions. Your miscellaneous itemized deductions, for example, are first subject to a two percent floor, then lumped in with the other itemized deductions and subject to the new three percent floor. The two percent floor on miscellaneous itemized deductions is discussed in Chapter 7.

Other Matters

Remember you — not your tax preparer — are responsible for reporting all the income you receive on your federal income tax return. Accordingly, you must keep accurate records of all the money you receive during the tax year. Otherwise, you may overlook something.

If you haven't already done so, make sure you let any financial institution you do business with know your taxpayer identification number — for most individual investors, it's your Social Security number. You do so by filling out Form W-9, *Request for Taxpayer Identification Number and Certification*, which the institution will send you.

If you do not properly supply your taxpayer identification number the institution may withhold a portion of your earnings for taxes. As a result, you may end up making a tax-free loan to the IRS for the amount withheld. In addition, you may find yourself subject to a civil penalty of $50.

Investment income is taxable to you in the year you receive it or constructively receive it. You constructively receive income when the amount is either credited to your account or made available to you.

In other words, you do not have to physically receive the money for it to be considered taxable income.

EXAMPLE

You own stock in XYZ Corp. On December 27, 199A, XYZ dividend income is credited to your brokerage account for remittance to you by the broker. However, due to the holiday weekend, your broker does not remit the dividend check to you until January 3, 199B.

Even though you don't receive the check until the new year, you still must report that amount as income in 199A. In the eyes of the government, you had constructive receipt of the money, since it was available to you on December 27, 199A.

Now, let's move on to what's taxable — and what's not — when it comes to your investments, beginning (in the next chapter) with the interest you receive.

2

INTEREST INCOME

- What types of investment interest are taxable?
- Do the reporting requirements vary for different types of investment vehicles?
- Can you defer taxes by electing when to receive interest?

The government wants to make sure you pay federal taxes on *all* your interest income. That's why it requires payers of interest, such as banks and savings and loans, to report the amounts of interest they pay (as well as to whom they pay it) to the federal government.

These institutions must mail you a Form 1099-INT, "Interest Income," by the last day of January in the year following the tax year in which you earned the income.

If you don't receive your Form 1099-INT within a few weeks of that date, telephone or write the institution and ask for a duplicate. Or if you do receive your form but disagree with the amount of interest reported, call for an explanation of why the amount listed is incorrect.

If you never received a Form 1099-INT, the institution should mail you a copy of it. Further, if you received an incorrect Form 1099-INT and the institution agrees the amount is wrong, it should issue you an entirely new "corrected" form. When you receive your new Form 1099-INT, though, make sure it is marked "corrected," so there's no confusion about which form is the right one.

If you continue to disagree with the amount listed, report what you think is the correct amount on your return and include an explanation of the change in your tax return.

TIP

You do not need to attach your Forms 1099-INT to your return — in this or any other case. Simply report your total interest income on line 8a of your Form 1040. If your total taxable interest comes to more than $400, complete Schedule B, "Interest and Dividend Income" (by separately listing the names of each payor and the amount of interest received from each one) and attach it to your return. Before signing your tax return, compare the amount of interest you report on your return with that recorded on all your Forms 1099-INT to ensure you haven't forgotten anything.

CAUTION

Failing to report all your interest income may subject you to an accuracy-related penalty equal to 20 percent of the tax due on the interest you failed to report. Also, you will pay interest on the additional tax accruing from the day your income tax return was due.

TAXABLE INVESTMENT INTEREST

A wide range of investment vehicles exist yielding taxable interest. The following list includes many of the sources of taxable investment interest.

Bank Accounts

What do you need to know — tax-wise, at least — about passbook savings accounts? You pay taxes on your interest in the year you are able to withdraw it. It's that simple.

Banks currently pay interest on passbook accounts at an annualized rate that is generally lower than the rate paid on money-market accounts. Often you can earn one to two percentage points more in interest by transferring your dollars to a money-market account at the same institution.

Some parents open savings accounts for their children, then list themselves as custodian of the account. Interest on these accounts is taxable to the child as long as the account legally belongs to the child and the parents don't use any of the funds to support the child.

However, unearned income — including interest income — of minor children under age 14 may be taxed at the parents' rates if that rate is higher. Once children reach the age of 14, though, their unearned income is taxed at their own rates.

Money-market accounts offer you liquidity; you may withdraw your dollars at any time. So they're a good place to maintain your emergency fund. You pay taxes on the interest you earn from money deposited in money-market accounts at banks and other financial institutions.

TIP

> When you shop for such an account you should look for an institution offering competitive rates of return *plus* frequent "compounding". Compounding is simply the concept of earning interest on interest.

Why frequent compounding? Frequent compounding such as daily compounding means your interest income adds up faster than with quarterly or annual compounding.

EXAMPLE

> You deposit $50,000 in a money-market account at a bank that compounds quarterly and pays you an annualized rate of 3 percent. At the end of the first quarter, your interest income comes to $375 — that is, $50,000 times 3 percent times one-quarter.
>
> In the second quarter, you earn interest not only on your $50,000 of principal but also on your $375 of interest income. So your interest income for the second quarter totals $378 — that is, $50,375 times 3 percent times one-quarter.
>
> Continue these calculations for the next two quarters and by the end of the year, your interest income adds up to $1,517 (vs. the $1,500 you would have earned through annual compounding).
>
> If you deposited your $50,000 at a bank that also pays you an annualized rate of 3 percent but compounds daily you would earn interest on your interest — plus, of course, your principal — every day of the year. In the above example, daily compounding would earn $9 more than the $1,517 you would have earned with quarterly compounding.

TIP

> Look for an institution that compounds interest on a 365-day year,

not a 360-day one. Once again, you will earn an (ever so) slightly higher yield with a 365-day year.

TIP

If you're a safety-minded investor, you may want to opt for a money-market account from an institution that is a member of the Federal Deposit Insurance Corporation (FDIC) or the National Credit Union Administration (NCUA). That way, your principal and any interest due you are added together and guaranteed (up to the amount of $100,000) if the institution goes bankrupt.

TIP

Dollars deposited in Individual Retirement Accounts (IRAs) are insured separately by the federal government up to $100,000.

EXAMPLE

You deposit $100,000 in a money-market account in your name at the local thrift where you also maintain your IRA and the institution later goes bankrupt.

The government gives you back only the $100,000 you deposited in the money-market account and not any interest due you because the amount would exceed $100,000. However, the government also returns to you the principal plus any interest due you on your IRA — up to $100,000.

CAUTION

Dollars you deposit in a bank and at one of its branches are not insured separately by the government. They're treated as deposits at the same bank. The same goes for deposits you make in different accounts in the same bank — they're added together and insured up to a maximum of $100,000. (Exceptions exist to this rule so you may want to ask you banker for clarification.)

To be safe, don't deposit more than $100,000 in all of your accounts at any one bank, including its branches.

Certificates of deposit

When the stock market is on the rise and interest rates are low, few investors find certificates of deposit (CDs) attractive investments. But the popularity of

CDs increases when the market is down, interest rates are high, or the economic outlook appears uncertain.

CDs are generally issued by banks and other financial institutions. You normally buy certificates of deposit for terms ranging from several days to several years. When you invest in a CD, your bank or other institution uses the deposit for a specified period of time and, in exchange, you receive a rate of interest competitive with other investments of similar risk.

If you cash out of your CD early, the bank will likely impose an early, or premature, withdrawal penalty that may be as large as the entire amount of interest due you.

CDs are available not only from banks but also brokerage firms as well. CDs offered by brokerage houses often pay a higher rate of interest than those issued by banks because brokers buy CDs in bulk from banks and can negotiate a higher rate of interest.

Most brokerages don't usually impose a penalty for early withdrawal because they make a secondary market in CDs. If you may need to cash out of your CD early, your broker will sell your certificate to another investor.

TIP

If you want to defer interest income on CDs from one year to the next, buy a certificate in one year that matures in the following year. Unless you receive interest — or interest is credited to your account and made available for withdrawal — during the current year, your earnings are taxed when you receive them — that is, when the CD becomes due.

This tax strategy applies *only* to certificates with a maturity of one year or less. With CDs of longer maturities, you report the amount of interest the certificate earns annually — even if you do not actually receive the cash.

TIP

When you withdraw money before maturity, the government treats the early withdrawal penalty as an adjustment to your gross income. That means you reduce your gross income for tax purposes by deducting the early withdrawal penalty.

Here's how to do the reporting for the early withdrawal penalty on your tax return:

- First, report the gross amount of interest received or credited to your account during the year without subtracting the penalty. The interest you receive and the early withdrawal penalty count as two separate transactions, and

- Then, you write off the penalty in full as an adjustment to your income on page one of your Form 1040.

You will find the amount you should deduct on your tax return on Form 1099-INT, in the box labeled "Early withdrawal penalty."

Another fact you should know is that many banks won't allow you to cash in a portion of your CD. When it comes to withdrawing your money, it's all or nothing. However, you may be able to withdraw interest you earn at any time during the term of the CD.

TIP

When it comes to investing in CDs, most banks and savings and loans set a minimum deposit amount as well as a minimum term of maturity. Sometimes investors even borrow money from the same bank or thrift to meet the minimum deposit requirement.

EXAMPLE

Your bank offers a $100,000, six-month CD that pays an annual yield of 4 percent. You invest in the CD — using $90,000 of your own money and $10,000 you borrowed from the bank that is offering the CD. Your annual interest rate on the loan is 8 percent.

The CD earns you $2,000 in interest but you receive only $1,600 — i.e., your $2,000 in interest income minus the $400 in interest (for one half year) on your $10,000 loan. The bank mails you a Form 1099-INT reporting $2,000 in interest income. It also mails you a statement listing your $400 in interest expense.

You include the $2,000 in your interest income for the year, and deduct the $400 in interest expense as an itemized deduction on Schedule A of your Form 1040.

CAUTION

If you don't itemize, you lose the deduction.

Annuities

Annuities offer you a host of benefits such as guaranteed principal, interest that accumulates tax-deferred, and monthly checks for the rest of your life. As savings plans sponsored by insurance companies, annuities promise to pay you a regular income typically starting the day you retire and running for the rest of your life. The size of these payments depends on your life expectancy, the amount of dollars contributed, and the interest rate used by the insurance carrier.

When it comes to annuities, the government imposes a whole host of complicated rules and regulations that are covered in detail in Chapter 14.

Dividends taxable as interest

Dividends on deposits in bank money-market accounts or certificates, savings certificates, cooperative banks, credit unions, savings-and-loan associations, and mutual savings banks are really interest—in the eyes of the IRS—and you must report them as such.

CAUTION

Interest earned on mutual fund money-market accounts is taxed as dividends, not interest. Dividend income is listed on a Form 1099-DIV. (Dividends are covered in Chapter 3.)

Report the income on your tax return as your bank or other financial institution reports it to you. Interest income is reported on a Form-1099-INT.

Foreign accounts

If you earn interest from bank accounts or trusts established outside the United States, the foreign country may require you to pay taxes on the interest you've earned, sometimes at much higher tax rates than those in the United States.

In addition, you are also required to pay taxes in the United States. In fact, as a U.S. citizen or resident, you must pay taxes on all your worldwide income.

If you're required to pay taxes in the foreign country, you are allowed to either deduct those taxes as "other taxes" on Schedule A of your Form 1040, or claim those taxes as a credit on Form 1116, "Foreign Tax Credit," which you attach to your Form 1040.

The credit is generally limited to the amount of U.S. tax attributable to foreign income. In other words, you pay tax on the income at the higher of the two tax rates.

TIP

It usually makes sense to claim the credit rather than the deduction, since credits reduce your tax dollar-for-dollar. Deductions, on the other hand, simply reduce the amount of your income subject to tax.

CAUTION

Calculating the foreign tax credit can be extremely complicated, so consult your tax adviser.

TIP

You must report foreign interest on your U.S. tax return in U.S. dollars. You should attach a schedule to your return that shows how you converted the foreign interest into U.S. dollars. Generally, use the exchange rate prevailing at the time the interest was paid to you or credited to your account. If interest was earned ratably throughout the year, you may use the average annual exchange rate.

CAUTION

If you have any foreign bank or financial accounts, complete Part III of Schedule B of your Form 1040 by answering the two questions about foreign bank accounts and foreign trusts. In addition, if the combined value of the accounts is more than $10,000 during any entire year, you must file Form TD F 90-22.1, "Report of Foreign Bank and Financial Accounts," with the Department of the Treasury by June 30 of the following year.

Frozen assets

If you deposited money at a savings and loan or other financial institution and it went bankrupt, do you pay taxes currently on the interest credited to your account — even though you can't withdraw the money?

The answer is no — the government allows you to exclude from taxes amounts credited to your account during the year, but which you were unable to withdraw by the end of the year. Any interest you exclude under this rule becomes taxable when it's available for withdrawal.

Gifts for making deposits

If you receive a gift for making a long-term deposit in a bank or other financial institution, the value of that item is taxed as interest income.

EXAMPLE

You open a money-market account at a local bank. The account earns you $1,600 in interest. In addition, you receive a free color television worth $300.

At the end of the year, the bank sends you a Form 1099-INT. It lists interest income of $1,900 — that is, the $1,600 of interest plus $300 for the television.

IRAs, Keoghs or 401(k)s

You do not pay taxes on interest earned from investments in an Individual Retirement Account (IRA) until you withdraw the money — usually at retirement. You also pay no taxes on interest earned on investments in a Keogh or 401(k) plan until you withdraw the money, again, usually at retirement.

CAUTION

The tax law caps your annual contributions to IRAs, Keoghs and 401(k)s. If you inadvertently exceed these limits, the rules require you to withdraw the excess plus any interest you've earned on the excess amount. This interest is subject to taxes. Furthermore, the IRS may assess you a penalty for contributing more than you should. For more details on IRAs and Keoghs, see Chapter 16 — "Retirement Basics."

Installment sales

An installment sale occurs when an asset is sold in one year and at least one payment is received in a later year. If interest is not provided on the deferred payment(s), and at least one of the deferred payments is due more than one year after the date of sale, a portion of payments made six months after the sale is treated as interest. In other words, if you don't charge interest at the minimum rate the government prescribes, you must treat a portion of the principal payment as interest. You also must pay tax on that interest in the year you receive the related payments.

Calculating the amount of interest is exceedingly complicated. If you find yourself in this situation, seek the help of a tax professional.

TIP

These rules don't apply to installment sales of $3,000 or less. For more information on the installment sales rules, see Chapter 5.

Joint accounts

If you and a friend are joint owners of a savings account, the tax law requires both of you to report the amount of interest attributable to the money you deposited in the account.

CAUTION

Financial institutions usually report interest income under the Social Security number of only one person, even if two or more people own the account. So, you face a potential problem by reporting only your share of income. The IRS may issue a deficiency notice to the person whose Social Security number is listed because he or she didn't report the full amount.

TIP

To avoid this problem, you must follow the procedure for reporting a nominee distribution.

EXAMPLE

You and your sister are joint owners of a savings account, and the interest the account earns is reported in your name and under your Social Security number. You should complete Form 1099-INT for her share of the interest no later than January 31 of the following tax year, and give Copy B to your sister.

You must also complete a Form 1096, "Annual Summary and Transmittal of U.S. Information Returns," and file it with Form 1099-INT no later than February 28 of the following tax year. On Form 1099-INT, list yourself as the payer and your sister as the recipient.

On line 1, Schedule B, of your Form 1040, include with your share of interest the amount of interest attributed to your sister. Then, several lines above line 2, subtotal the amounts listed on line 1.

Below this subtotal, write "nominee distribution" and list the amount reported to you but belonging to your sister. Then subtract this amount from the subtotal.

List the result — which is your share of the interest income — on line 2.

Market discount bonds

A bond is essentially a contract between an issuer (or borrower) and a bondholder (or lender). Corporations and various levels and agencies of government use bonds to raise money for a variety of reasons.

The bonds may sell at *par* — their face value or what the issuer will pay when the bond matures — and pay a market rate of interest each year which you report annually as interest income (unless the bonds are municipal — state or local — bonds). Or, they may sell at a discount or premium to par.

Market discount bonds, which can include both corporate and government bonds, have a coupon interest rate — in other words, a stated interest rate — of less than the prevailing market rate of interest on bonds of a similar quality and maturity. Therefore, these bonds usually sell for less than their stated redemption rice.

EXAMPLE

On July 1, 199A, a ten-year bond was issued for $10,000. It pays interest semiannually at a 6 percent rate and will be redeemed at maturity for its issue price of $10,000.

On July 1, 199C, the prevailing market rate of interest on similar bonds has increased. So, you may be able to purchase the bond from its original holder for $9,000. The difference between the bond's $10,000 stated redemption price and $9,000 — the price you paid — comes to $1,000 and represents the market discount. The discount, in effect, compensates you for the lower interest you'll earn over the life of the bond compared to similar bonds.

CAUTION

A bond could be originally issued at a discount — called "original issue discount" (OID). Then, because of rising interest rates, that bond could be subsequently sold with an additional discount — this time a market discount. The amount of market discount in this case is the excess of the original issue discount price plus the total OID includible in the income of all previous holders of the bond over the subsequent purchase price.

EXAMPLE

You purchase a bond for $24,000, and the bond has a stated redemption price of $25,000. The previous bondholder — who sold you the bond — acquired it at its original issue price of $23,000. By the time he sold you the bond, he had reported $1,500 of the total OID of $2,000 as income. Your market discount comes to $500 — that is, the issue price of $23,000, plus the $1,500 of OID reported by the previous bondholder, minus your $24,000 purchase price.

The treatment of OID is discussed later in this chapter. For now, you should simply be aware that OID generally represents the discount offered by the **issuer** of the bond. Market discount, by contrast, is the discount a subsequent bondholder offers. And the tax treatment accorded to each type of discount differs.

The tax treatment of market discount depends upon the date the bond was originally issued. As a general rule, for bonds issued before July 19, 1984 and purchased before May 1, 1993, the tax rules treat any gain you realize when you dispose of the bond as capital gain to the extent of the market discount. In addition, any gain in excess of the market discount would also be capital gain. A disposition includes not only a sale or exchange of the bond but also a redemption of the bond at its maturity date.

EXAMPLE

A bond was issued on January 1, 1984, for $50,000. You purchased this bond on July 1, 199A, for $45,000 (a market discount of $5,000). On July 1, 199E, you sell the same bond for $47,000. Your profit on the sale of $2,000 is treated as a long-term capital gain.

Different rules apply to bonds issued (i) after July 18, 1984 and (ii) before July 19, 1984 but purchased after April 30, 1993. For these bonds, any gain you realize when you dispose of the bond is treated as interest income — that is, as ordinary income, not capital gain — to the extent of the bond's "accrued market discount" through the sale date. You treat any additional gain as capital gain. (Of course, if you sell a bond you acquired at a market discount for less than its purchase price, you have a capital loss.)

The law gives you two choices for calculating accrued market discount.

- ratable accrual, and
- constant interest.

TIP

You need to run the numbers and determine which method is more beneficial to your tax situation.

Under the ratable accrual method, you treat the total market discount as accruing in equal daily installments over the period you hold the bond.

In other words, you divide the total market discount by the number of days after you acquire the bond through the bond's maturity date. Then you multiply that amount — the daily market discount — by the number of days that you actually hold the bond.

The result is the accrued market discount at the date you sell the bond. Of course, if you hold the bond until it matures, the accrued market discount equals the total market discount on the bond.

EXAMPLE

You purchase a bond on September 2, 199A, for $26,000. The bond matures 800 days later — on November 10, 199C — for $30,000. Your total market discount is $4,000.

Now, let's say that you decide to sell the bond on April 24, 199C — 600 days after you acquired it. Under the ratable accrual method, your accrued market discount would come to $3,000 — that is, $4,000 (total market discount) divided by 800 days (total days to maturity) times 600 days (the number of days you held the bond.)

The constant interest method is more complex (this method also applies to certain original issue discount (OID) bonds — a subject discussed later in this chapter).

In general, the constant interest method corresponds to the actual economic accrual of interest. You compute accrued market discount for each one-year period — beginning on the date you acquire the bond and each anniversary date thereafter — by multiplying your cost basis (what you paid for the bond) plus any previously accrued market discount, by the bond's yield to maturity. Then you subtract any interest actually paid on the bond during that period. (A discounted bond's yield to maturity — which your broker can calculate for you — will be greater than its stated interest rate because of the discount.)

Repeat this calculation for each subsequent period you hold the bond. When you sell the bond, you allocate accrued market discount for the one-year period that includes the sale date over the number of days you actually hold the bond during that period.

Under this method, accrued market discount for each one-year period will increase each year because of the compounding of the accrued market discount. Therefore, at any given disposition date, accrued market discount under the constant interest method will be less than under the ratable accrual method. And that means the government will tax less of your gain as ordinary income.

EXAMPLE

On January 1, 199F, you acquire a 10-year, 10 percent bond for $95,000. The bond was issued on January 1, 199A for its redemption price of $100,000. Your total market discount is, of course, $5,000. And you'll receive interest payments of $10,000 for each full year you hold the bond. The bond has a yield to maturity of 11.3653 percent.

For 199F, your accrued market discount using the ratable accrual method comes to $1,000 ($5,000 times 364 days divided by 1,826 days). Under the constant interest method, however, your accrued market discount would come to only $800 ($95,000 times 11.3653 percent, less $10,000).

Then, in 199G, your accrued market discount would again total $1,000 under the ratable accrual method. But it would total only $890 under the constant interest method ($95,000 plus $800 equals $95,800; $95,800 times 11.3653 percent minus $10,000 equals $890).

The table that follows compares the accrual of market discount under both methods:

CAUTION

Year	Ratable Accrual	Constant Interest
199F	$1,000	$ 800
199G	1,000	890
199H	1,000	990
199I	1,000	1,100
199J	1,000	1,220
TOTAL:	$5,000	$5,000

Once you elect to use the constant interest method for a particular bond, you may not change the election for that bond, although you may use the ratable accrual method for other bonds.

Thus, as we've seen, the government generally recognizes market discount as income when you dispose of the bond — either by selling it or redeeming it at maturity. And, depending on when the bond was issued and purchased, the income counts either as capital gain or as ordinary interest income.

A special rule lets you elect to report market discount as current income, rather than waiting until you sell or redeem the bond. That is, you report the accrued market discount — using either the ratable accrual or constant rate method — as interest income on your tax return each year you hold the bond.

TIP

One reason to recognize the income currently, rather than wait to pay the tax, is you may expect your tax rate to increase in future years and you want to take advantage of lower rates now.

TIP

Another reason might arise if you borrowed money to purchase the bond. In this case, you may want to recognize income currently to avoid a special rule limiting the amount of interest expense you may deduct each year on the loan.

This special rule generally provides that if your interest expense exceeds the interest income you earn on the bond during the year, you may only deduct an amount equal to the interest income plus the amount, if any, by which the "excess interest expense" (i.e., the interest expense in excess of the interest income) exceeds your accrued but unreported market discount for the year. In other words, once your interest expense exceeds your interest income you cannot deduct the amount of such excess to the extent of the accrued but unreported market discount for the year.

EXAMPLE

In 199A, you take out a loan to buy a market discount bond. You earn $5,000 of interest on the bond. In addition, your accrued market discount for the year — which you do not have to report currently — comes to $500. You pay interest of $6,250 on the loan needed to buy the bond.

You may deduct only $5,750 of that amount — that is, $5,000 (the amount of interest income) plus $750 ("excess interest expense" of $1,250, less accrued market discount of $500). The $500 you are not allowed to deduct becomes deductible when you dispose of the bond. Or, you can elect to deduct the excess in any other year to the extent that your interest income from the bond exceeds your interest expense on the loan in that year.

As noted, when you dispose of the bond, you can deduct any remaining disallowed interest expense. Your gain on the disposition of the bond is treated as ordinary income to the extent of such deductible interest plus accrued but unreported market discount. The IRS treats any additional gain as long-term capital gain for bonds issued before July 18, 1984 and purchased before May 1, 1993.

Thus, as noted in the tip immediately preceding the above example, if you elect to report your accrued market discount currently, you are not subject to any of these special interest disallowance rules. Therefore, in the above example, you could deduct the full amount of interest expense — $6,250 (subject to the investment interest expense limitations discussed in Chapter 6).

CAUTION

If you *do* opt to report this income currently, make sure to carefully evaluate the consequences. For instance, in the above example, the election gives you $500 more in deductions, but also $500 more in income. The bottom line on your tax return may not change.

CAUTION

The law states that you may not change your mind once you begin reporting your accrued market discount each year unless you get permission from the IRS to revoke the election you made.

There is one other special rule related to reporting income from market discount bonds.

Assume you *acquired* the bond after October 22, 1986 and the issuer of the bond makes a partial payment of the bond's principal to you before maturity. You must report the payment as ordinary interest income to the extent of the accrued but unreported market discount as of the payment date. The amount you report reduces the amount of remaining accrued market discount that you take into account when you dispose of the bond.

Return to the example on the constant interest method of accruing market discount (page 22):

EXAMPLE

On July 1, 199H, the issuer of the bond pays you $2,500 of the $100,000 face amount of the bond. If you accrued market discount under the ratable accrual method, the entire $2,500 would be taxable as ordinary interest income. That's because your accrued market discount at July 1, 199H, would be $2,500 ($5,000 times 912 days divided by 1,826 days). If you used the constant interest method, however, you would report only $2,184 — $800 plus $890 plus $494 ($990 times 182 divided by 365 days) — of the $2,500 as interest income. The remaining $316 would be tax free in the year received and would reduce your basis in the bond.

As always, there are exceptions to the rules. The following bonds are not subject to the interest income rules for market discount bonds:

- Bonds issued before July 19, 1984 and purchased before May 1, 1993, as discussed above;
- Short-term bonds — i.e., bonds with a fixed maturity date that doesn't exceed one year from the date of issue (see "Short-term obligations," later in this chapter);
- Tax-exempt obligations purchased before May 1, 1993 (see "Tax-exempt investments," later in this chapter);
- U.S. Savings Bonds (see "Savings bonds," later in this chapter); and
- Installment obligations (see "Interest on installment sales," earlier in this chapter).

Tip

If the amount of market discount totals less than one-fourth of one percent of the redemption price of the bond multiplied by the number of full years to maturity, you may disregard the market discount altogether — that is, you may treat it as zero. So any gain you recognize when you dispose of this bond is treated as capital gain rather than ordinary interest income. This rule also applies to OID.

Example

You pay $9,900 for a 10-year bond, issued four years ago for its redemption price of $10,000; your market discount is $100, and it is less than one-fourth of one percent of the redemption price ($10,000) multiplied by the number of full years to maturity (six years) — or $150. Therefore, you don't have to worry about calculating accrued market discount when you sell or redeem the bond. You treat any gain you recognize as capital gain.

Original Issue Discount bonds

Original Issue Discount (OID) bonds — including zero-coupon bonds — are **issued** at a discount from the face value of the bond.

Original issue discount is simply the difference between the price paid for the bond when it was originally issued and the amount the holder receives for the bond at maturity. A bond issued for $9,000 that promises to pay $10,000 in 10 years plus annual interest at eight percent, for example, has OID of $1,000.

You may buy OID bonds from a variety of sources — banks, brokerage houses, even the Federal Reserve. You can expect to pay a small sales commission — two percent is typical — when you purchase these bonds from institutions.

If you own OID bonds, you are generally required to report part of the discount as interest income on your tax return each year you own the bonds, even though you don't actually receive the money until you cash in the bonds at maturity (Note: This rule differs from the one for market discount bonds. In the case of those bonds, the law generally requires that you recognize the market discount as interest income — ordinary income — only when you dispose of the bonds).

How much of the discount do you report each year? The bond issuer or brokerage firm will calculate the amount of the discount you must report and mail you a Form 1099-OID, "Original Issue Discount," each year — if your discount for the year adds up to $10 or more. Your Form 1099-OID lists the taxable amount you must report.

TIP

There is no need to attach Form 1099-OID to your tax return, but you should keep a copy for your records in case you're audited.

How your broker or bond issuer calculates the taxable portion of your OID each year depends on the type of bond and when it was issued.

For bonds issued after 1954 and before May 28, 1969 (or before July 2, 1982, for government obligations), no OID is included in taxable income until the year you dispose of the bond by selling, exchanging, or redeeming it. Any gain you realize on the disposition is treated as ordinary interest income to the extent of OID accrued on a monthly basis. Generally, any additional gain is treated as capital gain.

You compute the amount of gain taxed as ordinary interest income by multiplying the total OID by the number of full months you held the bond. Then you divide the result by the number of full months from the date of original issue to the date of maturity.

If you dispose of the bond at a loss, the entire loss is treated as a capital loss. As a result, you have no OID to report.

For corporate bonds issued after May 27, 1969 and government obligations issued after July 1, 1982, you generally report a portion of the OID as interest income each year that you hold the bond. Your basis in the bond for determining gain or loss when you dispose of it is increased by the amount of OID you report.

EXAMPLE

You purchased a post-July 1, 1982, 10-year, $10,000 bond for $9,200 at original issue on January 1, 199A. Two years later, you decide to sell the bond. You've reported a total of $115 of OID as interest income on your 199A and 199B tax returns. Therefore, the basis of your bond for computing your gain or loss on the sale comes to $9,315—i.e., your issue price of $9,200 plus the $115 of OID you've reported as income.

As noted, the method your bond issuer or broker uses for determining the annual taxable portion of OID depends upon when the bond was issued. The annual taxable portion of OID on corporate bonds issued after May 27, 1969, and before July 2, 1982 is calculated as the ratable monthly portion of OID times the number of complete and partial months you held the bond during the year.

The ratable monthly portion of OID is the total OID divided by the number of complete months from the issue date to the maturity date of the bond.

EXAMPLE

You purchased a 10-year bond on July 15, 199A, with total OID of $10,000. The ratable monthly portion of OID is $83.33 ($10,000 OID divided by 120 months — the number of complete months from the issue date to the maturity date). The annual taxable portion of OID for 199A would be $460 ($83.33 times 5.5 months).

For corporate and government bonds issued after July 1, 1982, and before January 1, 1985, the annual taxable portion of OID is calculated using the complex "constant interest method," discussed earlier in this chapter under "Market Discount Bonds," that assumes annual compounding. A similar method is used for bonds issued after 1984, but semiannual compounding is assumed.

CAUTION

As discussed earlier, the bond issuer or brokerage firm will provide you with a Form 1099-OID that indicates how much OID to report as interest income each year. However, since the amount is calculated on the assumption that you held the bond for the entire year or through its maturity date, the amount may not be correct.

If you sell the bond during the year, you should report less OID as interest income. You may prorate the annual OID to the period you held the bond based on the ratio of days you held the bond to total days during the year. Or, you may use the tables found in IRS Publication 1212 "List of Original Discount Instruments." These tables show the daily portion of OID based on the constant interest method.

Using the amounts in these tables may mean you end up with a lower taxable OID than if you used the simple daily-proration calculation.

TIP

As discussed previously, the tax law gives you a break if your discount adds up to less than one quarter of one percent of the stated redemption price of the bond multiplied by the number of years to maturity. In such case, you don't need to currently report any of the OID as income on your tax return.

Your brokerage firm will make this calculation for you. So, if the bond meets the 0.25 percent de minimis test, the issuer or broker will report no OID to you. Before investing in a bond, ask the issuer or broker if it has OID.

TIP

There are other exceptions to the OID rules. For example, these rules do not apply to tax-exempt bonds, U.S. Savings Bonds, or to short-term obligations — such as obligations with a fixed maturity date not exceeding one year from the date of issue. Examples include Treasury bills and commercial paper.

There are a number of other rules you should know about when it comes to investing in OID bonds. If you acquire an OID bond from another holder — perhaps the original holder — you still have to worry about reporting OID.

However, how much you report depends on whether you acquired the OID bond with additional market discount (discussed earlier in this chapter) or with "acquisition premium" (discussed later in this chapter).

When you acquire an OID bond with additional market discount, you will recognize the remaining OID — the amount of OID not yet reported by the original holder — under the OID rules. In addition you will report the market discount under the general market discount rules.

EXAMPLE

You acquire a bond for $9,500. The bond has a stated redemption price of $10,000 and was originally issued for $9,000. The previous holder reported $600 of the total OID of $1,000. Your market discount comes to $100 — the issue price of $9,000 plus the OID already reported of $600, minus your $9,500 purchase price. You must also report the remaining $400 of OID over the remaining term of the bond.

However, you may find yourself in a situation where, instead of receiving an additional market discount on an OID bond, you must pay an "acquisition premium" for the bond. This circumstance would arise where interest rates on similar bonds are dropping.

The tax law defines acquisition premium as the excess of the price you pay for the bond over the sum of the bond's original issue price plus accumulated OID.

In the above example, assume you paid $9,800 for the bond. The acquisition premium would come to $200. That premium reduces the amount of OID you must report each year.

The rules for determining the amount by which the acquisition premium reduces reportable OID each year depends upon whether you purchased the bond before, on, or after July 19, 1984.

*T*IP

> To invest in OID bonds and avoid reporting a portion of your discount as interest income each year, buy these bonds with dollars deposited in an IRA or Keogh. That way, you're not taxed on the discount until the money is withdrawn from your plan, usually at retirement. (See Chapter 17 for more information on retirement accounts.)

Investing in zero-coupon and other OID bonds offers convenience. The amount you invest today will have grown to a fixed sum at a set date in the future.

You do not need to worry about reinvesting the interest you earn. In fact, you need only decide whether to buy the bond in the first place — and whether or not to sell.

*T*IP

> Sometimes bonds sell for more than their stated redemption price. The excess, or "premium," is generally reported as a capital loss when you redeem the bond at maturity. Similarly, if you sell the bond at a loss, the entire amount of the loss is treated as a capital loss, part or all of which is attributable to the premium.

If you pay more than the redemption price for an OID bond, you do not have to include any of the unreported OID in your income.

*T*IP

> If you acquire a bond — whether or not it is an OID bond — at a premium, you may elect to deduct, or amortize, the premium over the life of the bond rather than wait to claim a capital loss when you redeem or sell it. The amount you deduct each year reduces your cost basis in the bond for determining gain or loss when you dispose of it.

The way you deduct the premium depends on when you acquired the bond. Generally, for bonds acquired after 1987, you offset your interest income by the amount of the annual amortization deduction. For bonds acquired after October 22, 1986, and before 1988, report your annual deduction as investment interest expense on Schedule A of Form 1040, subject to the limits on investment interest expense we discuss in Chapter 6.

And for bonds acquired before October 22, 1986, you claim your deduction as a miscellaneous itemized deduction that is *not* subject to the two percent of AGI limitation.

CAUTION

If you acquire a tax-exempt bond at a premium, you may not deduct the premium currently. However, you must reduce your cost basis in the bond by the annual amortization amount.

TIP

The tax rules concerning OID are complex and often difficult to apply. If you have any questions, consult your tax adviser.

Savings bonds

If you think now is no time to take needless chances with your money, you may find United States savings bonds a safe and rewarding place to put your dollars.

TIP

Many taxpayers do not know it, but the tax they pay on their interest income varies with the type of savings bond — Series HH or Series EE — they buy.

With Series HH bonds, you pay taxes currently. That's because when you buy Series HH bonds, you pay face value, and your interest check is mailed to you twice a year by the government. Thus, you pay taxes on the interest as you receive it.

TIP

Series HH bonds replaced Series H bonds, which were issued through 1979. Any outstanding Series H bonds are treated the same as Series HH bonds.

When you purchase Series EE bonds, you buy them at a discount from their face value. When the bond matures, you collect the face value. The difference between the price you pay when you buy the bond and the amount you pocket when you redeem it is your taxable interest.

TIP

Series EE bonds replaced Series E bonds, which were issued through 1979. With Series EE bonds, you have a choice when it comes to reporting the interest. You may report it in the year you cash the bonds or in the year in which the bonds finally mature — whichever comes first. Or you may report the interest each year, but doing so doesn't make much sense in most situations.

In addition, the government allows you to switch from one method of reporting interest to another without permission. All you need to do is file Form 3115 with your tax return. On the form, specify the savings bonds for which the change is requested. And print on the top of page one of Form 3115, "Filed under Rev. Proc. 89-46."

You should know, however, that the year you change to the annual reporting method, you are required to report all the interest that's accrued on the bond to date.

CAUTION

You may not use different methods in the same year to report the interest on different bonds. You must use one method or the other for all the savings bonds you hold in any given year.

TIP

Report your interest income from your savings bonds in a year in which you have a low income or a low tax rate. But, only do so if you expect either your income or income tax rate to increase in a later year.

TIP

If you own Series E bonds, and you trade them for Series H bonds, or you own Series E or Series EE bonds and trade them for Series HH bonds, you're entitled to a break. The rules say that you pay taxes only on the accrued but unreported interest you actually receive in cash. If you roll all your interest over into more savings bonds in the manner described, you pay no taxes on the interest accrued through the trade date.

EXAMPLE

You own Series E bonds with a current redemption value of $10,887 that originally cost you $5,000. You trade them for $10,000 worth of Series HH bonds. You keep the remaining $887. You're taxed only on the $887 you actually received and not on any additional accrued interest (i.e., $5,000) that is, in effect, "rolled over" in the trade. Such accrued interest will be taxed when you receive it (e.g., when you ultimately sell your HH bonds).

This tax break applies only to Series EE or Series E bonds with a current redemption value of $500 or more.

When you redeem a savings bond at a bank or other institution, that institution must forward to you a Form 1099-INT if your interest is $10 or more.

Printed in box 3 of your Form 1099-INT is your taxable interest income — that is, the difference between the amount you paid for the bond and the amount you received. Often, though, this number is incorrect. One reason for this is that the institution assumes the interest you receive is entirely taxable to you at the time of redemption, even though you — or the original buyer — may have reported interest income from the bond each year.

If you find yourself in this situation, report the full amount of interest on Schedule B of Form 1040, then subtract the amount not currently taxable to you and explain why.

CAUTION

If you buy a savings bond and list yourself and your child as co-owners you, the buyer, must pay taxes on the bond's interest. This rule holds true even if you let your child redeem the bond and keep the proceeds. However, if you bought the bond in your child's name and did not list yourself as co-owner, the interest is taxable to the child.

TIP

If you live in a high-tax state — California, New York, or Massachusetts, for example — savings bonds may be tax-wise investments for you. The reason is that federal law specifically excludes interest on these bonds from state and local income taxes.

TIP

The tax law gives you a break if you're twenty-four years of age or older, invest in Series EE bonds issued after December 31, 1989, and use the proceeds to pay for *qualified* education expenses for yourself, your spouse, your child, or other dependent — see Chapter 17, "Investing In (Financing) Your Child's Education" for more details.

Short-term obligations

Any bond or note that matures in a year or less, including both corporate and government bonds, is considered a short-term obligation. You may purchase these obligations at a discount from their face value, and you realize the interest income when the obligation is paid. You are not subject to either the rules on market discount bonds or original issue discount (OID) bonds.

EXAMPLE

> In March 199A, you paid $9,400 for a short-term note that carries a face amount of $10,000. In February 199B, you receive payment of $10,000 for your note. You must report $600 in interest on your 199B return.

If you sell the short-term note at a gain before its maturity, you treat the gain as ordinary interest income to the extent of your ratable share of the discount at that date. Generally, you follow the rules we discussed earlier in the chapter for market discount bonds — that is, use either the ratable accrual method or the constant interest method — for determining your ratable share of the discount. Any gain that tops your ratable share is short-term capital gain. Any loss is treated as a short-term capital loss.

Stripped-coupon bonds

Special rules apply to stripped-coupon bonds — bonds where the right to receive interest has been "stripped" (i.e., separated from the underlying bonds and sold). Both the interest coupons and the principal are sold separately. The separate bond and the separate coupons represent the claim to receive payments on the due date. Stripped bonds include so-called zero-coupon instruments sold by brokerage houses under the names CATS or TIGRS. The U.S. Treasury also offers zero-coupon bonds under the name STRIPS.

When you buy a stripped bond (coupon), the spread between the amount you pay for it and its face amount is treated as original issue discount. Therefore, you must report a part of this spread as interest income each year. When you buy a stripped bond (coupon), you treat as OID the excess of the amount payable on the due date of the bond (coupon) over the amount you paid for it.

The rules to calculate the reportable OID depend upon when the bond or coupon was issued — after July 1, 1982 and before January 1, 1985, or after December 31, 1984. In both cases, you use the complex, constant interest method discussed previously. In the former case, however, you use annual compounding — i.e., you calculate OID for each one-year period beginning on the date you acquired the bond or coupon. In the latter case, you use semiannual compounding — calculating OID for each six-month period beginning on the acquisition date and six-month anniversary date.

Stripped-preferred stock

Stripped-preferred stock is treated in generally the same manner as a stripped-bond, mentioned above. The difference between the acquisition and the redemption price of stripped-preferred stock is classified as OID. A portion of the OID is accrued and included in the income of the holder of the stripped-preferred stock each year. The OID amount included in income is treated as ordinary income, but is not characterized as interest or dividends (the treatment for stock purchased before May 1, 1993). The taxpayer's basis in such stock is increased by amounts included in income under the OID rules.

Stripped preferred stock is defined as any preferred stock where the ownership of the stock has been separated from the right to receive any dividend (and the dividend has not yet become payable). The underlying preferred stock qualifies if the stock is limited and preferred as to dividends, does not participate in corporate growth to any significant extent, and has a fixed redemption price in order to qualify.

Tax-exempt investments

Interest you receive from tax-exempt investments such as municipal bonds or municipal bond mutual funds are free from federal income taxes.

Most states exempt bonds that are issued within their borders from taxes, too, so they are doubly tax exempt. Check with your tax adviser to find out how your home state treats these bonds.

If you live in a high-tax state, an investment in double tax exempt municipal bonds is more attractive to you.

EXAMPLE

You live in Minnesota and are taxed at a rate of eight percent. You are also in the 36 percent federal tax bracket and itemize your deductions. That means your combined tax rate — 36 percent plus 8 percent — is 44 percent.

However, although your combined tax rate is 44 percent, you deduct state income taxes on your federal return; therefore, your net federal and state marginal tax rate is 41.12 percent, not 44 percent. The 41.12 percent is calculated as follows:

Your net marginal rate is the sum of your federal tax bracket — in your case, 36 percent — plus your **effective** state tax rate, meaning your state tax rate after you calculate the benefit of deducting your state tax on your federal return.

To figure your effective state tax rate, multiply your actual state tax rate (8 percent in your case) times one minus your federal rate of 36 percent (0.64 percent). The result — 5.12 percent — is your effective (true) state tax rate.

Therefore, a Minnesota municipal bond that pays 5.75 percent is the equivalent of a 9.77 percent taxable yield. To arrive at that figure, divide the yield on the bond — 5.75 percent — by 0.5888 (one minus 0.4112 — your combined federal and effective state tax rates).

TIP

See the Introduction to this book for a chart comparing the taxable and tax-free investment yields.

TIP

Just as the tax law allows you to deduct state income taxes on your federal return, some states such as Missouri allow you to deduct federal income taxes on your state return. And that, of course, reduces your true federal tax rate.

TIP

Most states levy taxes on the interest from out-of-state municipal bonds purchased by residents. There are a few exceptions to this rule, so check with your tax adviser.

If you invest in a bond fund that purchases issues from a variety of states, your fund will send you a letter outlining the sources of its income. Then it's up to you to figure out on what portion of the interest from the fund you must pay state and local taxes.

Municipal bonds — like corporate bonds — are rated by services such as Standard & Poor's and Moody's, and the higher the rating, the lower the risk of default and the lower the interest rate will be.

TIP

Generally, tax-exempt interest is not recorded on a Form 1099-INT. Rather, you'll receive a letter from your financial institution detailing your earnings. For information purposes only, you must report those earnings on line 8b of your Form 1040.

If you do receive a Form 1099-INT for tax-exempt interest, be sure to report the interest on line 1 of Schedule B of your Form 1040. Then several lines above line 2, subtotal the amounts on line 1. Below this subtotal, write "Tax-Exempt Interest" and show the amount. Then subtract this amount from the subtotal. List the result, which is your taxable interest income, on lines 2 and 4. As noted, you must also list the tax exempt amount on line 8a of your Form 1040.

TIP

> The payment of interest and principal of some municipal bonds is insured. Compare the interest rates and the strength of the entity insuring the obligation to determine whether an insured bond is a worthwhile investment for you.

CAUTION

> The tax laws do not allow you to claim a deduction for any expenses, including interest, associated with producing tax-exempt income. That means that if you borrow money to buy shares in a tax-exempt bond fund, you may not deduct the interest you pay.

CAUTION

> Some municipal bond funds invest in so-called economic development bonds or industrial development bonds. These bonds are issued by state and local governments to finance private business activities — construction of a shopping mall or a manufacturing facility, for example.

Some of these bonds pay interest exempt from regular federal income taxes but subject to the alternative minimum tax (AMT).

The AMT is imposed at a rate of 26 percent (28 percent for adjusted alternative minimum taxable income in excess of $175,000). It is a completely separate tax system designed to ensure that everyone pays his or her fair share of tax. See Chapter 8 for more information on AMT.

If your municipal bond fund invests in private-activity bonds, it will notify you by mail each year of the proportion of its income derived from these bonds.

TIP

> If you invest in these bonds directly, you are entitled to write-off expenses incurred in purchasing them. But, as noted, the interest income on them is subject to AMT.

CAUTION

> Certain state and local obligations may be guaranteed by the federal government. If these obligations were issued after 1983, the interest on them will generally be taxable to you. However, interest isn't taxable on obligations guaranteed by the Federal Housing Administration, the Department of Veterans Affairs, and the Student Loan Marketing Association.

CAUTION

If you receive Social Security benefits, tax-exempt interest is taken into account in determining whether a portion of your benefits are taxable.

CAUTION

Income exempt from taxation in the United States doesn't necessarily escape taxation abroad. For example, interest on municipal bonds is tax-free here but if you are living and working in Germany, you can expect to pay taxes on those earnings.

Treasury bills, notes and bonds

You pay federal taxes on the interest you earn from any so-called U.S. debt obligations — including Treasury bills, notes, and bonds; however, these earnings are exempt from state and local taxes. Therefore, if you live in a high tax state, Treasury securities may be especially attractive to you.

EXAMPLE

You are married, file jointly, and are in the 36 percent bracket. You live in sunny Los Angeles, California, and invest $100,000 in a 52-week Treasury bill earning interest at an annualized rate of 3 percent.

Your tax liability adds up this way:

- You pay $1,080 in federal taxes on the $3,000 you earned from your T-bill — that is, 36 percent times $3,000; however
- You pay no state and local taxes on your T-bill earnings.

Therefore, your after-tax earnings on the T-bill equal $1,920, for an after-tax yield of 1.92 percent.

If you'd invested your $100,000 in a certificate of deposit also earning interest at an annualized rate of 3 percent you would have to pay $1,080 in federal taxes *plus* state and local taxes of $300 — a marginal state tax rate of 10 percent times $3,000. You would be allowed to deduct these state taxes on your federal return, and the benefit to you is $108 — that is, $300 times 36 percent.

Your after-tax earnings on the CD would come to $1,728 — $3,000 of interest income minus $1,380 of federal and state taxes, plus a tax benefit of $108 from your state tax deduction. The state taxes actually reduced your after-tax yield from 1.92 percent to 1.73 percent.

TIP

You can easily defer all the interest you earn to the following tax year just by purchasing a T-bill that comes due next year.

You generally pay a commission — usually 0.2 percent to one percent of the face amount — when you buy Treasuries from your bank or broker.

CAUTION

These commissions reduce the return on your investment.

TIP

You can avoid paying commissions by purchasing Treasury securities directly from a Federal Reserve Bank. The Federal Reserve Banks, acting as agents for the Treasury Department, sell U.S. government obligations to the public without sales commissions.

Treasury bonds, notes, and T-bills are also generally available after issuance by the U.S. government in a secondary market.

EXAMPLE

An investor may purchase, in September of 199A, a Treasury note of $10,000 at 4 percent due to mature in August of 199B. The investor can sell the note at any time prior to its maturity date. Therefore, through a secondary market, investors have an endless array of maturity dates and denominations to choose from for Treasury bonds and notes.

A Treasury note or bond is issued for maturities of more than a year. You may buy notes that mature in more than four years for a minimum of $1,000 and notes that mature in four years or less for a minimum of $5,000. (If you buy a Treasury note at a discount, the rules for OID bonds, discussed earlier, apply.)

By contrast, a T-bill is a short-term obligation issued in denominations of $10,000, and in multiples of $5,000 thereafter. They mature in 90 days, 180 days, or 52 weeks. Treasury bills are issued at a discount. The interest equals the difference between the discounted price you pay for the bills and the face value you receive at maturity. You report this interest income when you redeem the bill at maturity.

If you sell a Treasury bill before it matures, the selling price may be part interest and part short-term capital gain or loss.

EXAMPLE

On July 1, 199A, you buy a 180-day, $100,000 T-bill issued at $97,000. If you hold the bill until it matures on December 27, you will report $3,000 of interest income — that is, the $100,000 you collect when you redeem the bill less the $97,000 you paid when the bill was issued.

Assume, however, that you sell the T-bill on August 29, 199A, for $99,000. Your total gain, of course comes to $2,000 ($99,000 minus $97,000). Of that amount, $1,000 is ordinary interest income, and the remaining $1,000 is short-term capital gain.

To calculate the interest portion, you allocate your total discount — $3,000 — over the number of days you hold the bond during its maturity period. So, in our example, you divide $3,000 by 180 days — the total maturity period — to calculate the amount of interest the bill earns each day — in this case, $16.67. Then, you multiply that amount times 60 days, the number of days you actually held the bill, to get $1,000.

If you sold the T-bill for only $98,000, your gain would come to $1,000, and the entire amount would be treated as ordinary interest income.

Treasury securities are backed by the full faith and credit of the United States government, so they're among the safest investments around.

Treasuries aren't for everyone since you must have the cash to meet the minimum investment requirements. Also, because they're such safe investments, their interest rates are generally lower than other types of investments such as corporate bonds. But that's the trade-off — safety vs. a higher rate.

3

ALL THE NEWS ABOUT DIVIDENDS

- What are the reporting requirements for dividends?
- Does the tax treatment of various types of dividends differ?
- How can you use tax-wise strategies to defer income?

Dividends are distributions of money, stock, or other property paid by a corporation, partnership, or trust from its earnings.

However, not all dividends are taxed. This chapter discusses which distributions are treated as dividend income plus some tax-wise strategies for deferring dividend income. Below are a few of the basics.

The law generally requires any person or company that pays you $10 or more a year in dividends to send you a Form 1099-DIV, "Dividends and Distributions." This form must be mailed to you by the last day of January in the year following the one in which you received your dividend.

If you don't receive your Form 1099-DIV within a few weeks of that date, contact the payor and ask for a duplicate. If you receive a Form 1099-DIV but don't agree with the amount of dividend income listed, telephone or write the payor and explain why the number is wrong and ask to be issued a corrected form. Once you receive this new Form 1099-DIV, make sure it's marked "corrected." That way, neither you nor the IRS will get confused about which form is the right one.

If you are unable to resolve your dispute with the payor that issued the Form 1099-DIV, report what you think is the correct amount on your tax return and include with your return an explanation of why you think the amount you're reporting is correct.

There's no need to attach Form 1099-DIV to your return. You report the amount of dividends you received on line 9 of Form 1040.

Box 1a of your Form 1099-DIV includes the total amount of dividends and other distributions you received during the year. In box 1b is the amount of your ordinary dividends (this figure is included in the total in box 1a).

Box 1e has your investment expenses. You write these off as miscellaneous itemized deductions on Schedule A of your Form 1040. (See Chapter 7 for more information.)

If your dividends total more than $400, you must list the amounts you receive — and from whom — on Schedule B of your Form 1040.

If your brokerage firm collects your dividends for you, you receive a Form 1099-DIV from your broker — not from the corporation that paid the dividend — at the end of the year. Therefore, on your Schedule B, you should list your dividends as coming from your broker, not from the corporation.

Don't sign your return until you compare the total dividend income you recorded with all your Forms 1099-DIV to make sure you haven't forgotten anything. If you fail to report all your dividend income, you may be subject to a penalty.

The penalty equals 20 percent of the additional tax due. You also pay interest on the dividend income you fail to report — beginning on the day your tax return was due.

DIVIDEND INCOME

The following items constitute dividend income.

Dividends earned by your children

The tax law allows you to report dividend income your children receive on your tax return **only** if certain requirements are met:

- the child is under the age of 14 at the end of the tax year,
- his or her unearned income totals no less than $500 but no more than $5,000, and
- the unearned income consists of interest and dividends only.

To report a child's dividend income on your return, file Form 8814, "Parent's Election to Report Child's Interest and Dividends," with your Form 1040.

CAUTION

Your children must file their own returns if they make estimated tax payments or you make estimated tax payments in their names. Furthermore, if your children had any overpayment from the previous year's tax return added to the current year's tax return, they must file their own return. Likewise, your children must file their own returns if they're subject to backup withholding.

When it comes to reporting your children's income on your tax return, there are a host of pluses and minuses to consider.

On the plus side is less paperwork. When you include your children's income on your return, you file only one return—not two, three, four, or more.

You also may benefit, tax-wise at least, by reporting your children's investment income on your federal return.

For example, if your investment expenses add up to more than your investment income, you may write off investment expenses only to the extent of your investment income. In your case, that means you may not write off all your expenses on your current return.

You carry forward any investment expenses you are not able to deduct currently to offset investment income in future years. Now, add your children's investment income to your own and report it on your tax return. Your children's income boosts your total investment income and allows you to offset more of your investment expenses on your current return.

On the minus side, reporting your children's investment income on your return boosts your AGI, which, in turn, may reduce the deductions for certain items and increase your tax liability.

EXAMPLE

The rules allow you to deduct miscellaneous itemized deductions only to the extent that they exceed 2 percent of your AGI. If your AGI adds up to $90,000, you may write off only those miscellaneous itemized deductions exceeding 2 percent times $90,000 — or $1,800. If you add your children's income to your own, and your AGI climbs to $95,000, your miscellaneous itemized deductions must exceed $1,900 before they're deductible.

Another downside of reporting your children's income on your return is that doing so may make their income subject to state income taxes. Often the income children receive is so small that it isn't subject to state taxes, or if it is, it is a very low rate. Adding the income your children receive to your own makes it subject to state taxes or subject to a higher rate.

TIP

See Chapter 24 of *The Price Waterhouse Personal Tax Adviser* for more information about your children's taxes.

Dividends from estates, trusts, or partnerships

If you are the sole beneficiary of a trust or estate that earns dividend income, in most cases you pay taxes on the amount of income the trust or estate receives. However, in certain cases the trust or estate will pay the taxes. If you're not the sole beneficiary or you're a partner in a partnership, you pay taxes only on the portion that belongs to you.

Your fiduciary or partnership will report your dividend income to you each year on Schedule K-1. Your copy of Schedule K-1 and its instructions will tell you where to report items from it on your Form 1040.

Dividends from foreign corporations

Some foreign governments — but not all — withhold taxes from dividends paid by companies in their countries. And the taxes in these foreign countries can be as much as double what they are in the U.S. For example, the top rate in Japan is 50 percent, while the top rate in France is 56.8 percent and Spain, 53 percent.

Now, let's say you own 100 shares of stock in a Japanese corporation, and it declares a dividend of 50 cents a share. When you receive your check, it totals $42.50 — not $50 — because the Japanese government, under a treaty with the United States, withholds taxes at a rate of 15 percent from the amount due you.

TIP

If you receive a dividend taxed in a foreign country and the United States does not have a treaty with that country, the tax withholding rate will generally be 30 percent.

Box 3 of your Form 1099-DIV lists the amount of foreign taxes withheld on your dividends, and box 4 identifies the country that withheld these taxes.

If you receive a Form 1099-DIV with entries in these boxes, you have a choice. You may deduct the amount of foreign taxes withheld as an itemized deduction under "other taxes" on Schedule A of your Form 1040, or you may file a Form 1116, "Foreign Tax Credit," with your Form 1040 and claim a foreign tax credit for the taxes you've paid.

This tax credit reduces the amount payable on your tax return by taking into account the taxes you've paid to foreign governments.

TIP

Most people are better off — tax-wise, at least — claiming a foreign tax credit rather than taking an itemized deduction. That's because a credit reduces your tax liability dollar for dollar. A deduction, meanwhile, simply cuts the amount of your income subject to tax.

Calculating your foreign tax credit is exceedingly complicated and not something most taxpayers want to tackle alone. If you receive investment income from abroad, you may want to seek help from your tax adviser when it comes time to file your return.

The rules that govern dividends paid by foreign corporations also apply to dividends from mutual funds that invest in foreign securities.

Let's say that more than 50 percent of your mutual fund's assets are invested in foreign securities. In this case, it may pass on to you the right to claim a deduction or foreign tax credit for the taxes the fund has paid. You'll find this amount listed in box 3 of your Form 1099-DIV.

The tax law doesn't require all foreign corporations to provide you with a Form 1099-DIV.

Loans taxable as dividends

If you are a stockholder in a corporation and receive a low-interest or no-interest loan from that company, income is "imputed" to you. This income equals the interest you would have paid if the loan were made as an arm's length transaction. However, you report the imputed income as dividend, not interest, income.

Your imputed dividend income equals the amount of the outstanding loan times the applicable federal rate (determined by the IRS and based on an average rate the federal government pays on its borrowings).

TIP

You are allowed an offsetting imputed interest deduction subject to the limitations on the deductibility of interest. (See Chapter 6 for the details.)

CAUTION

The rules governing low-interest and no-interest loans are complicated. Consult your tax adviser if you are party to such a loan.

Mutual fund dividends

If you invest in a stock mutual fund, and it pays you dividends on the stocks you own, these dividends are taxable to you. (See Chapter 13 for more on mutual funds.)

Patronage dividends

Patronage dividends — those you receive from a cooperative — are usually taxable. These amounts are tax-free *if* they're a return of some of the money you spent at the cooperative. A farm cooperative is a case in point.

Example

> You purchase $5,000 worth of livestock feed from your local farm cooperative and don't use this feed in your trade or business or as part of an investment. At year's end, the farm cooperative mails you patronage dividends totalling $50. This amount isn't taxable to you as long as the amounts you spent were for personal items, because it is actually a rebate of some of the amount you spent at the cooperative during the year.

Short-term gains that are taxed as dividends

If you own shares in a stock mutual fund, which earns short-term capital gains by selling shares it held for one year or less, any net short-term gains passed along to you in the form of dividends are taxed as dividends. Thus, you may not use short-term capital gains passed through to you by a fund to offset any capital losses you may have. (Long-term capital gains are taxed as capital gains. For the details, see Chapters 4 and 5.)

Spill-over dividends

Spill-over dividends are those dividends declared in October, November, or December by a regulated investment company (i.e., a mutual fund) or real estate investment trust (REIT) but not paid to you until January of the following year.

CAUTION

> A special rule applies to spillover dividends. You must pay taxes on these amounts in the current tax year, as long as the company pays you your dividends in January of the following year.

EXAMPLE

You own 1000 shares of a mutual fund. On December 15, 199A, the fund declares a quarterly dividend of 50 cents a share. You receive a check for the amount due you — $500 or 50 cents times 1000 shares — on January 13, 199B. Under the rules, you must report the $500 you received as income on your 199A tax return, even though you didn't pocket the money until 199B.

Dividends paid in stock or cash

Usually, dividends paid in the form of stock aren't taxable as ordinary income. Dividends paid in cash are reported on your Form 1040.

TIP

If you buy a stock on or near the date a dividend is declared, make sure that you receive all the money due you. Sometimes, sales aren't recorded in time by the corporation paying the dividend, and it forwards the payment to the former owner.

If you don't receive a dividend that you know is due, check with your stockbroker. He or she will help you correct the situation.

Dividend reinvestment plans

Dividends are taxed as ordinary income to you even if you choose to reinvest these dollars in additional shares of stock.

The tax law allows you to deduct fees you pay to participate in dividend reinvestment plans. Don't make the mistake some taxpayers do, and subtract these fees from your dividend income. Report your dividends in full, then write off these fees on Schedule A of your Form 1040.

Dividends from restricted stock

Restricted stock is stock you get from your employer for services you perform. It is referred to as restricted stock because it is not transferable to someone else, usually for a specified period of time. Often restricted stock is forfeitable, also for a specified period of time.

You are not required to add to your taxable income the value of the stock when it's awarded to you. However, you must pay taxes on any dividends you receive. These dividends, though, are taxed as *wages*, not dividends.

Your employer includes these amounts with your wages and reports them on your Form W-2. If you also receive a Form 1099-DIV reporting the same dividends, list the dividends from your restricted stock on Schedule B of your

Form 1040 along with all your other dividends. Then subtotal the amount. Beneath the subtotal, write "dividends on restricted stock reported as wages on line 7, Form 1040," and subtract the amount of these dividends.

Dividends from stock held jointly

Let's say you and a friend own 1,000 shares of stock in XYZ Corp. You purchased the shares for $10,000, and each of you contributed $5,000 toward the purchase price. Now, XYZ pays you $500 in dividends.

Who reports that amount as income? The answer is both of you. Each of you contributed 50 percent of the purchase price of the stock, so each of you is entitled to 50 percent of the dividends. You both report $250 in income on your returns.

What if you contributed 80 percent of the purchase price and your friend 20 percent? You would be entitled to 80 percent of the dividends and your friend, 20 percent. And each of you would report the amount you'd receive on your personal tax return.

CAUTION

A corporation paying dividends will record the amount only to the Social Security number of one person on Form 1099-DIV. And that's a problem when it comes to joint ownership.

If the total is reported to your Social Security number and you list only a portion of the income on your return, the IRS will probably send you a deficiency notice. Therefore, when you file your return, report the full amount of dividends paid on Schedule B of your Form 1040. Write "amount attributable to others" or "nominee distribution" in the dividend section of your Schedule B.

Then, subtract the portion that went to the other person. Also list on Schedule B the Social Security number of the person who jointly owns the stock.

Dividends from taxable money-market funds

When you invest in a money-market mutual fund, you buy shares in that fund. In most cases, you receive one share for every dollar you invest. What's more, your dividends are paid in shares.

EXAMPLE

You invest $20,000 in a money-market fund that earns interest at an annualized rate of four percent. Your $20,000 buys you 20,000 shares. By the end of the year, your 20,000 shares, or $20,000, grows to 20,800 shares, or $20,800 — that is, your principal plus $20,000 times four percent.

Money-market funds pool the dollars people deposit to invest in short-term obligations of federal, state, and local governments, as well as corporations and banks. The interest net of allowable expenses they receive is passed along to you in the form of dividends.

These dividends are taxed as *dividends*, not as interest income. (By contrast, interest on a money-market account at a bank is taxed as interest.)

If you make the mistake of reporting these amounts as interest income, you're likely to receive a letter from the IRS asking for an explanation. So make sure to list your income from money-market funds in the *dividend* section of Schedule B of your Form 1040.

TIP

Money-market funds pay a rate of return that's typically higher than most money-market bank accounts. And that's their primary advantage.

You may want to subscribe to a publication that tracks the performance of money-market mutual funds to find the account with the highest yield.

TIP

Money-market funds also offer you liquidity — that is, you may withdraw your money at any time and without penalty. So they are a good place for your emergency fund or temporary excess funds.

To take money out, all you have to do in the case of many money-market funds is write a check or, in some cases, visit an automated teller machine. You also may transfer or wire money to your checking account.

Another plus of money-market funds is protection when interest rates rise. Short-term interest rates usually rise with inflation, and so do your earnings from a fund.

CAUTION

Money-market funds — unlike money-market bank accounts — are not insured by the federal government. Therefore, you may want to evaluate the credentials of the mutual fund company or brokerage firm and identify what types of securities it holds.

Look at the prospectus of your fund to determine what types of securities your fund holds. The prospectus lists the types of obligations in which the fund invests.

Dividends from tax-exempt money-market funds

To reduce taxable income consider investing in a tax-exempt money-market fund. The interest you receive — in the form of dividends — isn't taxable on your federal tax return.

TIP

There's only one way to know whether a tax-exempt fund is right for you, and that's to run the numbers. Compare the return you would earn on a tax-exempt fund with the return from one that's taxable. Here is a simple formula to help you compare investment returns.

Divide the interest you expect to collect from your tax exempt fund by one minus your marginal tax bracket expressed as a decimal — 0.31 for example. The table below shows the differing yields between taxable and tax exempt dividends (and only takes federal taxes into consideration):

Tax Exempt Yield	3%	4%	5%	6%	7%
Equivalent taxable yield:					
28% bracket	4.17%	5.56%	6.94%	8.33%	9.73%
31% bracket	4.35%	5.80%	7.25%	8.70%	10.14%
36% bracket	4.69%	6.25%	7.81%	9.38%	10.94%
39.6% bracket	4.97%	6.62%	8.28%	9.93%	11.59%

Here's another way to look at it. You're in a 36 percent federal tax bracket and an 8 percent state bracket, and you're faced with a choice — invest $10,000 in a taxable money-market fund yielding 7 percent or in a money-market fund exempt from federal and state taxes yielding 5 percent.

Which investment makes the most sense for you?

If you invest in the taxable fund, you'll receive $700 in dividends each year. But from that amount you'll have to subtract $288 in federal and state taxes (taking into account the tax benefit of deducting the state taxes on your federal return; see Chapter 2 for details). So, from your $700 of dividend income, you'll net only $412, for an after-tax yield of 4.12 percent (compared to the pre-tax yield of 7 percent). If you invest in the tax-exempt fund instead, you'll receive $500 in dividend income each year — all of it tax free.

4

CALCULATING GAINS AND LOSSES ON YOUR INVESTMENTS

- Which method for determining basis helps you best manage the tax on your capital gains?
- When can you claim a capital loss?

Capital gain is the profit you make when you sell a capital asset. Almost everything you own including your investments is a capital asset. Stocks, bonds, mutual fund investments, gold, silver, antiques, personal residences, gemstones, and oriental rugs all fall into the capital assets category.

A long-term capital gain is the profit you make when you sell a capital asset that you've held for more than a year. A short-term capital gain, on the other hand, is the profit you make when you sell a capital asset that you've held for a year or less.

Long-term capital gains are generally taxed the same as ordinary income, such as salaries, interest, and dividends — with one exception. For taxpayers in the 31, 36 or 39.6 percent tax brackets, long-term capital gains are taxed only up to 28 percent. Short-term capital gains are taxed at the same rate as ordinary income.

The tax law requires investors to keep track of long-term capital gains and categorize them on their tax returns. The law also requires investors to keep track of short-term capital gains.

In this chapter, we run through the rules governing capital gains. For purposes of determining whether a gain is long- or short-term, you start counting from the day *after* you purchase an investment, and you include in the holding period the day you sold that investment.

EXAMPLE

You purchase 100 shares of ABC Corp. on January 30, 199A. As the rules require, you start counting your holding period on January 31. Now, say, you sell your shares for a profit on January 30, 199B. Your gain is short-term because you did not hold the stock for more than a year.

For securities traded on a public exchange, the holding period for tax purposes begins on, and the gain is taxable as of, the respective trading dates, not the settlement dates.

EXAMPLE

You sell some stock on the New York Stock Exchange on December 27, 199A. The rules of the stock exchange say that the trade closes with delivery of the stock five trading days after the sale — in your case, January 6, 199B. That's the same day you receive payment from the stock you sold.

The gain is reported in 199A — that is, the year the stock is traded — even though you did not receive the cash on the sale of the stock until 199B.

Your brokerage firm will send you a Form 1099-B "Proceeds From Broker and Barter Transactions," listing the proceeds from all your sales for the year based on the trade date. It's best to rely on this document for information when tax filing time rolls around, rather than on your brokerage statements.

Why? If you buy or sell stock near the end of the year, these trades may not appear on your December statement, and, as a result, you may overlook them.

But you should reconcile the information in your records with what's reported on your Form 1099-B.

If your Form 1099-B is incorrect, contact your brokerage firm or other financial services institution, and ask it to issue a corrected form. It is important that amounts shown on Form 1099-B be included in the proceeds reported on your Schedule D "Capital Gains and Losses" of Form 1040. If they don't match, the IRS will likely send you a notice and may assess a penalty for negligence if you have failed to report income.

You should be aware of the concept of netting because the law requires you to net your capital gains and losses. That is, you calculate your net capital gain or loss by first subtracting your short-term capital losses from your short-term capital gains, then subtracting your long-term capital losses from your long-term capital gains. Next, you combine your net long-term capital gains or losses with your net short-term capital gains or losses. The result is your net capital gain or loss.

EXAMPLE

	Long-term capital gain	capital loss	Short-term capital gain	capital loss
Greg	$500	(200)	300	(100)
Joanne	600		100	(900)
Jim	500		100	(400)

Greg will report a net long-term capital gain of $300 and a net short-term capital gain of $200. Joanne has a net long-term capital gain of $600 and a net short-term capital loss of $800, yielding a net short-term capital loss of $200 that may offset ordinary income. Jim has a net long-term capital gain of $500 and a net short-term capital loss of $300. Jim will report a $200 net long-term capital gain on his tax return.

CALCULATING YOUR BASIS

Basis is generally the amount you pay for an asset plus certain expenses such as sales commissions.

Basis is used to figure gain or loss on the sale or exchange of an asset. In other words, basis is subtracted from the sales proceeds to determine the gain or loss.

For each investment sold or exchanged during the year, a taxpayer must know:

- The number of shares bought
- The amount paid per share
- The date of each purchase
- The total dollar amount of the purchase, including items such as commissions and fees
- The number of shares sold or exchanged
- The price received per share from the sale or exchange
- The date of each sale or exchange
- The total dollar amount received from each sale or exchange

Most of this information may be obtained from personal records, monthly statements, and Form 1099-Bs from brokerage firms or financial institutions.

If less than all of the investment in a particular stock, bond, or other security is sold, you must also identify which shares were sold so you can determine the proper basis to use. There are two different methods to identify the shares sold.

Selling specific shares

If you know how many shares you bought when you purchased them, and how much you paid, the law requires you to use the specific share method. This method may give you a choice about whether to realize a gain or a loss.

EXAMPLE

You own 565 shares of stock in XYZ Corp. You purchased 250 shares at $10 a share in February 199A, 15 shares at $15 a share in January 199B, 200 shares at $14 a share in July 199B, and 100 shares at $12 a share in August 199B. Assume your broker holds your shares for you.

Now, you tell your broker on June 1, 199C, to sell the 200 shares you purchased in July 199B at $14 a share. Because you specified the shares to sell, figuring your basis is easy. In this case, it's $14 a share — the price you paid for them.

If you sell the 200 shares for $11 per share, you report a short-term capital loss of $3 per share — that is, your $11 selling price less your $14 basis. Your total loss comes to $600 — $3 times 200 shares. Since you owned the shares less than a year, your loss is a short-term one.

You may use your $600 loss to offset some capital gains you may have had from other transactions. If you had no capital gains, the rules say you can subtract the $600 from your ordinary income. There's a limit on how much capital loss you may deduct each year from your ordinary income. (More on this topic later in this chapter.)

TIP

It's important that you have a record of your instructions to sell specific shares. So make sure to keep a copy of your dated letter to your broker or fund.

CAUTION

Such instructions are only effective if the stock is held in "street name" — that is, the stock is held for you in the name of the broker or fund. **If the shares sold are held in your name, it does not matter what the instructions were — the actual certificates delivered are the ones that are considered sold.**

First in, first out

Where there are no records concerning the purchase of a stock, bond, or other investment, a taxpayer may have to use the first in, first out (FIFO) method (i.e., the first bought is the first one sold).

EXAMPLE

Using the facts in the previous example, you sell 200 shares of XYZ for $11 a share. Under the FIFO method, the shares you sell are considered the first ones you purchased — meaning the shares you purchased in February 199A.

You paid $10 a share for that stock, so that's your basis. Your gain, then, is $1 a share — your selling price of $11 minus your $10 basis — or a $200 long-term capital gain.

You can see what a difference FIFO makes — and not necessarily for the better. With FIFO, you must post a $200 long-term capital gain, while with the specific-share method (discussed above), you're able to claim a $600 capital loss.

Exceptions

There are a few exceptions to the rules governing basis. For example, if you receive stock as a gift, your basis is the basis of the stock to the donor at the time of the gift. In other words, the donor's basis becomes your basis.

What if you sell the stock at a loss? Then your basis is the lesser of the donor's basis or the fair market value of the stock on the date the gift was made.

A wash sale is a sale of stock at a loss either 30 days before or after you make another purchase of the same (or substantially identical) stock. Your basis in the new stock is what you paid for it; however, it's increased for any loss that is disallowed. See Chapter 5 for more on wash sales.

With Original Issue Discount securities, your basis is the amount you paid for the securities plus the interest income that accrues annually. (For more information on Original Issue Discount, see Chapter 2.)

Finally, if you inherit stock or some other capital asset, your basis is either the fair market value of the asset on the day the person died or its value six months after the person's death if the executor of the estate chooses that date to value the estate.

Your stock basis can also be affected if the corporation issues stock dividends, declares a stock split, makes a capital distribution, or undergoes a reorganization. If you find yourself in one of these situations, you may want to consult your tax adviser. The rules are complicated, and you may need professional help.

If you disposed of a mutual fund investment, see chapter 13 for information concerning the calculation of the capital gain or loss.

Capital Losses

The rules allow you to use your capital losses to offset your capital gains plus $3,000 of ordinary income. Also, the rules let you carry forward (indefinitely, until utilized) any capital losses you aren't able to deduct currently to future tax years.

Example

Your capital losses for the year come to $8,000, and your capital gains total $1,000. The difference between the two — $7,000 — is your net capital loss.

You may use up to $3,000 of this amount to offset your ordinary income. So, if your taxable income is $50,000, you could reduce it by $3,000. As for the remaining $4,000, you may carry forward this amount to offset income in future years.

Capital losses that you carry forward retain their "character"; that is, short-term capital losses remain short-term capital losses, and long-term capital losses remain long-term capital losses.

Caution

Don't make a common mistake and *lump* your capital *losses and gains* from passive investments, such as limited partnerships, with your other capital losses without first taking the passive loss rules into account. The law imposes special restrictions on the deductibility of passive losses. In most cases, you may deduct your capital losses from passive activities only to the extent of your passive income. See Chapter 9 for more information on passive losses.

Capital losses on collectibles

If you invest in jewelry, coins, stamps, antiques, or the like, and you incur capital losses on the sale of these items, the tax law allows a deduction only if the following conditions are met:

- you must prove that your primary purpose in purchasing the item was to make a profit, and
- you must show that you didn't purchase these items purely as a hobby or for your personal enjoyment.

TIP

Maintain detailed records on the purchase and sale of collectibles. Your reputation as an investor is your best defense upon an IRS audit.

Capital losses when your income is zero

If you had zero or negative taxable income before you deducted your capital losses, you may be able to carry forward all or a portion of your losses to next year.

EXAMPLE

You're single, and your taxable income — before you subtract your capital losses but after you claim your personal exemption — amounts to a $250 loss. Your net capital loss for the year adds up to $3,000.

To calculate how much of your capital losses you may carry forward to next year, add back to your taxable income — in your case, a $250 loss — your personal exemption of $2,350. The result is taxable income of $2,100.

You subtract $2,100 from $3,000 and the result — $900 — is the amount you may carry forward to next year (note that your taxable income for the current year is zero).

Capital losses on bonds bought at a premium

There may be instances when you pay a premium for a bond; that is, you pay more for it than its face value at maturity. This situation normally occurs when market interest rates fall below the interest rate of the bond. For information on the tax treatment of the premium, see Chapter 2.

5

GETTING THE MOST FROM YOUR CAPITAL GAINS

- Which strategies save taxes on capital gains and losses?
- When is business property treated as a capital asset?
- How does the use of installment sales effectively defer taxes?

What else do you need to know about capital gains? Let's take a look at some lesser-known facts about how capital gains and losses affect certain investments and, more importantly, some tax-saving strategies.

BUSINESS PROPERTY

If you invest in a business — a partnership or S corporation, for example — you are likely to have "Section 1231 gains and losses" reported to you on your Form K-1. Net Section 1231 gains receive long-term capital gain treatment.

Although property used in a trade or business is not considered a capital asset, the law provides that real estate or depreciable property used in a business that has been held for more than one year is Section 1231 property. All or a portion of the gain during a taxable year from the sale of Section 1231 property may be treated as Section 1231 gain (i.e., receive long-term capital gain treatment). Some of the gain may be considered ordinary income if it relates to prior depreciation expense. The partnership or S corporation will perform these calculations for you and the amount that is reported on your K-1 as Section 1231 gain or loss will be the amount eligible for Section 1231 treatment.

On the other hand, a net Section 1231 loss is deductible as an ordinary deduction without regard to the limitations on long-term capital losses. There may, however, be other limitations on deducting a Section 1231 loss — see, for example, the discussions on passive activities in Chapter 9 and at-risk rules in Chapter 18.

As a general rule, to determine whether there is a net Section 1231 gain or a net Section 1231 loss, add up all your Section 1231 gains for the year and then subtract all your Section 1231 losses. If the result is positive, you have a net Section 1231 gain. If the result is negative, you have a net Section 1231 loss.

CAUTION

If you did not deduct Section 1231 losses in the previous five years, all of the current-year Section 1231 gain will be treated as a long-term capital gain. But if you were able to deduct Section 1231 losses during that time period, only the portion of the gain which exceeds the prior year losses is treated as a long-term capital gain and the balance is treated as ordinary income.

Once a prior year Section 1231 loss is applied against a later Section 1231 gain — also known as being "recaptured" — causing that Section 1231 gain to be treated as ordinary income, it does not need to be recaptured again when additional Section 1231 gains are realized in subsequent years.

EXAMPLE

You had a Section 1231 gain of $400 reported on your K-1 from XYZ Partnership in the current year. You had no other Section 1231 gains or losses during the year. When you look back at your income tax returns for the five previous years you discover that the only net Section 1231 gain or loss was two years ago. In that year, you reported a Section 1231 loss of $500. Since your current year Section 1231 gain was less than that amount, it will all be treated as ordinary income.

Assume further that it's now a year later and you have a Section 1231 gain of $300. Since only $400 of your Section 1231 loss from two years ago was recaptured in the previous year, you must still recapture an additional $100 in the current year. Thus, you would have $100 of ordinary income and $200 of long-term capital gain.

INSTALLMENT SALES

An installment sale occurs when an asset is sold in one year and at least one payment is to be received in another year.

EXAMPLE

You purchased unimproved land in 199A for $60,000 and sell it in 199G for $100,000. The new owners agree to pay you over a two-year period; that is, they will make payments to you of $50,000 in 199G and 199H.

Under the installment sale rules, the taxable income you report in any year is based upon the amount of cash received during the year.

In 199G, your taxable gain from the sale is $20,000 — that is, one half the total gain since you received one half the selling price in 199G. You report your profit as long-term capital gain and pay taxes at your ordinary rate but not to exceed 28 percent.

CAUTION

You cannot report gain from the sale of stocks, bonds, or other securities that are publicly traded using the installment sale method. Also, the installment sale rules do not apply to most dealer dispositions or to sales of inventory, or if a sale results in a capital loss. For other installment sales, however, the law requires you to use the installment sale rules unless you make an election on your tax return to report all of your income in the year you make the sale.

CAUTION

If you sell an asset on the installment method, the sales price is more than $150,000 and total installment obligations exceed $5 million at the end of the year, you should consult your tax adviser. In this case, you may be required to pay interest on the amount of tax which is postponed under the installment sale rules.

LIKE-KIND EXCHANGES

A like-kind exchange is an exchange of one item for another that's similar. Like-kind exchanges are tax-free if the property received and given is used in a business or is held for investment.

CAUTION

A sale followed by a reinvestment in like-kind property does not qualify for this special treatment.

For example, assume that you trade gold bullion for Canadian Maple Leaf gold coins. Since you're exchanging gold for gold, your trade qualifies as a like-kind exchange and isn't taxable. Similarly, if you exchange one piece of rental real estate for another, that transaction also qualifies as a like-kind exchange.

Although seemingly inconsistent, when U.S. currency is converted into foreign currency, any profits are taxable. In other words, exchanges of currency do not qualify as like-kind exchanges.

This same rule applies to exchanges of partnership interests. Thus, when you trade an interest in one partnership for an interest in another, any gain is taxable.

Likewise, exchanges of inventory, stocks, bonds, notes, certificates of trust, securities, and chooses in action do not qualify as like-kind exchanges and are taxable.

The term "chooses in action" refers to a right or claim to personal property that the taxpayer does not have in his or her possession.

For example, you loan $2,000 to your brother-in-law and he gives you a promissory note representing the loan. This note is a chooses in action.

Other items that do not qualify as like-kind exchanges include exchanges of gold bullion for silver bullion and of male livestock for female livestock.

Under the rules, a taxpayer has 45 days from the date of disposition of one asset to *identify* another one to receive in exchange (e.g., in a signed document sent to the other party). Otherwise, the trade is taxable even if the asset was identified on the 46th day.

In addition, the taxpayer must complete the exchange through the receipt of replacement property by the earlier of 180 days from the date of the ownership transfer of the property or of the due date, including extensions, of his or her tax return for the year in which the exchange takes place.

EXAMPLE

It's July 13, 199A, and you transfer a parcel of farm land to another person in what is to be an exchange transaction. You have until August 27 (45 days from date of transfer) to properly identify a new piece of property to receive in exchange. Then, you have until January 9, 199B, (180 days from date of transfer) to actually receive the property and acquire title. If you meet these deadlines, the exchange is tax-free.

CAUTION

If you participate in a like-kind exchange, you should consult your tax adviser as the rules are complex.

PROPERTY SETTLEMENTS

When you transfer ownership of capital assets from one spouse to another in cases of divorce, the transaction isn't taxable — as long as neither spouse is a nonresident alien. The transfer must occur within one year from the date the marriage ends or, if the transfer is made under a divorce or separation agreement, it may not occur more than six years after the marriage ceases.

SHORT SALES

A short sale occurs when someone sells stock which he or she either does not own or does not want to transfer. The seller borrows identical stock — from a broker, for example — to deliver to the buyer. At a later date, the seller "covers" the short sale by either delivering the stock owned or acquiring identical stock and delivering it to the lender. The seller recognizes a capital gain or loss measured by the difference between the basis of the stock delivered and the proceeds received from its sale.

TIP

It is possible to report a current year paper profit on your stocks and have it taxed next year. In effect, you freeze a profit (or loss) and postpone the tax by using a technique known as a "short sale against the box." To do this, go to your broker and tell him or her you want to arrange a short sale.

EXAMPLE

On December 1, 199A, you own 1,000 shares of stock in XYZ Corporation with a basis of $10,000 and a current value of $30,000. The stockbroker allows you to borrow another 1,000 shares, using your existing shares as collateral. You then sell the borrowed shares, thus fixing your profit.

Sometime in 199B, you cover the short sale by delivering your original shares to the broker in repayment.

The result? The profit on the 199A short sale becomes next year's taxable income. From a tax standpoint you achieve a significant benefit because the tax on the sale is deferred.

CAUTION

If you borrow stock that you do not own to sell short (in which case you have simply a short sale, not a short sale against the box), you have the potential for unlimited losses if the price of the stock increases substantially before you acquire the shares to close the sale.

TIP

If the price of XYZ stock drops before you close the short sale by delivering the stock, you can "buy in" the short position and retain your low basis stock.

EXAMPLE

On January 12, when your short position is still "open" — that is, you haven't delivered stock to the lender — the value of 1,000 shares of XYZ drops to $20,000. You may want to buy in the short position by acquiring 1,000 new shares to cover the short position.

In this case you would recognize a capital gain of $10,000 ($30,000 sales price less the $20,000 cost of new XYZ shares), rather than the $20,000 gain you would have recognized if you had delivered the original shares. And the original shares would keep their basis of $10,000 and their long-term holding period.

STOCK OPTIONS

The buyer or the "holder" of an option has the right within a stated time period to buy or sell a specified amount of the underlying property at a stated price. The amount paid for a put or call (defined below) is called the "premium." The seller or "writer" of an option is obligated to sell or buy the underlying property at the stated price if the option holder exercises the option. Options are available on a multitude of assets.

The tax rules are generally the same for all options other than "Section 1256 contracts." A Section 1256 contract is any of the following:

- regulated futures contracts,
- any foreign currency contract,
- any nonequity option including options on commodities,
- commodity futures contracts, and
- debt instruments and broad-based stock indexes.

If you invest in Section 1256 contracts, you should consult your tax adviser regarding the special rules that apply. However, this discussion will cover only the tax aspects of noncompensatory put and call options on stock.

Puts

A put is an option to sell. As the holder of a put, you have the right to require the writer to purchase the underlying stock from you at the stated price.

If you buy a put and later exercise it, the premium you paid for the put reduces your proceeds from the sale of the underlying stock when you calculate your gain or loss on the sale of the stock. If your put expires before it is exercised, you generally recognize a short-term or long-term capital loss depending on how long you held the put before it expired.

If you are the writer of a put, you don't recognize income when you sell it. If the holder of a put you wrote allows it to expire, you generally recognize a *short-term* capital gain at the date it expires. The gain equals the premium received.

If the put is exercised and you — the writer of the put — have to buy the underlying stock, the premium you received for the put reduces your basis in the stock you buy. In this case, your holding period for the stock begins on the day the stock is bought — not on the day you sold the put.

If you write a put and want to cancel the put before it expires or is exercised, you may buy an identical put — that is, "buy in" the put. In this case, you would have a *short-term* capital gain or loss equal to the difference between the premium paid for the buy-in and the premium received on the sale.

TIP

Rather than selling stock short against the box, you may choose to buy a put. Similar to a short sale against the box, you are able to lock in a gain, but the tax on the gain is deferred until you exercise the put.

The disadvantage of buying a put is the option price in a put is usually less than the current market value of the underlying stock. And you have to pay for the put. But if you buy a put, rather than a short sale against the box, you may take advantage of future increase in the stock value.

EXAMPLE

You own 1,000 shares of APJ Corporation which you bought several years ago for $8,000. On December 3, 199A, 1,000 shares of APJ is worth $25,000 so you buy a put to lock in your gain. If the value of 1,000 shares of APJ soars to $40,000 on January 21, 199B you may choose not to exercise the put and sell your APJ stock on the market. Had you sold short APJ on December 3, you couldn't avail yourself of its subsequent price rise.

Calls

A call is an option to buy. If you are the holder of a call, you may require the writer to sell stock to you at the stated price. If you exercise a call you hold, the premium you paid for the call is added to the price you pay for the stock to determine your basis in the stock used to calculate the gain or loss when you later sell the stock.

If a call you hold expires, the premium you paid is generally a short-term or long-term capital loss depending on how long you held the call.

To briefly review these complex rules, you could sell a put or call you hold before it expires. If you do, you generally recognize a capital gain or loss. The amount of the gain or loss depends on what you paid for the put or call and how much you sold it for. The general rules for the determination of holding periods apply to the sale.

If you write a call, you do not recognize income when you sell it. If the holder of the call lets it expire, you generally recognize a *short-term* capital gain at the date it expires equal to the premium received.

If a call you write is exercised and you must sell the underlying stock to the holder, the premium you received for the call increases your sales proceeds when you calculate the gain or loss on the sale of the stock. In this case, the gain or loss is long-term or short-term depending how long you held the stock — not when the call was sold.

You may also buy in a call you write if you want to cancel it before it expires or is exercised. You do this by buying an identical call. In this case, you would have a *short-term* capital gain or loss equal to the difference between the premium paid for the buy-in and the premium received on the sale.

TAX-EXEMPT INVESTMENTS

Tax-exempt investments are not always tax-free. When a taxpayer sells or exchanges tax-exempt bonds or shares in a tax-exempt fund and posts a profit, he or she is taxed on the gain.

Similarly, when an investor shifts money between municipal bond funds, it's the same as selling shares in one fund and buying shares in another. Thus, any profit on the transaction is taxable as a capital gain.

CAUTION

Tax-exempt bonds purchased after April 30, 1993 at a market discount will generate some ordinary income upon disposition. Also, certain tax-exempt bond mutual funds may report ordinary income to shareholders if tax-exempt bonds are purchased below par.

INVOLUNTARY EXCHANGES

An involuntary exchange or involuntary conversion is the sudden loss of an asset and the receipt of insurance or other compensation (property) to replace it. Rental property destroyed by fire qualifies as an involuntary conversion, as well as land seized by a state highway department for use in the construction of a road.

If an asset is lost through an involuntary conversion and the taxpayer is compensated for it, the law says you must report the excess of the compensation over your basis as income on your tax return unless the money is reinvested in similar property generally within two years after the year compensated (certain exceptions apply to a personal residence).

EXAMPLE

You and your partners invest in an Ohio wheat farm. The U.S. Army Corps of Engineers announces plans to build a dam, and your farm is needed for the project.

The Corps agrees to pay you and your partners $100,000. If you and your partners reinvest the $100,000 in another farm in a timely way, none of you has to report that amount as income on your tax returns.

But if you and your partners decide to use the money to invest in stocks or bonds, you must report the excess of the $100,000 over your basis in the farm as taxable income on your tax return.

SMALL BUSINESS STOCK

To encourage investment in small businesses, the law allows taxpayers to deduct from ordinary income (e.g., wages, salaries, etc.) losses of up to $50,000 ($100,000 if married filing jointly) on so-called small business stock. Thus, if your stock qualifies as small business stock, losses aren't subject to the annual $3,000 capital loss limitation.

Stock of a small business corporation with total capital of not more than $1 million qualifies as small business or Section 1244 stock. The stock must be acquired directly from the corporation. Also, small business stock cannot be convertible into other securities of the corporation.

A company must meet a number of other requirements for its stock to qualify as Section 1244 stock. It is advisable to ask a company whose securities you're considering purchasing if its stock qualifies under these rules.

TIP

You should also know that the $50,000 ceiling on losses is per taxpayer per year (or $100,000 if married filing jointly). So if you're considering selling Section 1244 stock that will produce a loss of more than $50,000 in one year, you may want to stagger the sale of these shares over more than one year.

EXAMPLE

You're married, file jointly, and you've invested $200,000 in 1,000 shares of Section 1244 stock. You plan to sell the stock at a loss of $150,000.

If you sell all your shares in 199A, you deduct only $100,000 from your ordinary income. The remaining $50,000 is treated as a long-term capital loss; that is, you may use it to offset your capital gains but the excess may be written off only at the rate of $3,000 a year.

TIP

A better idea is to sell enough of your stock in 199A to generate a $100,000 loss, then sell the remaining stock in 199B. That way, the entire loss is deductible from your ordinary income much sooner. (You file Form 4797, *Sales of Business Property*, with your tax return to report your loss from Section 1244 stock.)

Capital Gains Exclusion for Small Business Stock

Individual taxpayers who hold qualified small business stock issued after August 10, 1993 which is held for more than five years can exclude up to 50 percent of gain on its disposition. Thus, investors acquiring such stock will be able to first take advantage of the exclusion in 1998. The other half of the gain is treated as capital gain, taxed at a maximum rate of 28 percent. To qualify, the stock must be acquired directly by the taxpayer (or indirectly through a "pass-through" entity such as an investment partnership) at its original issue.

TIP

This exclusion reduces the effective tax rate on qualifying gains to 14 percent (50 percent of gain taxed at a 28 percent tax rate), as long as the investor isn't subject to the AMT (see below).

For investors to qualify for the exclusion, the stock must be acquired in exchange for money, property other than stock, or as compensation for services.

What kind of stock qualifies for this tax break? Basically, small businesses with $50 million or less of capitalization qualify. The business can't be involved in the performance of personal services (e.g., health or law) or in the finance, banking, leasing, real estate, farming, mineral extraction, or hospitality industries. Other types of businesses, such as investment companies, are also disqualified. Other eligibility restrictions and special rules apply as well.

CAUTION

There is a limit to the available exclusion. Gain eligible for the exclusion is limited to the greater of ten times the investor's basis in the stock or $10 million.

TIP

Losses on qualifying stock are not limited to 50 percent but are subject to the general capital loss limits. If the stock qualifies as Section 1244 stock (discussed earlier in this chapter), part or all of the loss on its sale or disposal will generally be classified as ordinary (i.e., fully deductible against ordinary income.)

CAUTION

One half of any exclusion claimed is considered to be a preference for alternative minimum tax (AMT) purposes. See Chapter 8 for more information on AMT.

Rollover of gain from sale of publicly traded securities into specialized small businesses

To further spur investment in small businesses, certain taxpayers including individuals may elect to roll over capital gains realized on the sale of publicly traded securities where the sales proceeds are used to purchase common stock or a partnership interest in a specialized small business investment company (SSBIC) (a partnership or corporation licensed by the Small Business Administration) within 60 days of the sale of the securities.

Investors may take advantage of this rollover election on sales of publicly traded securities on or after August 10, 1993. However, the rollover is limited to $50,000 each year for individuals (lifetime cap of $500,000).

CAUTION

This gain rollover results in only a deferral of taxation, since an investor's basis in SSBIC common stock or partnership interest is reduced by the amount of capital gain not recognized.

TIP

Before electing rollover treatment, consider offsetting the capital gain against any capital losses that otherwise may not provide a current benefit.

WASH-SALE RULES

The wash-sale rules prevent a taxpayer from selling stock, including stock in a mutual fund, at a loss, writing off the loss on his or her tax return, then immediately buying the stock back.

These rules provide that a loss may not be deducted if, within a period beginning 30 days before the sale of a security and ending 30 days after that date (a period of 61 days), the taxpayer acquired or entered into a contract or option to acquire "substantially identical stock or securities."

Moreover, the Supreme Court has ruled that a taxpayer may not take a loss if his or her spouse purchases identical shares. The rules don't apply, however, if the new stock or security is received through a gift, bequest, inheritance, or tax-free exchange.

EXAMPLE

On September 15, 199A, you bought 1,000 shares of XYZ stock for $10,000. On March 22, 199B, you bought an additional 1,000 shares of XYZ for $9,750. On April 15, 199B, you sold the 1,000 shares you purchased on September 15 for $9,000.

Since you bought 1,000 shares of the same stock within the period beginning 30 days before the date of the sale and ending 30 days after that date, you may not claim a $1,000 loss on your return.

However, the basis of the shares you retained is increased by the amount of the loss, thereby reducing the gain, if any, on their ultimate sale. Also, the holding period of the shares you sold is added to the shares you retained. Thus, the shares purchased on March 22 would have a basis of $10,750 ($9,750 plus $1,000) and the holding period would be increased by seven months.

WORTHLESS SECURITIES

A capital loss can be claimed in the year securities (e.g., stocks, bonds, etc.) become worthless. Determinations of whether stock has become worthless, and if worthless, the year in which it ceased to have value, are questions of fact, and the burden of proof is on the taxpayer. Thus, you should consult your tax adviser before claiming a deduction on worthless securities.

CAUTION

Mere shrinkage in value of stock of a corporation through market fluctuations or otherwise does not entitle you to a loss deduction, and, in such case, the loss is allowable only upon the disposition of the stock.

CONVERSION TRANSACTIONS

If an investor is essentially in the economic position of a lender with respect to certain transactions involving dispositions of property, there are rules which require capital gains recognized on the disposition of property to be recharacterized as ordinary income. Consult your tax adviser for more information.

STATE TAXES ON CAPITAL GAINS

Some states tax long-term gains differently than short-term capital gains. Consult your tax adviser for the rules applicable in your state.

CAPITAL GAINS THROUGH MUTUAL FUNDS

For a discussion of the capital gain that your mutual fund passes along and retains, see Chapter 13.

6

THE RIGHT WAY
TO WRITE OFF
INTEREST

- How can you maximize your mortgage interest deduction?
- When is investment interest deductible?
- How do you "trace" interest on a multi-purpose loan?

Interest — the cost of borrowing money — is probably the most complicated of all deductible expenses. It's complicated because some interest costs are deductible, some are not, some are only partly so, and the situation changes from year to year.

Interest charges fall into a number of categories — personal interest, business interest, and so on. In this chapter, we look at the ones investors are most likely to claim and provide tax-saving strategies for each. Let's start, though, with a few words about leverage.

LEVERAGED INVESTMENTS

Leverage is using borrowed money to make an investment. The objective of leverage is to earn more income (through investing the borrowed funds) than your net-of-tax interest cost. Your goal is to deduct your interest and enhance the return on your investment because your total return is measured only on the amount of your own money invested.

EXAMPLE

You pay out $20,000 to buy 2,000 shares of a stock selling for $10 a share. If the price of the stock rises to $15, the value of your holdings climbs to $30,000. Your gain is $10,000 — equal to the market price of $30,000 minus your $20,000 purchase price. Therefore, your return is 50 percent ($10,000 divided by $20,000).

If you had purchased 4,000 shares of stock at $10 a share for $20,000 in cash and $20,000 in credit, you would have $40,000 worth of the same stock. Then, if the stock price goes up to $15 a share, the value of your holdings would equal $60,000. You pay back the loan, and what have you got? $20,000 more than your original investment of $20,000. And your gain is 100 percent — not 50 percent.

That's how leverage — in a best-case scenario — works; but leverage carries risk, too. Let's say — as in the example above — you bought 2,000 shares of XYZ stock at $10 a share. Instead of the stock rising to $15 a share, it plunges to $5 a share.

If you sell your shares, you post a $10,000 loss — your original investment of $20,000 minus the $10,000 you received for your shares.

However, if you had purchased 2,000 shares with your own money and 2,000 shares on credit and, again, the stock plummets to $5 a share, your loss adds up to $20,000. You sell the shares and receive $20,000 — just enough to repay the loan. Thus, your entire original cash investment of $20,000 is gone.

Does it make sense for you to leverage — or borrow — to make an investment? The answer may be yes if your after-tax rate of return on the leveraged investment tops the after-tax cost of borrowing.

You also must weigh the risks of investment. So, as with any investment, it's more an economic decision than a tax decision.

INTEREST DEDUCTIONS — THE BASIC RULES

Interest is deductible in the year it's paid. If you pay by check, the day you mail or deliver the check is the date of the payment.

If you pay by telephone or wire transfer, the day the money is transferred is the date of payment. The date of payment is listed on the statement your bank or other financial institution mails you each month.

Prepaying interest is not helpful — from a tax standpoint, at least. For example, you borrow $5,000 on June 1, 199A, to purchase 500 shares of stock in a high technology company. In December, you pay eleven months of interest.

Under the rules, you may write off interest payments for seven months — meaning those you made for June through December of 199A. Interest you prepaid for January, February, March, and April of 199B isn't deductible until you file your 199B return.

If you're thinking about deducting interest on money you borrowed on your life insurance policy, it also pays to know the rules.

The tax rules tell you if you file your return using the cash basis of accounting — as almost all of us do — you may only write off interest on these loans when payment is actually made. For example, you're not entitled to a current deduction for interest if the insurance company deducted the interest in advance from the amount of the loan, or you didn't make interest payments when due and the insurance carrier added the interest due to the loan.

If you borrow money to make interest payments, the IRS says you may not deduct any interest you pay with borrowed funds unless you borrow from a different lender. If you take out a loan from the same lender, then there is no deduction until the loan is repaid.

You may not write off interest on a debt unless you're legally liable for it — that is, you're a party to the loan. In other words, the interest payments you make on your brother-in-law's loan aren't deductible on your return, unless you're personally liable for these amounts.

It would be a better idea to give your brother-in-law the cash to make the interest payment, so he, at least, can write off the interest; otherwise, the deduction is lost.

You also may not write off interest on a debt unless — according to the tax code — a "true debtor-creditor relationship" exists.

EXAMPLE

You and your husband loan your son $5,000 to help him make the downpayment on his first house. "Thanks, Mom and Dad," he says and promises to repay you someday. Meanwhile, you're not holding your breath until that day comes. There is no loan repayment schedule and nothing is in writing. In this situation, he may not deduct any interest payments he makes to you because no true debtor-creditor relationship exists.

Now, let's change this scenario slightly. Your son borrows $5,000 from a local bank to purchase some stock, and you cosign the note. Both of you are legally liable for the loan, and whoever makes the interest payments is entitled to an interest deduction.

CAUTION

If you make payments for your children, the IRS may consider it a gift. Consult your tax adviser if you're considering assisting your children in this manner.

RULES FOR DEDUCTING INTEREST EXPENSE

As you read the pages that follow, keep in mind that there are only two ways to reduce the cost of borrowing:

- share the cost with the government, or
- pay a lower rate of interest.

So when it comes time for you to borrow, "you better shop around". Interest rates vary from one institution to another, and so do the fees — such as points — charged to lend you money.

Mortgage interest

If you borrowed money to purchase a home, the mortgage interest is 100 percent deductible on your Form 1040 — as long as you incurred the debt on or before October 13, 1987. However, if you signed your mortgage loan after that date some restrictions may apply.

For example, you may deduct mortgage interest only on principal amounts to purchase a home of up to $1 million. Any interest paid on the principal portion of your mortgage in excess of $1 million is not deductible.

Additionally, interest on home-equity loans is deductible only up to $100,000 of principal. However, this interest is deductible regardless of how the money is used — unless the loan proceeds are used to purchase a tax-exempt investment (for alternative minimum tax purposes, interest on a home-equity loan is generally not deductible — see Chapter 8 for more details).

Say, for example, you borrow money on your home-equity line to make an investment. The interest is still deductible as mortgage interest.

The rules require that the mortgage be secured by the property — be it a house, a cooperative apartment, a condominium, a house trailer, or a boat. Trailers and boats, though, must include basic living accommodations — for example, space for sleeping as well as cooking and bathroom facilities.

TIP

The IRS has indicated that a single debt may qualify as partially acquisition and partially home equity indebtedness. The IRS provides the following example: "If a taxpayer incurs a debt secured by his qualified residence and uses a portion of the debt proceeds to refinance an existing acquisition indebtedness and uses the remaining portion of the debt proceeds for purposes other than the substantial improvement of the residence, the portion of the debt used to refinance the acquisition indebtedness will qualify as home equity indebtedness, subject to the $100,000 limitation on home equity indebtedness." Under these circumstances, the maximum limitation on acquisition indebtedness would be $1,100,000 (maximum acquisition indebtedness plus the maximum home-equity loan limit).

Business interest

Business interest is, generally, 100 percent deductible. If you're faced with a choice of borrowing to make an investment or to raise capital for your business, borrow for your business. That way, you're guaranteed to get a deduction for the entire amount of interest paid.

Investment interest

Interest on money you borrow to make an investment is probably tax-deductible depending on the type of investment.

The general rule is that your deduction of investment interest in any one year is limited to the amount of your investment income. In other words, if you don't make money on your investments in any specific year, you may not deduct the interest on your investment loans.

EXAMPLE

You are an active investor and earn $15,000 in taxable dividends and interest from various stocks and bonds during one year. If you borrowed money to purchase some of those investments, you may write off up to $15,000 in interest expenses.

If your investment-interest expenses for the year add up to more than $15,000, the rules allow you to carry forward the amount not deducted indefinitely.

EXAMPLE

Your investment interest expense for the year totals more than $15,000 — $20,000, say. You may write off $15,000 of the interest against your current year's investment income, and you may carry forward the $5,000 balance into next year or beyond. In other words, you may carry forward the $5,000 until you generate enough investment income — from dividends, interest, and capital gains — to offset the deduction.

TIP

You can convert investment interest to deductible home-equity interest by borrowing against your first or second home. Interest on the loan is totally deductible as long as your home-equity debt doesn't top $100,000.

Subsequent to 1992, a taxpayer may elect to include any portion of net long-term capital gain (LTCG) as investment income for purposes of determining the investment interest limitation. (Note: Prior to 1993, no election was required and net LTCG was always included as investment income in the determination of the investment interest limitation). Any portion of LTCG included in investment income for this reason is subject to ordinary income rates which may be greater than the LTCG rate of 28 percent.

EXAMPLE

You have the following items to consider in your 199C tax return (which is subsequent to 1992):

Interest income	$5,000
Dividends	8,000
Net LTCG	25,000
Investment interest	20,000

Prior to 1993 you would have been able to deduct the full amount of investment interest. In 199C, you will be limited to an investment interest deduction of $13,000 unless you elect to include a portion of the net LTCG in the determination of the investment interest limitation.

If you elect to include $7,000 of the net LTCG as investment income, all your investment interest will be deductible. However, by doing this $7,000 of the LTCG will lose its character as such and be taxed at ordinary income tax rates. Only the remaining $18,000 of net LTCG will be taxed at a maximum rate of 28 percent.

TIP

Remember that unused investment interest may be carried forward indefinitely. It may make sense to forego the election to include net LTCG if the investment interest carried forward may be usable in the near future. Consult your tax adviser and run the numbers.

CAUTION

You are not allowed to deduct interest on money you borrow to invest in tax-exempt municipal bonds or tax-exempt municipal bond funds. And in this case it doesn't matter if the loan qualifies as home-equity debt. The interest still isn't deductible.

If you borrow money and use half of it to invest in tax-exempt bonds and the other half to purchase stock, you may write off the interest on the part that goes to purchase stock. However, the interest on the part used to buy the tax-exempt bonds is not deductible.

CAUTION

Interest expense on money you borrow to buy single-premium life insurance policies, endowments, or annuities is not deductible.

This restriction includes contracts on which you pay almost all the premiums within four years of the date you purchase the policy, as well as contracts on which you deposit an amount with the insurance carrier to cover future premium payments.

If you're a partner in a partnership and your partnership purchases some stock on margin, your portion of the related interest is passed along to you on a Schedule K-1. You are allowed to deduct this interest as investment interest.

Now, suppose you're a shareholder in an S corporation and your S corporation purchases stock on margin. The interest — as in the case of a partnership — is passed along to you and deducted on your personal return as investment interest.

CAUTION

Don't let the tracing rules trip you up. These rules require you to deduct interest based on how the proceeds from the loan were used.

EXAMPLE

You borrow $25,000 and deposit the money in your NOW account. You use the proceeds to buy some stock, a car for your son, and a computer for your business. This loan — according to the tax law — produces three kinds of interest:

- the interest on the money you use to purchase stock is investment interest,
- the interest on the dollars used to purchase the car for your son is personal interest, and
- the interest on the money that goes to purchase a computer for your business is business interest.

Usually, when you take out a loan, you either use the proceeds at once for a particular purpose, or you deposit them in your checking or savings account for a time.

If you deposit the proceeds in an account containing some of your other funds, the interest on the loan is classified as investment interest. And it remains investment interest until you take the money out of your account and use it.

What's more, if you want the interest classified by how you actually use the loan proceeds, you must spend the money you borrow within 30 days before or after the money you borrow is actually deposited into your account. You're asking for trouble if you wait longer than 30 days. If you wait more than 30 days, the law requires you to base your interest deduction on the first purchase you make from your account which may not have been what you intended for the loan proceeds.

EXAMPLE

You borrow $20,000 on January 2 to buy some stock in a high-technology company. You deposit the money in your NOW account which already has a balance of $25,000.

On February 6, your car breaks down. So you buy a new one for $20,000. On February 10 — 40 days after you took out the loan — you buy the stock. You fork over $20,000 for 2,000 shares of XYZ Corp. How is the interest treated for tax purposes?

Interest on the entire $20,000 loan is treated as investment interest until February 6, when you buy a new car. Then the interest on the $20,000 you borrowed is treated as personal interest — in other words, as if you'd borrowed the money to purchase the car.

Now, here's another scenario. Your balance in your personal savings account is $15,000. You then borrow money to invest in an interest-bearing bond. Six months later, you sell the bond and use the proceeds to pay off all your credit cards.

The interest is treated as investment interest for the six months you owned the bond. Then it's personal interest because you used the money to repay your credit cards.

TIP

An easy way to have kept your deduction as investment interest — and fully deductible from your investment income — was to have used the money in your savings account to pay off your credit card bills.

Personal interest

The interest on charge accounts and loans that you take out strictly for personal reasons — car loans, let's say — is not deductible.

Since personal interest is not deductible you may be better off using some of your dollars to pay off your consumer debts rather than investing them.

How do you know what makes the most sense for you? We've included a chart below that illustrates how much you need to earn on an investment — given your tax bracket and the interest you're paying on your loan — before that investment makes financial sense for you.

PRE-TAX COST OF BORROWING *

		\multicolumn{8}{c}{Interest Rate}							
		5%	6%	7%	8%	9%	10%	11%	12%
		Equivalent Pre-tax Return on Investment							
Tax	15%	5.9	7.1	8.2	9.4	10.6	11.8	12.9	14.1
Bracket	28%	6.9	8.3	9.7	11.1	12.5	13.9	15.3	16.7
	31%	7.2	8.7	10.1	11.6	13.0	14.5	15.9	17.4
	36%	7.8	9.4	10.9	12.5	14.1	15.6	17.2	18.8
	39.6%	8.3	9.9	11.6	13.2	14.9	16.6	18.2	19.9

* This ignores any potential impact of the itemized deduction limit and the personal exemption phaseout discussed in Chapter 1.

TIP

Here's an idea for writing off consumer interest: Borrow the money from yourself — from your own savings. Then, pay back the principal plus interest just as you would a bank. You're effectively getting a deduction on your loan interest because you're not reporting interest income on the amount you took out of the account.

PASSIVE ACTIVITY INTEREST

Passive activities, which we cover in detail in Chapter 9, are generally businesses in which you don't materially participate in the management. Passive activity interest — that is, interest expense on loans used to purchase a passive activity — is deductible only from passive activity income. You may not write it off against wages, salaries, or any other income.

The tax law says you're not entitled to a deduction if you don't report any passive income. But — here's the good news — you may carry forward passive interest that you're unable to deduct to offset passive activity income in future years.

What's more, in the year you sell or dispose of a passive investment, you may deduct the interest related to that activity that you weren't previously able to write off.

7

How To Make Your Deductions Work For You

■ How to tell what is deductible as an investment expense?

■ How the different limitations work against you?

■ How municipal bonds take the deduction out of investment expenses?

Y ou can often lower your income taxes by itemizing deductions on your tax return. The rule of thumb for any taxpayer is, if you can itemize and the deductions (net of all limitations) exceed the standard deduction, you should.

In this chapter, we cover investment-related miscellaneous itemized deductions — expenses subject to the two percent floor.

What is the two percent floor? Take your adjusted gross income (AGI). Multiply by two percent. This number is the floor. Add up your miscellaneous itemized deductions. If their sum is greater than two percent of your AGI — and you itemize — you may deduct the difference.

For example, if your AGI totals $200,000, two percent of this sum equals $4,000. Your miscellaneous itemized deductions come to $6,000. If you itemize on your return, you may deduct $2,000. This amount will be added to your other itemized deductions.

Don't confuse the 2 percent floor on miscellaneous itemized deductions with the 3 percent floor on all itemized deductions (see Chapter 1). To calculate your allowable deductions, you first determine the amount of miscellaneous deductions you can take by applying the 2 percent floor. Then you add in this result with other itemized deductions that are subject to the 3 percent floor discussed earlier.

INVESTMENT-RELATED MISCELLANEOUS DEDUCTIONS

The tax law allows you to write off as miscellaneous itemized deductions those expenses you incur that are associated with your investments — as long as those investments produce taxable income.

If all your money is in tax-exempt bonds, you are not entitled to a deduction for investment-related expenses.

What if your money is in taxable *and* tax-exempt bonds, and you cannot identify the expenses associated with each type of investment? You are required to perform this simple calculation. First, add up your income from the taxable bonds and income from the tax-exempt bonds, then add these two numbers together. Next, divide your taxable bonds income by the total bond income. The result is the percentage of investment expenses you may deduct, subject to the two percent floor.

EXAMPLE

Your taxable interest for the year adds up to $4,800, and your tax-exempt interest comes to $1,200; your expenses total $500. Your expenses don't specifically relate to the type of income your investments produced, so the rules require you to perform the following calculation.

Add up your interest income — that is, your taxable interest of $4,800 plus your tax-exempt interest of $1,200 — to get $6,000. Next, divide your taxable interest — $4,800 — by your total interest income — $6,000 — to get 80 percent. That's the amount of your expenses attributable to your taxable bonds, 80 percent of $500, or $400. The 20 percent remaining — $100 — is attributable to your tax-exempt bonds and not deductible.

How to lower your tax bill

The following alphabetical checklist will help you take advantage of investment-related deductions that could lower your tax bill. Remember, some portion of deductions such as these may be allocable to tax exempt income and, therefore, not fully deductible. Furthermore, these expenses will be subject to the 2 percent floor.

Accounting fees

Do you use an accountant to keep track of your investments or help you with your tax matters or investment planning? The fees charged by the accountant are deductible.

Administration fees for an IRA

You may deduct trustee fees you pay in connection with your Individual Retirement Account (IRA) — as long as the fees are billed separately and not paid with dollars deposited in the IRA account.

Remember that these expenses belong on Schedule A of your Form 1040 — *not* on line 24 of your 1040 where you claim your IRA contribution.

CAUTION

Do not make the mistake some taxpayers do and deduct capital expenses, such as the commissions you pay a broker, as IRA administration fees.

Commissions you pay when you buy and sell stock in your IRA account are capital costs, and the rules require you to add them to your basis when it comes time to calculate your gain or loss. (See Chapter 4 for the details on figuring your basis.)

CAUTION

You also may want to think twice before you allow trustees to take their fees out of dollars you contributed to your IRA. Why? Doing so will reduce the money accumulating in your IRA.

Bank fees

Fees that banks charge you to service your investment-related account are deductible, but you may not write off check-writing expenses, even if you have an interest-bearing account.

Likewise, you may write off fees that banks or brokers charge you to collect interest and dividends on the taxable bonds and stocks you own.

Clerical help and office rent

You may deduct office expenses, such as rent and clerical help, you incur in connection with managing your taxable investments.

CAUTION

The tax law will not allow you to deduct home office expenses if you use your home office to monitor your investments. Why?

Although you have a profit motive, investment activities on your own behalf are not considered a trade or business.

You also may not write off the cost of a security system installed to protect investments — for example negotiable bonds or art objects — from theft.

Computers

You can deduct through depreciation the cost of a computer which you use to keep track of your investments; but, you may write off *only* that portion of the use attributable to investments.

For example, if you pay $5,000 for a computer and use it 60 percent of the time for managing your investments. The law allows you to depreciate 60 percent of the cost of the computer.

That means that you can write it off gradually over five years or more.

TIP

If you'd like more information on deducting the cost of your computer, see Chapter 18 of the *Price Waterhouse Personal Tax Adviser* or ask the IRS for a free copy of Publication 534, *Depreciation*.

Custodial fees for dividend reinvestment plans

Some companies charge custodial fees when dividends are automatically reinvested in additional shares. Fees paid for holding shares acquired through a plan and collecting and reinvesting cash dividends are deductible.

Fees that companies charge for keeping individual records and providing detailed statements of accounts may also be written off. And, you may deduct monthly service charges you paid to a bank or other financial institution to participate in an automatic investment plan.

Investment adviser fees

Fees paid for investment advice are deductible. But what if you pay for investment advice and aren't able to itemize? You lose the deduction.

Investment club expenses

If you belong to an investment club that is organized as a partnership, expenses your club incurs in producing investment income and managing its investments are passed along to you on a Schedule K-1. Report your portion of these amounts as a miscellaneous deduction on Schedule A of your Form 1040.

Legal fees

Fees paid to attorneys for assistance with investments are deductible *only* if they aren't part of the cost of acquiring or defending title to an investment.

If, for instance, you use an attorney to help you buy stock in a company, the fee isn't deductible. Rather, it's part of the capital cost of purchasing the stock.

The fee is added to the basis in the property when you sell the stock and calculate your gain or loss. (See Chapter 4 for more on basis.)

You also may not write off attorney's fees related to your tax-exempt investments.

Mutual fund fees

Not all miscellaneous expenses are subject to the two percent floor. For people who invest in publicly-traded mutual funds, shareholder expenses incurred by the fund aren't subject to the two percent floor.

Postage, supplies, and safe deposit box rental

You may deduct the cost of postage and supplies that are related to managing your investments. The cost of renting a safe-deposit box, provided the box is actually used to store taxable investments or papers related to these investments, may be deducted.

If the box is used only to store jewelry and other personal items or tax-exempt securities, the safe-deposit box fee isn't deductible.

Proxy fights

If you wage a proxy fight opposing management of a company in which you are a stockholder, the IRS allows you a deduction for your expenses.

Proxy fights waged for personal reasons are one exception to this rule. Say, for example, as a shareholder in a pharmaceutical company, you wage a proxy fight to halt its practice of testing drugs on animals. Your expenses aren't deductible because the fight is for personal reasons.

Seminars and conventions

The costs of attending investment-related seminars and conventions, including travel and meal expenses, are not deductible.

Service fees

Service fees paid to a broker, a bank, a trustee, or other agent to collect your taxable interest or dividends on shares of stock are deductible. Remember, though, that the fee paid to a broker to buy investment property, such as stocks or bonds, is not a service fee but a capital expense — and is not deductible.

Stockholder meetings

Transportation and other costs of attending stockholder meetings of companies incurred by shareholders are not deductible. However, these expenses may be written off if you're a shareholder and an officer or director of the company and the company is not reimbursing you.

Subscriptions

Subscriptions to investment-related publications are deductible, but the tax law will not allow the write off of multiple-year subscriptions in a single year.

For example, assume you pay a three-year subscription to an investment newsletter— a hefty $900 — in year 1. Under the rules, you may not deduct $900 on your year 1 return. Rather, you write off $300 in year 1 and $300 in each of the next two years.

Tax-related expenses

If you pay someone for help with most tax matters, those fees are deductible. Thus, you may deduct legal or accounting fees for tax advice, as well as tax planning and tax return preparation fees.

You may write off appraisal fees, as long as they're related to tax matters such as fees paid to determine the fair market value of property donated to charity.

Also deductible are fees you pay for determining, collecting, or refunding a tax — including income tax, estate tax, gift tax, sales tax, or property tax. And the cost of tax preparation and planning books — including this one — is also deductible.

You may also write off the cost of contesting a tax assessment — even if you lose — and of obtaining a private tax ruling from the IRS.

TIP

> You write off tax preparation fees in the year that you pay them. So, you claim a deduction on your year 2 return for fees paid in year 2 for preparing your year 1 return, as well as any fees paid for an early start on your year 2 return.

Telephone expenses

The law allows a deduction for the cost of investment-related telephone calls. These expenses include long-distance and cellular telephone charges. You may not write off any portion of your basic monthly charge for the first telephone in your home.

Transportation

If you prefer doing business in person and not on the telephone, you may have incurred transportation costs. The costs of driving to your stockbroker's office — including parking fees — are a deductible investment expense.

Besides our alphabetical checklist, there are several general strategies to use in maximizing your itemized deductions.

"Bunching" deductions

You can bunch deductions in one year by accelerating or deferring payments that are due early the following year. This way, you may exceed the standard deduction — and itemize — at least every other year. For example, you might pay in December investor adviser fees that are due in January.

Giving your investments away

Here's another strategy to keep in mind. Say you receive $2,000 a year for an investment that costs you $500 a year to maintain. You give the $1,500 annual profit to your son to help pay his college expenses. Because your $500 of miscellaneous expenses don't exceed two percent of your AGI, you receive no benefit.

Consider transferring ownership of the investment to your son. He gets the money to cover his college costs and, since his AGI is less than yours, he may be able to deduct the $500 of investment expenses. Remember, though, when you give away the investment, you give it away forever.

Married, but filing separate tax returns

If both you and your spouse have income from a job, business, investments, etc., it may pay to file separate tax returns, particularly if the total taxable income for one of you is much different than the other. Since the miscellaneous itemized deduction limitation or floor is keyed to a specific income level, a different "net" deduction will result when income is lower. Although the net deductions for both spouses may be greater due to lower income of one spouse, the tax rate might be lower so the tax benefit will be lower too. And other factors and limitations come into play when you and your spouse file as "married filing separately". Thus, you must "run the numbers" to be sure filing separate returns is a good idea.

CAUTION

If each spouse does not pay an expense with his or her own funds, the expense may be deemed to have been paid half by each spouse. You may lose the ability to get more benefit by deducting the expense all on one return that way.

8

UNDERSTANDING THE ALTERNATIVE MINIMUM TAX

- When are you subject to alternative minimum tax (AMT)?
- Are other tax years affected by AMT?
- What strategies help you avoid the AMT?

Through the use of deductions, deferrals, and credits, you may significantly reduce the income tax you owe.

However, a separate tax system, the alternative minimum tax (AMT), is designed to ensure that you pay your fair share of taxes. How does the AMT work?

You calculate the amount of tax you owe under the regular system and the amount you owe under the AMT system. Then you compare the two results and pay the higher amount.

Not everyone is liable for the AMT. However, you may be subject to the AMT if you have taken a number of deductions in the following categories:

- State and local real-estate taxes, income taxes, and personal property taxes

- Passive investments such as oil and gas limited partnerships and real estate

- Interest on a refinanced mortgage where the amount refinanced is greater than the original mortgage (that is, interest on the amount of debt that exceeds your original debt)

- Home equity interest (where the loan proceeds are not used to improve your home)

- Miscellaneous deductions

If you claimed a number of deductions — particularly in the above categories — there is a good chance you'll have to pay the AMT.

But other circumstances may also expose you to an AMT liability. For example, you may have exercised incentive stock options (ISOs) (see chapter 15) or invested in what are known as private-activity bonds. (State and local governments issue these bonds so they can raise money for private purposes such as helping small businesses build factories. Because of the AMT potential they may offer a slightly higher interest rate than other municipal bonds.)

CAUTION

If you just can't tell whether you will be subject to the AMT, you must "run the numbers."

This chapter helps you:

- determine how much of your income is subject to the AMT;
- determine if an exemption may help you offset some AMT taxable income;
- calculate tentative minimum tax and the minimum tax credit; and
- develop strategies to minimize AMT.

STEP 1: AMT INCOME

First you must calculate exactly how much of your income may be subject to the AMT. This amount is called alternative minimum taxable income, or AMTI. To begin, take your regular taxable income and make the following adjustments.

Standard deduction and personal exemptions

For purposes of AMT you cannot claim the standard deduction or a deduction for personal exemptions. So you must add these items back to your regular taxable income.

Itemized deductions

The AMT system prohibits many itemized deductions allowed under the regular tax system. Therefore, when calculating your AMTI, you must add most of these deductions back to your regular taxable income.

Specifically, you must add back:

- real estate and personal property taxes, state and local income taxes, and medical expenses that total less than 10 percent of your AGI (as you may recall, for regular tax purposes, you may deduct medical expenses that are more than 7.5 percent of your AGI); and

- other miscellaneous deductions — professional dues and tax preparation fees, for instance.

TIP

Since you are not allowed to deduct state and local income tax payments for AMT purposes, you don't have to report any state and local tax refund as income when calculating AMTI.

However, you may claim some itemized deductions for AMT purposes:

- investment interest that does not exceed your investment income;
- casualty losses; and
- home mortgage interest.

CAUTION

If you refinanced after July 1, 1982 for more than the outstanding balance on your mortgage, interest on the excess is not deductible for AMT purposes.

TIP

Although you may not deduct any investment interest in excess of investment income, you may carry forward indefinitely — until fully utilized — any of this interest expense you're unable to deduct for AMT purposes in the current tax year.

Also, the rules are different than the regular tax rules when it comes to interest you incur when you refinance your home mortgage or take out a home-equity loan. Under the AMT, you may deduct interest only on that part of the refinanced mortgage that does not exceed your outstanding mortgage before you refinance.

CAUTION

If you take out a home-equity loan to avoid the rules on deducting personal interest (e.g., you use the loan proceeds for personal purposes), the AMT rules may prohibit you from deducting this interest. You usually may not deduct interest on home-equity loans for AMT purposes. (See Chapter 6.)

TIP

The law does allow an exception to this rule. If you use the money you receive from the home-equity loan to pay for major home improvements or renovations, the interest is deductible for AMT purposes.

TIP

If you have interest expense on a loan — home equity or otherwise — where you use the money for a trade or business, you may deduct the interest on the loan for AMT purposes.

CAUTION

If you buy a luxury boat, and it qualifies as a second home, there is a good probability that the interest on the money you borrow to purchase the boat is deductible under the regular tax system. However, you may not deduct this amount under the AMT system because, according to the AMT rules, a boat doesn't qualify as a dwelling unit.

TIP

The three percent floor on itemized deductions discussed in Chapter 1 does not apply for AMT purposes. Therefore, all itemized deductions allowable for AMT purposes — for example, cash contributions to charity — are fully deductible.

Passive activities

Passive activities come in many forms, including an investment in a limited partnership or rental property (see Chapter 9).

The IRS considers any investment passive if it constitutes a trade or business in which you do not materially participate in managing (i.e., investing as a limited partner).

The passive activity rules are the same for both regular tax purposes and AMT purposes. You can generally deduct losses from passive activities only to the extent you have income from other passive activities. You may carry any nondeductible ("suspended") losses forward to future years and offset passive income in future years.

Only in the year you sell or otherwise dispose of your interest in the passive activity will these suspended losses be deductible against other income (for example, wages, interest, and dividends). In addition, any loss incurred when you dispose of the interest is similarly deductible in the year of the disposition.

CAUTION

The amount of the passive loss carryforward or the amount of the deductible loss from a passive activity is not necessarily the same for both regular tax and AMT purposes.

Some items, such as depreciation deductions, may be written off faster for regular tax purposes than for AMT purposes.

EXAMPLE

You invested in a limited partnership in which you do not materially participate and it produces a regular tax loss of $800 in the current year. If you have no other passive income, you will not be able to currently deduct the passive loss for regular tax purposes.

Some of the $800 loss occurred because the property owned by the partnership was depreciated using an accelerated method over a shorter life. The AMT rules say that you may depreciate property only using the straightline method over a longer life, which gives you a lower depreciation deduction in the early years that the property is owned.

The partnership recalculates its depreciation deductions for AMT purposes. Instead of the $800 loss reported to you for regular tax purposes, it reports $200 of income for AMT purposes. This means that for AMT purposes, you realized $200 of income on the same investment that produced the $800 loss for regular tax purposes.

You would also have an $800 passive loss carryover from the current year for regular tax purposes, but no AMT passive loss carryover.

Stock options

Incentive stock options (ISOs) are a valuable employer-provided benefit because when you exercise them, you usually pay less for the stock — sometimes much less — than the stock's fair market value. According to the tax code, this difference between the price you pay upon exercise of the option and the stock's fair market value (FMV) at the date of exercise — the "bargain element" — is not subject to regular tax.

CAUTION

The bargain element of an ISO is treated as an "adjustment" for the AMT.

An adjustment is similar to an AMT "preference," because it receives favorable tax treatment under the regular tax rules but not under the AMT rules. Both adjustments and preferences are commonly grouped together and called AMT preferences.

In the year you exercise your options, generally you must add back the bargain element to your AMT income. This difference (i.e., FMV minus the cost upon ISO exercise), however, becomes part of the stock's cost basis for AMT purposes. Therefore, when you finally sell the stock, your gain — for AMT purposes — is less than it is for regular tax purposes.

EXAMPLE

In 199A, your company grants you 1,000 ISOs at an option price of $11. You exercise the options early in 199C. The fair market value of the stock when you buy it comes to $61 a share. You have a tax "preference" of $50,000 for 199C — the difference between the option price ($11,000) and the fair market value ($61,000) — which is added back to your regular taxable income to determine AMTI. By late 199D, you're ready to sell the 1,000 shares, which you do for $71 a share. Your gain for regular tax purposes totals $60,000, i.e., $71,000 less your option price of $11,000.

For AMT purposes, however, your gain totals only $10,000 — $71,000 less $61,000, your AMT basis for the shares (the $11,000 option price plus the $50,000 bargain element you had to add to your AMT income in 199C).

CAUTION

If you are an insider — (i.e., meaning an officer, director or significant owner of a corporation under the jurisdiction of the Securities and Exchange Commission — usually any public company) special rules apply to your ISOs. See Chapter 15 for a discussion of these special corporate insider rules.

TIP

Never put tax considerations in front of economic considerations when it comes to investment decisions. If it makes economic sense — including the tax impact — to exercise your options now, then do so.

Depreciation

For AMT purposes you must add back to (or subtract from) your regular taxable income the difference between the depreciation you claimed for regular tax purposes and depreciation you calculated using alternative depreciation.

EXAMPLE

In December 199A, you bought the land and building where you have an office. The price came to $125,000. You allocate $100,000 to the cost of the building and $25,000 to the cost of the land.

When you file your 199B return, you write off depreciation for the building. You decide to use the straightline method over 31.5 years to calculate this deduction resulting in $3,175 of depreciation for 199B.

For AMT purposes, you depreciate the building under the alternative method. You must depreciate real property — the building — using the straightline method over 40, not 31.5 years. So your depreciation deduction would come to $2,500. The difference between the two methods, $675, is the amount you must add back to your income for AMT purposes.

Assume that 32 years have gone by. You have fully depreciated the building for regular tax purposes. Under the AMT rules, you may still deduct $2,500 each year in years 33 through 40. You no longer must add back depreciation since it has been fully depreciated. Instead, you may claim an additional deduction from your AMT income.

CAUTION

One exception to this rule exists. It applies to real property and leased personal property placed in service before 1987. You must add back to your regular taxable income the excess of the depreciation you claimed using the accelerated method over the old straightline depreciation. However, you may not later subtract the difference between the straightline method and accelerated depreciation when straight line depreciation exceeds the accelerated depreciation.

Other preference and adjustment items

There are a number of other preference and adjustment items AMT purposes.

1) *The excess of percentage depletion over the tax basis of property that generates the mineral deposit.*

EXAMPLE

You own a 10 percent partnership interest in an oil and gas operation. In 199A, your proportionate share of the percentage depletion is allocated to you. Depletion is a deduction reflecting the fact that the operation decreases in value as the oil and gas is produced because the oil and gas is being removed.

Your share of the percentage depletion on the gross income of the oil and gas operation totals $20,000. Your share of the adjusted basis of the land that produces the oil and gas comes to $15,000. The tax preference comes to the $5,000 difference, the amount you must add back to your AMT income.

2) *Interest on tax-exempt "private-activity" bonds issued by state and local governments after August 7, 1986.* You pay no tax on the income from these bonds under the regular tax system. But you do pay tax under the AMT system. However, the AMT rules let you write off the interest expense you incur to buy these bonds. The regular tax rules, by contrast, do not let you deduct this interest.

3) *Excess intangible drilling costs that total more than 65 percent of the net income from productive oil and gas wells.* The adjustments you must make when you own shares in oil and gas partnerships are quite complicated. Furthermore, in 1990 Congress enacted certain AMT relief provisions related to oil and gas investments that are equally as complicated. So consult your tax adviser if these are part of your investment portfolio.

4) *Research and experimental expenditures.* For purposes of the regular tax system, you may write off these expenses in the year you incur them. The AMT rules, however, require you to capitalize the R&E expenses and deduct them over 10 years. You deduct 10 percent of the R&E costs each year of the 10-year period.

TIP

The law does provide a planning opportunity to avoid treating R&E expenses as a preference item. You may deduct them over 10 years for regular tax purposes, the same as for AMT purposes.

The downside of this strategy is you get a much smaller deduction each year for regular tax purposes. Therefore, you must do a calculation and determine which method of treating these costs saves you the most tax.

STEP 2: EXEMPTION

After you've made all the adjustments to your regular taxable income and accounted for all tax preference items, what's left is your AMT income, or AMTI.

The law allows you to reduce your AMTI by these exemptions:

- $45,000 for married taxpayers filing a joint return; $22,500 for married taxpayers filing separate returns; and
- $33,750 for single taxpayers.

CAUTION

You may have to reduce your exemption if your AMTI is high. You reduce it by 25 percent of the amount by which your AMTI exceeds:

- $150,000 for married taxpayers filing jointly;
- $75,000 for married taxpayers filing separately; and
- $112,500 for single filers.

As a result, you will not be allowed any exemption if you and your spouse file jointly and your AMTI exceeds $330,000. As a single taxpayer, your ceiling comes to $247,500.

EXAMPLE

You and your spouse file jointly and your AMTI comes to $213,725. Your exemption falls from $45,000 to $29,069, calculated as follows:

Take your AMTI of $213,725 and subtract $150,000, the threshold for joint filers. The answer: $63,725. Then multiply this amount by 25 percent. The result comes to $15,931. Next, subtract $15,931 from the $45,000 AMT exemption to arrive at $29,069.

STEP 3: TMT AND MTC

The AMT calculations are almost finished. To compute your AMT, take your adjusted AMT income, as determined above, and multiply it by the AMT tax rate of 26 percent (28 percent for adjusted AMTI in excess of $175,000). The result you obtain — after you have subtracted any foreign tax credits the law allows (recomputed for AMT purposes) — is your tentative minimum tax (TMT).

Compare your TMT to your regular income tax. (Again, first take any allowable foreign tax credits for both regular tax and AMT purposes.) If your TMT is larger than your regular tax, you must pay the difference — the AMT — in addition to your regular tax but subject to what's known as the minimum tax credit (MTC).

The MTC is a credit for AMT taxes you paid in earlier years to the extent your AMT liability resulted from income being "accelerated" for AMT purposes. In other words, the AMT rules sometimes merely require you to report income **sooner** than you would have to for regular tax purposes. To the extent an AMT liability is paid for this reason, you can claim a credit for such AMT in future years.

One example is paper profits you "realize" when you exercise ISOs. Since under the AMT system you pay taxes on this income earlier than you otherwise would under the regular system, you have already paid a portion of your regular tax liability. In a later year, the MTC can reduce your regular tax liability by the amount of AMT taxes you paid in prior years.

In computing your AMT income, you've made adjustments to your regular taxable income that fall into one of two categories. These adjustments are either "deferral items" or "exclusion items." Deferral items, as the name suggests, only **defer** your regular tax liability until later. They will not **reduce** the amount of regular tax you owe permanently.

Exclusion preferences and adjustments, on the other hand, are items for which you never have to pay regular taxes. There are only four exclusion preference items:

- all itemized deduction adjustments,
- the percentage-depletion preference, and
- the tax-exempt bond preference item.

Everything else counts as a deferral preference item. And as we have seen it is only the deferral items — which accelerate income for AMT purposes — that give rise to the MTC.

To calculate your MTC, recalculate your AMT adding back only the exclusion preferences to your AMT income. Your MTC equals the difference between this adjusted AMT and the AMT you calculated using both the exclusion and deferral preferences (limited, of course, to the total AMT you paid for the year). Thus, your MTC is the amount of AMT attributable to deferral items only.

You may carry this credit forward indefinitely (although you may not carry it back) to offset your regular tax liabilities in the future. You may not reduce your regular tax, however, to an amount lower than the TMT in the year you carry forward this amount.

EXAMPLE

In 199A, you pay $16,000 in AMT. The entire amount results from your exercising incentive stock options which count as a deferral tax preference item. So the $16,000 now qualifies as your MTC carryover.

In 199B, you calculate a regular tax liability of $61,000 and a TMT of $59,000. Therefore, you may use $2,000 of that $16,000 MTC carryover from 199A to reduce your 199B tax payment.

CAUTION

If you must pay the AMT year after year or your AMT liability and your regular tax bill are similar, the minimum tax credit doesn't help you much at all.

STEP 4: STRATEGIES

It is important to think about both short-term and long-term strategies when you plan for the AMT. Your short-term strategies should involve accelerating or deferring income and deductions. But you must also consider the impact of the minimum tax credit. Long-range planning requires you to focus on the kinds of investments you make.

EXAMPLE

You've invested heavily in real estate or oil and gas limited partnerships over the years. In fact, these are practically your only investments. You suspect you may have to pay the AMT either this year or in future years. What should you do? It may make sense, subject to other economic considerations, for you to shift your money into corporate bonds, say, or stocks or mutual funds. The reason? These investments do not have any effect on the AMT.

TIP

Similarly, focus on the kind of tax treatment you elect for rental property and other depreciable assets. You might want to choose, for regular tax purposes, the longer alternative method of depreciation. If you do, you won't be required to add to your AMT income the difference between accelerated depreciation and alternative depreciation.

Of course, such a strategy may not work when it comes to preferences from limited partnership investments. With these investments, you don't have much influence over decisions.

TIP

Always assume you might be liable for the AMT. Then run the numbers each and every year.

It is important to project your tax situation two years out. That's because the actions you take this year affect your AMT situation next year.

TIP

Remember, you can't wait to worry about the AMT until you're ready to send in your tax return. The rules say that you must pay 90 percent of the tax you'll owe for the current tax year or if you qualify 100 percent of the prior year's tax shown on your return in withholding and estimated tax payments. That means you may have to pay more in estimated taxes if you're subject to the AMT.

9

Making Sense of the Passive Loss Rules

- What is a passive activity?
- Why are material participation tests important?
- What happens when I sell a passive activity?

When our legislators passed the Tax Reform Act of 1986 governing passive activities, their intent was to discourage tax shelters, but the rules went far beyond that simple goal.

If you're a shareholder in an S corporation, a shareholder in a closely-held or personal service corporation, a self-employed person, a partner in a partnership, or a beneficiary of a trust or an estate, you're potentially affected by these rules.

The same is true if you own rental real estate or rent out other types of property such as video tapes, hotel rooms, or tools. As a result, you may face burdensome restrictions and paperwork requirements.

The rules governing passive activities and passive losses are pretty complex. Here in this chapter we detail these rules with a view towards demystifying them.

Defining the Terms

What's a passive activity? In the eyes of the IRS, a passive activity is any trade or business activity in which you invest but aren't a material participant (regularly, continuously, and substantially involved in its operation), or rental activities for most people (i.e., for those who are not real estate professionals).

CAUTION

Limited partnership investments are almost always passive, because limited partners almost never materially participate in managing the trade or business of the partnership.

Investment activities can generate two kinds of income.

- Passive income (or loss), meaning income from a trade or business or rental activity.

- Portfolio income, which includes interest, dividends, annuities, royalties, and so on.

Income from personal services — that is, payment you receive for services rendered — and retirement plans is nonpassive income.

Why are these distinctions important? Because as a general rule, only like activities may offset one another. Passive activity losses, for instance, may offset only passive activity income. Or, put another way, your passive activity losses may not reduce taxable income from nonpassive sources — salary or portfolio income, for instance.

EXAMPLE

You're a doctor in private practice, and you invest in a real estate limited partnership in 199A. In 199B, the partnership produces a $10,000 loss. Meanwhile, net income from your medical practice adds up to $120,000, and your interest income from other investments is $5,000.

Because your limited real estate partnership is a passive investment, the losses it generates can't offset your nonpassive medical practice income or portfolio income. So under the law, your adjusted gross income (AGI) comes to $125,000.

What's a Passive Rental Activity?

The IRS generally considers all rental investments, with the exception of those listed below and those made by real estate professionals (discussed later), to be passive regardless of whether you materially participate. And rental activities include any investment that generates income from payments for the use of tangible property, rather than for services.

Included, then, are real estate rentals, equipment leasing, and rentals of airplanes or boats — as long as no significant personal services (flying or fishing lessons, say) are provided in making the property available to your customers.

EXCEPTIONS FOR CERTAIN RENTAL ACTIVITIES

The tax law provides several exceptions to the passive activity rules for individuals and businesses whose main activity is renting either personal or real property.

Exception 1 — The average rental period of your property is seven days or less. You usually determine the average rental period by dividing the total number of days you have rented the property by the number of rental periods. (But the calculation becomes more complicated if you charge more rent for some units in the same complex — for example, you collect more for the handful of chalets nearest the slopes of your ski resort. See your tax adviser if your property falls into this category.)

A rental period is defined as a period during which a customer has a continuous or recurring right to use the property.

This exception exempts most hotels, motels, and bed and breakfasts from the rental property rules, as well as such businesses as short-term auto rentals, tuxedo rentals, and video cassette rentals.

Exception 2 — The average rental period is 30 days or less and you or someone you hire provides significant personal services to your rental customers. An example of this type of rental includes resort accommodations.

CAUTION

In the eyes of the IRS, significant personal service does not include routine repair, maintenance, security, and trash collection nor services required for the lawful use of the property. In addition, significant personal services must be performed by individuals, so telephone and cable services aren't included.

The IRS has stated that in determining what services are significant, all relevant facts and circumstances must be taken into account. These include the frequency of services provided, the type and amount of labor required to perform the services, and the value of the services relative to the amount charged for the use of the property.

Exception 3 — Extraordinary personal services are provided by the owner of the property without regard to the average period of customer use.

Extraordinary personal services are those provided in connection with a customer's use of the property, but the "rental" is incidental to the receipt of the services. For example, a patient in the hospital is renting the bed, but the bed rental is merely incidental to the major service of the visit, which is hospital care. Therefore, hospitals are not subject to the rental activity limitations.

Exception 4 — The rental of the property is incidental to a nonrental activity of the taxpayer. Take, for example, a developer who has constructed a condominium. During the marketing period, some of the units are temporarily rented. Under these circumstances, the rental won't be considered a rental activity.

Exception 5 — Property is customarily made available during defined business hours for the nonexclusive use of various customers. A golf course, for example, might qualify under this exception. While golfers pay a fee to use the course, the course is available during defined business hours and for the nonexclusive use of various customers.

Exception 6 — Property you provide to a partnership or S corporation if you own an interest in that partnership or S corporation. This rule applies to any property that you may own that you provide to your business. It can include buildings and equipment.

CAUTION

When your rental investment meets one of the exceptions, your income isn't automatically deemed nonpassive. Instead, you determine whether you must treat your business as a passive activity by running through the material participation rules (described later in this chapter).

Exceptions for Real Estate Professionals

After 1993, the 1993 Tax Act provides some relief from the passive loss rules for certain rental real estate activities. Generally, these relief provisions are aimed at real estate professionals adversely affected by the Tax Reform Act of 1986.

Under these provisions, losses and credits from rental real estate activities in which the taxpayer materially participates, which would otherwise be treated as passive regardless of such material participation, are generally not subject to the passive loss limitations if certain eligibility requirements are met. These requirements focus on demonstrating "material involvement" in the real estate businesses for which the taxpayer performs services including minimum annual time commitments.

Generally, individual taxpayers are eligible if:

- More than half of all the personal services they perform during the year are for real property trades or businesses in which they materially participate and

- They perform more than 750 hours of service per year in those real estate activities.

A real property trade or business means any real property development, redevelopment, construction, reconstruction, acquisition, conversion, rental, operation, management, leasing or brokerage trade or business.

EXAMPLE

Jim spent 1200 hours working as a self-employed real estate broker during the year and 800 hours employed as an insurance salesman. In addition, Jim spent 200 hours managing four houses that he rents out, performing substantially all the services related to the management and maintenance of the houses. Jim suffered a $40,000 rental loss on the houses during the year.

Because Jim materially participated in real estate trades or businesses for more than 750 hours (in fact, 1,400 hours) and more than 50 percent of his time spent performing personal services was in real estate trades or businesses (1,400/2,200), Jim may deduct the full $40,000 loss related to the rental real estate activities.

CAUTION

Personal services you perform as an employee are not treated as performed in a real property trade or business unless you own at least 5 percent of the business. And, if you do not own at least 5 percent of the business, such services will effectively count against you in determining if more than 50 percent of your time was spent in real estate trades or businesses.

Material participation has the same meaning as under the general passive loss rules discussed below (i.e., the taxpayer must be involved in the operations on a regular, continuous, and substantial basis). Also as under the general rules, an interest as a limited partner in a limited partnership generally is not treated as an interest in which a taxpayer materially participates.

TIP

This is a limited relief exception designed to be available only to real estate professionals. The passive loss limitations (discussed above) continue to apply to all other taxpayers.

CAUTION

Because of the eligibility requirement that limits the availability of the relief to those who devote at least 750 hours per year to real

estate trades or businesses and more than half of their total working hours during the year to real estate activities, it may be difficult
for many individuals not already qualifying to modify their circumstances sufficiently to become eligible.

TIP

The relief should be available to married couples if at least one of
the spouses satisfies the service requirements.

EXAMPLE

Tom is a 25-percent owner of a real estate brokerage business in
which he worked as an employee for 900 hours during the year.
Tom also worked as a bookkeeper for 600 hours. Tom's wife Cindy manages an apartment building she owns and spends 550
hours during the year managing the building. The apartment
building suffers a $80,000 rental loss for the year.

Since Tom materially participates in the real estate business for
more than 750 hours *and* more than 50 percent of the personal
services he performs are in real estate activities, all of the real estate
losses from rental real estate activities of both Tom and Cindy in
which either materially participates are deductible in full on their
joint return. Thus, the $80,000 loss is deductible in full.

CAUTION

Rental real estate losses are only deductible if either spouse (or
both spouses) materially participates in the activity. In the above
example, if neither Tom nor Cindy materially participated in the
operation of the apartment building, it would fall under the general rental real estate rules discussed earlier in the chapter.

PASSIVE TRADE OR BUSINESS

Now you know what's automatically passive when it comes to rental activities. But what's passive when it comes to a trade or a business or when it comes
to a rental activity that meets one of the above exceptions?

Under the activity rules, you must first determine whether your involvement with many trades or businesses constitutes a single activity or multiple
activities.

How do you determine whether these trades or businesses are a single
activity or multiple activities?

Beginning in 1992, the rules that define an activity were changed. Prior to 1992, the rules were long, complex and difficult for taxpayers to understand and apply.

CAUTION

These complex rules applied for 1991 and prior years and, in some circumstances, they applied for 1992. Consult your tax adviser for more information on these complex rules.

Under the new rules, which generally apply to 1992 and future years, you must apply a so-called "facts and circumstances" test to identify and segregate businesses into separate activities. Each separate activity must represent an appropriate economic unit.

To determine whether multiple trades or businesses qualify as a single activity or multiple activities, consider:

- Similarities and differences in the types of businesses,
- The extent of common control of the businesses,
- The extent of common ownership of the businesses,
- The geographic location of the businesses,
- The interdependencies of the businesses.

EXAMPLE

You own part of a bakery and part of a movie theater in Rochester, New York and part of a bakery and part of a movie theater in Philadelphia. Depending on the relevant facts and circumstances, you may group all four businesses into a single activity, split them into two activities — a movie theater activity and a bakery activity, or a Rochester activity and a Philadelphia activity, or treat the businesses as four separate activities.

You can probably group these activities in a manner which is most advantageous to you as long as you can substantiate that the grouping is an appropriate economic unit. However, grouping a movie theater and a bakery together probably requires more interdependence than just location. If the businesses have the same customers or employees, or are accounted for with the same set of books and records, the argument that they comprise an appropriate economic unit will be easier to substantiate.

EXAMPLE

Jake is a partner in a business that sells non-food items to grocery stores (partnership A). Jake also is a partner in a partnership that owns and operates a warehouse (partnership B), which is in the same industrial park as A. The two partnerships are under common control. The predominant portion of B's business is warehousing goods for A, and B is the only warehousing business in which Jake is involved.

Jake can treat A's wholesale trade activity and B's warehousing activity as a single activity as they represent an appropriate economic unit.

Keep in mind a few special rules. You cannot group rental activities with nonrental activities, nor can you treat the rental of personal property and the rental of real property as a single activity (unless the personal property is provided in connection with the real property). There are exceptions to these special rules, so consult your tax adviser.

CAUTION

Once you have grouped your businesses into activities, you must continue to use that grouping unless a significant change occurs in the facts and circumstances surrounding them.

CAUTION

If the IRS believes you grouped businesses in a way designed to get around the passive activity rules, it may regroup them to prevent tax avoidance.

TIP

Since rental real estate is usually passive (subject to the exceptions outlined previously), it usually pays to treat each rental property as a separate activity. The reason? It may help when it comes time to dispose of or sell one or more of the properties, because you can use (i.e., deduct) in the year of disposal or sale any suspended losses from prior years (losses greater than passive income) that are attributable to the property or properties sold that you have incurred through that time. The same is true, of course, with nonrental real estate activities. (We discuss the treatment of suspended losses later in this chapter.)

TIP

Say you dispose of a substantial portion of an activity. You may be able to treat the disposed portion as an activity separate from the portion you retained. Doing so may allow you to deduct in the year of disposition the suspended losses attributable to the disposed portion.

MATERIAL PARTICIPATION

If you pass the material participation test, your trade or business (or your rental activity that fell into one of the exceptions) will not be classified as passive. The rules say that you materially participate in a rental or trade or business if you're involved in its operations on a "regular, substantial, and continuous basis." But what does that phrase really mean?

The IRS has devised seven tests to help you tell whether you're a material participant in an activity.

IF YOU SAY YES, YOU ARE A MATERIAL PARTICIPANT

1. Do you spend more than 500 hours in the activity annually?
2. Does your participation (or that of your spouse) represent substantially all of the participation by anyone in the activity?
3. Did you participate in the activity for more than 100 hours but not less than anyone else?
4. Did you spend more than 100 hours each on two or more activities and a total of more than 500 hours on all of them?
5. Have you been a material participant in the activity for any five of the last ten years?
6. If the activity is a personal service business, have you materially participated in any three previous years?
7. Do the facts and circumstances of your activity indicate you are a material participant?

If your involvement satisfies just one of these, you're a material participant. If you don't satisfy any, your investment is considered passive.

CAUTION

Passing any one of these tests may be bad news if you wanted the activity to generate passive income or loss. If you're counting on an activity to give you passive income to help offset passive losses, planning may be required to avoid meeting any of the material participation tests.

CAUTION

You may be a material participant one year and a passive investor the next. It's not enough to satisfy one of the tests in just any one year. The IRS requires you to reevaluate your participation annually.

Test 1 — More than 500 hours of participation. If you spend more than 500 hours in an activity during the year, you're a material participant for the year. When applying this test, you may count any work that you do in connection with the activity even if it is not the type of work normally done by owners as long as it is not performed to circumvent the passive activity rules.

Moreover, say your spouse also performs the work of an owner or performs work not ordinarily done by an owner, but the work is not done to avoid the passive activity rules (a facts and circumstances test — the IRS may challenge you on this one). In this case, you may add his or her participation to your own for purposes of this rule — and the other material participation tests outlined in this chapter.

TIP

It doesn't matter if your spouse isn't a part owner of the business or whether the two of you file a joint return for the year. If the total hours the two of you worked tops 500, you meet the requirements of the first test, and your investment isn't subject to passive activity rules.

EXAMPLE

Patrick and Meghan, a married couple, together put in more than 500 hours of work managing a restaurant that Meghan owns.

They meet the requirements of Test 1. But if Patrick's work had consisted of dish washing, a job that owners don't usually perform and the purpose of his taking on this task was to avoid the passive loss rules, his hours wouldn't count toward the 500-hour threshold.

CAUTION

For purposes of this test and the ones that follow, you are not allowed to count the number of hours you spend in your capacity as an investor, unless you're directly involved in the day-to-day management or operations of the business.

What's the role of investor? The IRS says it includes studying and reviewing financial statements, preparing or compiling summaries or analyses or monitoring the finances or operations of the business in a nonmanagerial capacity.

Test 2 — Substantially all participation. If your participation, or the participation of you and your spouse, represents substantially all of the participation by anyone, including nonowners, in an activity for the year, you're a material participant.

Test 3 — More than 100 hours of participation and not less than anyone else. This two-part test requires you to spend more than 100 hours during the year operating the business and to spend more time than anyone else, including nonowners, working in the business.

Test 4 — More than 500 hours worked in several activities with more than 100 hours in each. This test itself isn't complicated, but the consequences can surprise you. The test says that if you spend more than 100 hours on each of two or more activities and a total of more than 500 on all of them, you're a material participant in each of those business ventures.

EXAMPLE

Joseph, a full-time attorney, invested in several real estate limited partnerships. He expects these investments to lose money for several years.

Joseph is also a general partner in two other, very profitable separate activities — an auto parts store and a dry cleaning business.

He spends about 300 hours per year in the auto parts store and about 250 hours per year in the dry cleaning business. Both businesses have several full-time employees.

Joseph hopes to write off the passive losses from his real estate investments against the income from the dry cleaning and auto parts businesses.

After all, he figures, he isn't involved in either of the businesses for more than 500 hours, and others spend more time than he does working there.

But Joseph has a problem. Since his participation in each of these businesses comes to more than 100 hours and his total participation tops 500 hours, he meets the requirements of the fourth test.

So, under the tax rules, he's a material participant in both the auto parts store and the dry cleaning business. And the income from these businesses isn't passive. The result: Joseph can't use his passive real estate losses to offset the income from his two part-time businesses.

What if you invested in two businesses and both are posting a profit and your hours spent on both of these activities don't exceed 500 hours? A special rule applies if you have profits. Suppose you participate 140 hours in one business and 160 hours in the other.

Under test four, you aren't a material participant, but because of the special rule your profits aren't passive either. The IRS treats them as nonpassive income because you spent more than 100 hours participating in each business and the businesses were profitable. Therefore, you may not use these earnings to offset any of your passive losses.

Now, let's change the scenario. Say the two businesses are operating in the red. You lose again because the losses will now be treated as passive losses.

Test 5 — Material participation in any five of the last ten years. If you've been a material participant in a business for any five of the most recent ten years, the IRS considers you a material participant in the business for the current year — no matter how limited your actual involvement.

What's the point of this test? This rule is designed to prevent people from shifting income from the passive to nonpassive category — or vice-versa — just to reduce their tax liability.

EXAMPLE

Joe is the sole owner of Joe's Tool and Die, a very profitable sole proprietorship. He's also an investor in several real estate limited partnerships.

These limited partnerships produce sizable losses, which Joe wants to offset against the profits from his business.

Joe worked full time in his business since he started it ten years ago. But he has decided to reduce the amount of time he spends in the tool and die business beginning in the current year so he can pursue other opportunities.

Since Joe reduced his involvement, he thought his income from the business would be passive. Unfortunately, the fifth test would apply.

He has been a material participant in the business since he started it or nine out of the last ten years. Consequently, even though he doesn't materially participate in the business currently, the IRS treats him as a material participant.

Test 6 — For personal service businesses, material participation in any three previous years. Say you have materially participated in a personal service business — law, engineering, accounting, architecture, health, consulting, performing arts, actuarial science, and so on — in any three preceding years. What are the tax consequences?

Under this test you're considered a material participant for the current year and into the future.

Therefore, once you've been a material participant in, for instance, an architectural firm for *any* three years, any income you receive from the firm in the future is nonpassive no matter how few the number of hours you work for the firm.

The IRS considers residual fees, for instance, that inactive partners might receive from a personal service firm as nonpassive income.

Test 7 — Facts and circumstances. This test is easy to state, but difficult to apply. It says simply that the facts and circumstances in any specific case will be the determinant of whether you are a material participant.

Unfortunately, the IRS hasn't issued much guidance on how it will look at facts and circumstances. Still, it does have a few guidelines.

First, you may not automatically add, as time spent in the business, the number of hours you devote to management. You may include your management hours only if no one else performs and gets paid for managing the business, and no one else spends more time than you managing the business.

Second, you must devote at least 100 hours to the business during the year to qualify under the facts and circumstances test.

If your participation comes to fewer than 100 hours, you aren't a material participant in the business under this test regardless of any other facts and circumstances.

EXAMPLE

Assume you are the sole owner of a small company that provides word processing services. Your business is organized as an S corporation, and it is the only company in which you have an ownership interest. Your son is in charge of the day-to-day operations, but you are actively involved in consulting, arranging financing, and monitoring the corporation's financial success. You spend about 400 hours a year in these efforts. In fact, your financial analysis is used regularly in the actual decision making process of the business. In year 1, your business reported a loss. Do you report this loss as a passive loss?

The answer? It depends. You spend only 400 hours a year on the business — that is, you fail to meet the 500-hour material participation test.

The only material participation test that you might pass is the facts and circumstances test. As mentioned above, the IRS has yet to issue guidance on what criteria would allow the losses to be treated as nonpassive for purposes of the facts and circumstances test. However, the IRS is slated to issue further guidance on this test.

Can limited partners materially participate in a business? Generally they can't because state laws normally prohibit limited partners from being active in a business. And limited partners who do become active risk losing their limited liability.

Since limited partners do not normally participate in limited partnerships, the material participation tests we just discussed don't apply.

THERE'S ALWAYS AN EXCEPTION!

Three situations where limited partners are considered material participants:

- The first exception deals with the first test, the 500 hour test. Even limited partners are material participants if they put 500 hours or more into the business.

- The second exception relates to tests five and six. If a limited partner meets either the any five-of-ten year test or the any-three-previous year test, he or she is a material participant regardless of the limited partner designation.

- A third exception applies to people who are both general and limited partners in the same activity. The IRS considers them, on balance, to be general partners who must go back through tests one through seven above to determine whether they are material participants.

TIP

Although the law doesn't require it, anyone who anticipates that material participation could be an issue should keep a daily log of the hours put into a business. If the decision is a close call, the log could tip the balance.

LOSSES

Losses incurred in the current year from passive activities are good for offsetting your profits from other passive activities.

If you don't have profits from passive activities, you may carry your passive losses forward and use them to offset passive income in future years. The passive losses that you carry forward are called suspended losses. And you must keep track of suspended losses from each of your passive activities from year to year.

EXAMPLE

In 199A you have invested in three limited partnerships — A, B, and C. All these partnerships are passive investments and, under the tests, are considered separate activities.

Partnerships A and B each generate $10,000 in losses this year. But partnership C rewards you with a $5,000 profit. In total, you lost $15,000 on passive investments — that is, $10,000 plus $10,000 (or $20,000) minus the $5,000 profit.

The passive loss rules won't allow you to deduct your $15,000 on your current tax return. So you carry forward the suspended loss to future years.

The losses from partnerships A and B are used *pro rata* — meaning in proportion — against C's $5,000 passive income, resulting in $7,500 of suspended loss you can carry forward for each partnership, A and B.

To do the calculation: Multiply the suspended loss of $15,000 by the ratio of each partnership's loss to their total losses.

Partnership A's suspended loss is $7,500 — that is, $10,000 (A's loss) divided by $20,000 (A's loss plus B's loss) or 0.5 times $15,000.

Now, say the year is 199B. Partnership A earns a $20,000 profit. Partnership B once again generates a $10,000 loss, and partnership C posts another $5,000 profit. You have a net $15,000 profit for the year ($20,000 from A plus $5,000 from C minus $10,000 from B).

You carry forward your total $15,000 loss from 199A from partnerships A and B and apply it against 199B's $15,000 profit. The result? You've reduced your income from passive investments in 199B to zero.

Remember, you may carry forward these suspended passive losses indefinitely.

Moreover, when you sell a passive investment, the law allows you to use (deduct currently) all suspended losses from the activity you sold right away. You use these losses to offset not only your passive income but also any other income including earned income, or wages, and portfolio income as well.

You add suspended losses from an activity you dispose of this year to any current losses from the same activity and any losses you incur at the time you dispose of the activity. All these losses will be allowed in full, first as an offset against any net income or gain from all your other passive activities, then as an offset against any other income including wages and portfolio income.

Alternatively, if you still have current year net passive income after offsetting your passive income with the losses of the activity you sold, you may use suspended losses of other passive activities to offset the remaining passive income. But remember, unlike the activity you sold, you can only use suspended losses of activities you still own to reduce your net passive income to zero.

EXAMPLE

The year is 199B, and you decide to unload Partnership A (see example above). On June 30, you sell your entire interest to your neighbor, Lisa.

For the first six months of 199B, partnership A produces income of $2,000. And, when you sell, you realize a gain of $1,500. Partnerships B and C don't produce any income or loss during 199B. Your only other source of income: your $120,000 salary.

You would obviously like to use at least some of your suspended losses to reduce your hefty income. And you may. In fact, you may (or, to be precise about it, you must) use all your suspended loss from partnership A in 199B. But you must determine the suspended losses you're allowed as follows:

- Start by adding the following: the amount of your suspended loss from the previous year (in your case, $7,500); the amount of your loss from the current year (none); and the amount of loss you realize when you dispose of or sell the activity (none).
- Now, subtract from the result your net income from all your passive activities (in your case, $3,500).
- You may use the resulting amount — a $4,000 loss — to offset your salary.

What about the $7,500 suspended loss from partnership B? It's still suspended and will carry forward to 199C. You may not deduct it in 199B against your salary. The reason? You didn't dispose of your interest in B.

CAUTION

If selling your passive activity results in a loss and the passive activity was a capital asset the loss on the sale is treated both as a passive loss and as a capital loss subject to the capital loss rules (see Chapter 4 for more information on capital losses).

What can be done if there are substantial excess passive losses? Perhaps you should consider a Passive Income Generator (PIG). Or what if the investment yielded substantial deductions in the early years you owned it but now is generating only paper profits — known in tax lingo as phantom income? For more information on passive losses, see Chapter 10.

GIFTS

When you give away an interest in a passive activity to a friend or relative, you lose your right — forever — to claim (deduct) the suspended losses. Instead, the recipient of your generosity must add these suspended losses to his or her basis in the investment.

What if, later on, the recipient sells the investment at a loss? Then, for purposes of determining the donee's loss, his or her basis is limited to the fair market value of the interest on the date you made the gift. So if the fair market value on the date of the gift is less than the donee's basis (including the suspended losses), part or all of the suspended loss will be lost forever as a deduction.

EXAMPLE

Alex owns an interest in a limited partnership which he gifts to his sister Samantha. Alex had a basis of $1,000 and suspended losses related to the limited partnership of $5,000 on the date of the gift. The fair market value on the date of the gift is only $4,000; and Samantha's basis is now $6,000.

If Samantha later sells the interest for $3,000 (assuming no other activity which would have impacted Samantha's basis), the basis for determining her loss is limited to $4,000 (the fair market value on the date of the gift). Thus, $2,000 of Alex's original basis and suspended losses is lost forever.

Moreover, sales you make to related parties — relatives, your closely-held corporation, and so on — will also not let you immediately use your suspended losses. In such instances, however, unlike the gift discussed above, you do carry forward the suspended losses until the related party disposes of the investment in a taxable transaction. Upon such disposition, you get to deduct the suspended losses.

EXAMPLE

You sell your limited partnership interest to your father. You won't be able to use (deduct) the suspended losses from the partnership when you make the sale. Instead, you continue to carry these losses forward as suspended losses until your dad sells the investment to an unrelated party, at which time you may deduct the suspended losses.

What if you generate passive income from other activities before your father sells the investment? In that case, you can use the suspended losses of the activity you sold your father to offset the passive income of the activities you still own.

INTEREST EXPENSES

The law says that if an investment is a passive activity, interest expense on loans associated with that investment isn't subject to the personal or investment interest limits.

Instead, the rules say you may write off such passive activity interest only to the extent of your passive activity income. If you report no passive activity income, you may not claim a deduction.

But you may carry forward your passive activity interest indefinitely. In other words, you may use the interest you carry forward to offset passive income in future years. And in the year you dispose of a passive activity, you may deduct all passive activity interest that you hadn't been able to deduct before. In essence, this passive activity interest is treated just like it was a passive loss.

And it makes no difference whether the interest expense is "inside interest" — that is, interest incurred by the limited partnership itself (other than interest expense it incurs in its trade or business) — or "outside interest," that is, interest on money you borrow to invest in the limited partnership.

What does this rule mean? When you borrow money to purchase a passive activity investment, the interest expense is offset against your income or added to your loss from the investment to determine your overall passive income or loss from the activity.

The one exception to this rule applies to passive investments that earn portfolio income, such as a real estate partnership earning interest income on its excess cash reserves. In these cases, you must classify a portion of your interest expense (to the extent of your portfolio income) as investment interest, and it is subject to the investment interest limits.

EXAMPLE

You're a new limited partner in ABC Partnership in 199A. And, for 199A, you have a passive loss before interest expense of $10,000. In addition, the ABC partnership itself incurs $2,000 in interest expense (that is not incurred in its trade or business) allocable to you. ABC reports no portfolio income.

The partnership isn't required to treat any of its interest as investment interest. The entire $2,000 is added to your passive loss for the year. You don't need to treat this amount separately as investment interest on your return.

What if ABC did have portfolio income? In this case, the partnership must trace the debt proceeds and allocate the interest expense accordingly. If all (or a portion) of the debt proceeds which generated the interest expense was used by ABC to purchase securities, all (or a portion) of the $2,000 of interest expense must be allocated to the portfolio income. ABC would then report this amount — to the extent of your portion of the portfolio income — as investment interest separately to you. And you would have to treat it as investment interest expense on your return.

What if you loan money to the partnership or it loans money to you? Proposed regulations would permit you to treat a portion of the interest income generated by such lending transactions as passive, rather than portfolio, income.

Usually, losses you take from your passive investments won't have an impact on your investment interest limitations. See Chapter 5 for more information about interest deductions.

CREDITS

The same rules that apply to losses apply to credits. You may use tax credits passed along to you by shelters only to offset the tax on the net income from these investments.

EXAMPLE

You would owe $50,000 in tax if you disregarded your net passive income. But you would have to pay $80,000 if you took into account both your net passive income and your other taxable income.

So the amount of tax that you attribute to your net passive income comes to $30,000. Therefore, you're allowed to take credits from your passive investments up to $30,000.

This provision applies mostly to a tax shelter that passes along such tax credits as energy credits, rehabilitation credits, or research and development credits.

Like losses, you may carry forward suspended and unused credits to a future tax year. However — unlike losses — you can't use credits to offset tax on earned income and portfolio income when you sell your shelter.

In these cases, however, you may increase your basis by the amount of any suspended credit to the extent of any original basis adjustment before you sell. Basis adjustments were required, for example, when claiming the investment tax credit (under prior law). This provision gives you a lower gain or higher loss when you sell your property. You may no longer carry forward the suspended credit to offset other passive income.

SPECIAL CIRCUMSTANCES

Following are some special circumstances an investor may face when it comes to the passive activity rules:

Abandoning property

Say last year you invested in a building. This year you lose your only tenant, and it is virtually impossible for you to sell the building or convert it for use by someone else. Is there some way you can dispose of it, so you don't have to treat your loss for the year as passive?

You can abandon the property. The law considers abandonments as dispositions under the passive loss rules. So you may claim your entire loss in the current year.

Also, if you abandon your building the suspended loss rules let you deduct all the losses you have been carrying forward in the year the abandonment occurs.

How do you abandon an investment?

Your building will be considered abandoned if you can prove that you originally had a profit motive for investing in the building, and the property became useless. You must also show that you have permanently deserted the building and discontinued trying to rent or sell it.

CAUTION

Just not using the building — or a decline in its value — isn't conclusive evidence that you have abandoned your property. You must show that you have actually forsaken it. For example, the IRS would consider cutting off utilities, boarding up windows, and canceling insurance as proof of abandonment.

The law can be tricky, though, when it comes to abandoning property. If you plan to go this route, consult your tax adviser beforehand.

Installment sales

Assume you owned a limited partnership interest in a piece of rental real estate. You sold out years ago on an installment-sale basis, and you are still receiving income. Is this income passive?

The answer is yes. The income is treated as passive, even if the passive-loss rules weren't in place when you sold your partnership. However, any interest income received would be treated as portfolio and not passive income.

Paired investments

As their name implies, paired investments are limited partnerships with two distinct businesses. One business generates income and, hopefully, cash. The other business generates losses — at least for tax purposes — to offset that income.

Paired investments are just another variation on the tax shelter theme.

CAUTION

Invest in one of these vehicles only if it makes economic sense.

Both rental and nonrental operations

Assume you are a partner in a partnership that owns a hotel. In the hotel lobby are five commercial stores that the partnership leases to tenants. These commercial rentals make up 10 percent of the gross income of the hotel and are considered insubstantial in relation to the hotel's trade or business activity. Are the rental operations of the commercial stores considered a separate rental activity from the operations of the hotel?

The answer is no. The rental operations of the commercial space don't constitute a separate activity from the hotel because the rental activity is insubstantial in relation to the hotel's trade or business activity.

As a result, the operation of the hotel and the rental of commercial space may constitute a single activity. The hotel operations are dominant — that is, they contribute 90 percent of your revenues — and accordingly, the rental operations aren't necessarily considered a separate activity.

10

Do Tax Shelters Still Exist?

- How do the passive loss rules affect tax shelters?
- Which strategies should you use for "burned-out" shelters?
- What are the tax benefits in oil and gas investments?

Had we written this chapter years ago, the topic of tax shelters could easily have taken up half this book. We would have discussed topics such as solar energy property, real estate, cattle breeding and feeding, orchards, and windmill farms — all potential tax shelters.

Now, the at-risk rules and, more importantly, the passive activity rules of the 1986 Tax Act have all but slammed the door on these investment options. And in the years after the 1986 Tax Act, tax audits — and subsequent court decisions prompted by those audits — have taken away a great number of shelter benefits.

The courts have ruled, for example, that many "businesses" organized as shelters weren't operated with the goal of making a profit and had no substance.

Also, the courts have said, investors often were too aggressive in claiming big deductions on their tax returns. As a result, some taxpayers have had to pay back taxes on audit, including interest and, at times, penalty charges, when their shelter deductions were denied.

What's left when it comes to tax shelters? The answers, generally, are rental real estate for some taxpayers, building rehabilitation and low-income housing for other taxpayers (all discussed in Chapter 11), and working interests in oil and gas properties.

You may use losses generated by these investments to offset your regular income — subject to certain limitations. The effect of this dramatic change in the law on investment strategies has been enormous.

In the past, you no doubt decided whether to invest in a tax shelter based on the rate of return — a rate of return that included substantial tax write-offs.

These days, a traditional tax shelter generates what are known in the tax code as passive income and losses. As discussed in Chapter 9 losses from passive investments offset only gains from passive investments but not income from other sources, such as wages or salary, except in the year you dispose of the tax shelter.

Now that the tax rules have changed, investors should look to limited partnerships for solid economic returns in the form of cash flow and appreciation potential.

Today, high cash returns are almost a prerequisite to making these investments worthwhile. If the economics of an investment don't have a reasonably good probability of making a return on the money invested, tax reasons will provide little, if any, additional incentive.

Investors are also demanding protection from total loss, since tax benefits are less substantial. Therefore, many shelters now promote themselves as safe investments and offer risk protection through guarantees of income, protection from losses, and promises of cash returns.

CAUTION

You should view these guarantees, however, merely as added benefits, not as reasons to invest in a deal. If times get tough, many guarantors may default. And in good times, you probably won't need the guarantees.

CAUTION

Because of the changes in the shelter market, you should not purchase new shelters without carefully considering how they might help or harm you.

LEVERAGING YOUR PASSIVE INVESTMENTS

It used to make sense to leverage your tax shelter investment to the greatest extent you could; that is, it paid to borrow as much money as possible. The reasons?

Investors could obtain significant deductions with only a minimal cash investment. Also, they could deduct fully the interest paid on any borrowed funds.

Now, however, you may want to minimize leverage in your passive investments to reduce your interest expense. When you do minimize leverage and cut your interest expense, you also may end up creating passive income, perhaps breaking even in operations or at least reducing your passive losses.

It is possible your investment will produce positive cash flow in excess of the passive income. This can happen as a result of noncash deductions, such as depreciation and depletion, that do not require a cash expenditure.

WORKING WITH EXISTING TAX SHELTERS

What about those shelters that you purchased in years past? If acquired before the 1986 Tax Reform Act, the tax law allowed deduction of a portion of those losses through 1990 but not beyond. (See Chapter 9 for more information on passive losses.) Losses for shelters acquired after October 22, 1986, the Act's enactment date, are restricted as to use. (Certain exceptions, however, apply to investments in rental real estate. See Chapter 11 for details.)

However, here are some ideas that may help you use your losses currently and minimize your tax liability.

Passive income generators

If you have substantial passive losses from old tax shelter investments, consider passive income generators, or "PIGs."

PIGs are, in effect, reverse tax shelters. A PIG may generate a positive cash flow as well as taxable passive income.

Among the more common types of PIGs are limited partnerships that operate ongoing, profitable businesses such as a ski resort, golf course, or conference center. The benefit of these investments is that the income they generate is passive, and passive losses may be used to offset this passive income.

But how do you know which PIGs might make sense for your circumstances? First, you should know that many PIGs are syndicated — that is, they're offered to the public through public offerings — and are actively marketed by brokers. However, special rules may limit the benefits from such syndicated offerings. These rules will be covered shortly when Master Limited Partnerships are discussed.

Once you've decided that a passive income generator may help you at tax time, compare a specific PIG to other investments and consider the investment merits of the PIG exclusive of any associated tax benefits.

Using the same methods, compare rates of return. Also, take a look at how the deal and the promoter stack up against others in the same industry. Make sure to include in your analysis any fees that might be involved in buying or selling both investments.

If you're interested in investing in PIGs, you should have no trouble finding them. Your investment adviser, stockbroker, or financial planner will know the names of some of these partnerships. You may also run across names of PIGs in financial publications.

Use of passive losses by corporations

The law allows a corporation to use passive losses to offset its regular business income. And, it makes no difference if the corporation is closely held. If you own a profitable corporation that isn't organized as a personal service corporation or an S corporation, transfer ownership of investments that generate passive losses to your corporation.

CAUTION

This strategy doesn't make sense if your passive investments currently generate income (not losses), or will do so in the not-so-distant future. That's because the income a corporation earns is taxed twice — once at the corporate level, then again when the income is passed along to you in the form of dividends.

Another drawback is that if the shelter has phantom income (discussed below), such income may be triggered upon transfer.

TIP

If you're the owner of a profitable corporation but don't materially participate in business operations, another alternative is to elect S corporation status. Since you don't materially participate, your income from the S corporation is passive. And you can use your passive losses to offset profits from your S corporation.

Remember, you add together income and losses from all your passive investments. So, if you find yourself locked into some older investments that you expect will generate passive losses, invest in vehicles that generate passive income to offset your losses.

CAUTION

Make sure your investments make economic sense apart from the tax benefits.

Phantom income

In the past, tax shelters were structured so that investors could claim tax deductions — accelerated depreciation, say — in the early years of ownership. However, these deductions diminished over time, often leaving the shelter with only paper profits or phantom income.

A shelter that generates no further losses and may produce taxable income but doesn't generate cash is known in investment circles as a "burned-out" shelter.

The phantom income generated by this burned-out shelter usually occurs when you sell or dispose of the shelter. Phantom income is, in fact, passive income. You must report on your return an amount of income on the sale or disposition that exceeds — often by a considerable amount — the sales proceeds you actually receive. In other words, the phantom income represents a "reversal" of those tax shelter deductions you took in prior years.

TIP

Invest in a new tax shelter that generates passive losses to offset phantom income from your "burned-out" shelter if you have no other passive losses to offset the phantom income.

TIP

Or, sell the investment, but be warned that you'll usually have to sell at a deep discount. Besides losing money on the sale, disposing of the investment may create taxable — and phantom — income for you. Selling the shelter, however, may help you minimize the amount of phantom income that you'll have to report on your tax return.

Master limited partnerships

Interests in master limited partnerships — that is, MLPs or publicly traded partnerships — are traded on public exchanges, just like shares of stock. So, they're much more marketable and much more liquid than other types of partnerships. How do you treat — for tax purposes — income and losses from these partnerships?

Originally, these publicly traded partnerships were thought to provide passive income to investors with passive activity losses. These investors could then use the losses to offset their income. The partnerships came under congressional scrutiny, not only because they offered this opportunity to save on taxes, but also because they paid no tax (instead, the individual partners paid tax on their share of any profit) while having many common characteristics of publicly traded corporations.

As a result of congressional action, the tax law now treats net income from publicly traded partnerships as portfolio income. Investors may not use this income to offset passive losses from other investments.

Further, losses from publicly-traded partnerships are treated as suspended losses. Investors may subtract these losses only from net income from the same partnerships. You may deduct any unused suspended losses when you dispose of the interest in the partnership.

Moreover, the IRS taxes publicly traded partnerships formed after December 17, 1987, as corporations. Therefore, profits and losses no longer flow through to the partners.

There is, however, an exception to the corporate treatment rules. If 90 percent of the partnership's gross income comes from interest, dividends, real-estate rents, gains from the sale of capital assets, income or gains from certain oil and gas activities, and gains from the sale of certain trade or business assets, the IRS will still treat the MLP as a partnership.

Oil and gas

Investing in oil and gas partnerships may trigger the passive loss rules, depending upon the type of liability you incur. However, investors still may reap tax benefits by investing in a working interest in oil and gas properties (working interests are discussed in more detail below). Lawmakers made an exception to the tax-shelter (i.e., passive loss) rules for working interests in oil and gas properties when an investor's liability is not limited, even though the investor does not materially participate in the venture.

There are different ways to invest in oil and gas. One way is through a stake in a limited partnership known as an oil or gas program. The purpose of oil and gas programs is to explore or drill for oil or to purchase producing wells. Usually these programs come in the form of joint ventures or partnerships. Because they are limited in liability, partners in such programs are subject to the normal limitations on losses from passive activities.

Who offers these programs? They are put together and offered to investors either by independent oil companies or by oil investment managers. These programs come in four basic varieties — exploratory, development, balanced, and income.

Exploratory programs try to discover new petroleum reserves. Since exploration usually takes place in untested areas, the success rate is often very low or nil. Moreover, an exploratory well must be developed after it is discovered. So, more money from investors may be required before the partnership ever produces positive cash flow.

CAUTION

If everything goes well, the return on capital may be extraordinary. But it may take a long time to collect on your investment. Also, these investments are very risky.

Development programs set up wells near existing oil reserves in areas where production is already underway; therefore, chances of success are higher than in exploratory programs. Also, you can expect a faster return on your investment than with exploratory programs. As you might expect since the risk is lower, the return on your capital is often less than you would get with successful exploratory programs.

Balanced programs include both exploratory and development wells in about the same proportion. They try to combine the advantages of high yields produced by successful exploratory wells with the early cash flow and lower risk of development wells.

Unlike either exploratory or development programs, income partnerships purchase producing properties rather than develop drilling sites, so the risks are much less. Income programs also don't offer the same tax benefits. Most of their tax write-offs come from the depletion of their oil reserves rather than from development costs.

The principal advantage of these programs is that you get income over the life of the oil well, which might be 10 years, or the gas well, which might last 15 years. As the oil or gas is removed from the well, the income falls until the well is abandoned as commercially unproductive.

If you're thinking about an investment in an oil and gas partnership, look for a reputable financial adviser who has experience in evaluating these programs. Ask for an in-depth review of the investment.

Another way to invest in oil and gas is, as mentioned above, through a "working interest." A working interest or operating interest is one in which the partners pay a share of development and operation expenses.

Your losses in these partnerships aren't subject to the normal limitations on losses from passive activities, so you may deduct them from your regular income. And you don't have to participate in the actual operations yourself to do so.

CAUTION

To be exempt from the passive activity rules, a working interest cannot limit liability. This rule applies even if the investment is made through a partnership or S corporation. For many people, unlimited liability is reason enough to steer clear of these investments.

What's deductible on your tax return if you own a working interest in an oil or gas well? Day-to-day operating costs, for one; intangible drilling costs, for another.

Intangible drilling costs are the expenses incurred in drilling and developing a well, except for equipment. They include amounts spent for core analysis, engineering, management, and geological studies. They also include the costs of drilling a dry hole.

The tax law provides you with a choice when it comes to intangible drilling costs. They may be written off currently, or capitalized and written off through depletion.

While intangible drilling costs are deductible for regular tax purposes, they may be limited when it comes to the alternative minimum tax (AMT).

TIP

If you're subject to the AMT, you may want to elect to write off intangible drilling costs in equal installments over 60 months. By doing so you deduct only a portion of the intangible drilling costs in the current year. The rest is deductible in future years. As long as the AMT does not apply in those years you get the benefit of these additional write-offs.

If the AMT does apply, complicated adjustments may limit the benefit of the intangible drilling cost deduction. So consult with your tax adviser if you're in an AMT position and have investments in oil and gas properties.

Depletion is also deductible for regular tax purposes but it may not be when calculating your alternative minimum tax liability. The AMT will limit depletion to the amount of basis in the property.

Depletion represents the write off of the cost of obtaining mineral rights. The depletion deduction is the higher of the amount calculated under the cost method or the percentage method.

With the cost method, depletion is determined by comparing production sold during the taxable year with the total available production of the property.

EXAMPLE

You acquire the right to drill for oil in a 10-acre site in Oklahoma. You hire a geologist who estimates that the maximum amount of oil on your site is one million barrels. In the first year, you pump and sell some 100,000 barrels of oil from the property.

What is your depletion deduction? If you use the cost method, you may claim as depletion one-tenth of the amount you paid to acquire the reserves. The percentage method of depletion lets you claim as depletion a fixed percentage of your revenues from the sale of oil or gas. That figure is generally 15 percent.

A 25 percent depletion rate applies to marginally producing wells of independent producers who typically offer limited partnership interests. However, this provision applies only if crude oil prices fall below $20 per barrel. Again, if you invest in oil and gas, talk with your tax adviser.

If you use the percentage method, the rules generally will not allow you to claim depletion deductions that exceed 65 percent of your taxable income from all sources. However, you may carry forward depletion deductions you aren't able to deduct in the current year to future years.

There are other limitations if you use the percentage method for depletion. Depletion deductions are also limited to 100 percent (formerly 50 percent prior to 1991) of the taxable income from each property. Taxable income — in this case, at least — is calculated before the depletion deduction, and the limitation is figured on a property-by-property basis.

Any depletion taken reduces the tax basis in the property; however, unlike cost depletion, percentage depletion can be claimed in excess of your tax basis in the property. Moreover, taking percentage depletion in excess of basis does not increase the gain computed at the time of the sale of the property.

Depreciation is another deduction that may be claimed for a working interest in an oil or gas well. To depreciate an expense means to write it off in installments over time. Depreciation allows you to write off the cost of tangible assets — drilling rigs, and so on — over a period of time, or "life," designated by the IRS. Usually, you write off these costs using what is known as the straightline method or alternatively, you may use an accelerated method.

Depreciation — as with depletion and intangible drilling costs — is deductible for regular tax purposes, but different rules apply when it comes to the AMT.

Still another deduction that may be claimed is for so-called surrendered leases. These are leases acquired but abandoned or forfeited. The remaining cost of acquiring these leases is written off in the year of abandonment.

If you own a working interest in an oil or gas well, report your profit or loss and claim your deductions on Schedule C of your Form 1040.

CAUTION

You may be liable for self-employment taxes on your net income from a working interest in an oil or gas well. Sometimes you are liable for the tax even if you own a fractional interest through a partnership — five percent, say — and do not even play an active role in operations. The reason? The partnership is engaged in the active conduct of a trade or business.

CAUTION

When you sell a working interest in an oil or gas well, a portion of the gain may be classified as ordinary income, not capital gain income. This may occur if you previously wrote off intangible drilling costs (either though current expensing or capitalizing and amortizing), or if you took any depletion deductions that reduced your leasehold basis in the property.

The IRS takes back or recaptures certain deductions previously taken. That is, it requires you to report a portion of the gain as ordinary income, not capital gain income. The amount of the gain that is treated as ordinary income equals the total of certain deductions previously claimed.

EXAMPLE

You sell your working interest, your gain adds up to $5,000, and these deductions come to $4,000. The tax law says $4,000 of your gain is taxed as ordinary income. The excess gain — $1,000 — will likely be treated as a gain from the sale of trade or business property and may ultimately be eligible to receive capital gain treatment.

11

THE TAX BENEFITS OF RENTAL REAL ESTATE

- What are the rental real estate, passive activity and "at-risk" rule limitations?
- How do you report rental real estate activity on your tax return?
- What are the rehabilitation and low income housing credits?

Before investing in rental real estate it is important to understand the tax risks and rewards of such an investment. In this chapter, we provide this information with respect to rental real estate that you actively participate in managing. Why is it important that you actively participate in the rental activity? If you satisfy certain requirements or for tax years after 1993 if you are considered a "real estate professional" under the tax law (see Chapter 9 for a complete discussion of the definition of "real estate professional" and the passive loss rules), you may be entitled to certain tax breaks and be able to avoid the passive loss rules.

ACTIVE PARTICIPATION

You are an active participant in a rental real estate activity as long as you make significant and bona fide management decisions *and* own at least a 10 percent stake in the property. The management decisions that count include deciding

---

on rental terms, approving tenants, and approving major expenditures. As long as you make these decisions, it's acceptable to the IRS if you use a rental agent to execute them for you.

Unless you are a real estate professional, participation in a rental real estate activity is usually classified as a passive investment, regardless of your level of activity. Generally, losses from passive investment are only deductible to the extent of income generated by other passive investments you may hold.

Accordingly, if the expenses you incur relative to the rental property — mortgage interest, depreciation, utility bills, insurance, repair costs, and so on — exceed your rental income, the resultant net loss is generally deductible only to the extent you have income from other passive investments.

However, you may carry forward any passive losses you cannot use currently (known as "suspended losses") and deduct them in future years — as long as you have enough passive income in those future years. When you sell your property, you are entitled to deduct any remaining unused (i.e., suspended) losses against any passive or nonpassive income you report on your tax return.

When AGI is under $150,000

A special exception to these passive loss rules exists for taxpayers with adjusted gross income (AGI) less than $150,000.

This exception allows you to deduct rental real estate losses of up to $25,000 from your regular income as long as you satisfy two conditions:

- you meet certain income guidelines, and
- you actively participate in the operation of your rental property.

The income guidelines provide that as long as your AGI is $100,000 or less — figured before you subtract any rental or passive losses — you may deduct from your ordinary income up to $25,000 in rental losses from residential or commercial rental property.

You begin to lose the benefit of this exception as your AGI exceeds $100,000 and the benefit is entirely phased-out for AGI in excess of $150,000.

If your AGI is between $100,000 and $150,000 you must reduce the $25,000 limit by 50 percent of the amount by which your AGI exceeds $100,000.

EXAMPLE

Your AGI totals $140,000; that is, it tops $100,000 by $40,000. To determine the amount of additional loss you will be entitled to deduct you multiply 50 percent times $40,000, and subtract the result — $20,000 — from $25,000. In this case, you may deduct

$5,000 in rental losses from your regular income, as long as you actively participate in managing the property. If your losses exceed $5,000 you must treat the excess the same as you treat other passive losses (i.e., you may only deduct these losses to the extent of your passive income).

The $25,000 limit applies cumulatively to all your rental property. It does not matter how many rental buildings you own, the maximum loss you are allowed to claim as an offset against regular income may not exceed $25,000 in total in each tax year.

AT-RISK RULES

Another area of the tax law that you must consider when investing in rental real estate involves the "at-risk" rules. The at-risk rules apply to investments in real estate after 1986 and serve to limit the amount of rental real estate losses you may deduct to your "total at-risk investment."

Your at-risk investment is the cash you've contributed to your rental real-estate venture plus any money you've borrowed for the venture (to the extent that you're personally liable for the loan) plus the adjusted basis of any property you've contributed.

In other words, your losses may not exceed the total amount for which you're at risk. However, the law does carve out an exception for real estate.

So-called nonrecourse financing — for which you have no personal liability — qualifies for at-risk purposes, if it meets the following three conditions.

- The financing must be secured only by real property; that is, the real estate itself.
- The debt must be true debt — not convertible debt or disguised equity — meaning debt that's in reality an ownership share.
- You must have obtained the financing from a qualified lender — defined as a bank or a savings and loan. A related party such as a family member or a corporation or partnership in which you hold a greater than 50 percent interest may also qualify. However, if you obtain financing from a related party, the debt must be "commercially reasonable" and "substantially similar" to loans made to unrelated parties.

TIP

To ensure that a related party note will qualify as at-risk, sign a note that's payable on demand or on a specified date or dates and that carries a market rate of interest.

CAUTION

Be aware that the definition of a qualified lender does not include seller financing. So, you're subject to the at-risk rules if you use seller financing, unless that financing is recourse financing — in other words, a loan in which you assume personal liability for the debt.

If you own rental real estate you report your rental income and expenses on Schedule E of your Form 1040. If you own more than three rental properties, you may use multiple Schedules E.

RENTAL INCOME

Generally, rental income must be reported when rental payments are received.

CAUTION

If a tenant pays his or her rent in advance you are required to report that income in the year you receive it.

EXAMPLE

A tenant in an apartment building you own signs a two-year lease requiring her to pay you $5,000 annually in rent. But on the day she signs the lease, she hands you a check for the full amount of $10,000. You must report that $10,000 as income in the year you receive it, even though half of that amount is rent for a future year.

TIP

Security deposits normally do not count as income in the year received if you're required by law to pay interest on those amounts.

However, if you maintain the right to refund a security deposit or apply it to a future year's rent, then it generally counts as income in the year it's paid.

TIP

To avoid treating some security deposits as current year income, word your lease agreements so that security deposits are "equal to" one month's rent, not "in lieu of" the last month's rent.

CAUTION

The fair market value of property or services you receive in lieu of rent also counts as rental income. One way to determine fair market value of property is by getting an appraisal from a qualified real estate appraiser.

CAUTION

If a tenant wants to pay to cancel his or her lease, the amount received must be reported as rental income.

CAUTION

Payments received under an insurance policy that reimburses you for lost rent — say as the result of a fire or some other casualty — must be reported as rental income.

RENTAL EXPENSES

Advertising

The cost of advertising that a property is available for rent is deductible from gross rental income.

Commissions

Rental commissions are deductible from gross rental income.

CAUTION

The rules state some commissions are deductible; however, they require others to be added to the basis of the property.

For example, commissions paid upon the sale of rental property are effectively added to the basis of the property in that they are subtracted from the proceeds from the sale to calculate gain or loss. As for commissions paid upon the purchase of rental property, these costs must be added to the cost basis of the property purchased and may be depreciated.

Depreciation

Depreciation is generally the most significant tax break you get from rental property. You are allowed to recoup the cost of your investment by deducting a portion of your purchase price each year. This gradual write-off, depreciation, is intended to take into account the effects of wear and tear and decay on the property.

There is one restriction, however. You may write off *only* the cost of buildings, not the underlying land.

The cost of residential rental property may be recovered on one schedule — 27.5 years — and commercial property on another — 31.5 years for property placed in service before May 13, 1993 and 39 years for property placed in service on or after that date. Furthermore, the straightline method of depreciation must be used.

The law says depreciation deductions may begin once the property is "placed in service," but not before. This simply means that the building is on the rental market or ready for its intended use.

The law also requires the use of the so-called mid-month convention. This rule applies to both residential and commercial investments.

The mid-month convention means that the first year's depreciation deduction must be calculated from the middle of the month in which you place your property in service. It applies even if the property is placed in service on the first or last day of the month.

EXAMPLE

You and a colleague buy a small office complex (39 year property) on August 1 of a given year in a nearby suburban development. The property costs you $500,000 — $400,000 for the building and $100,000 for the land.

Assume you do some minor repairs and then place the property in service on September 1 of the same year.

Even though the complex was placed in service on September 1, the mid-month convention says the property is placed in service on September 15. You and your colleague together may deduct three and one-half months of depreciation, or $2,991 in the year you place the property in service.

The deduction adds up this way: You take the cost of the building — $400,000 — and divide it by 39 years, the number of years over which you must depreciate commercial property. Then you divide the result — $10,256 — by 12 months and multiply by three and one-half months.

TIP

While the mid-month convention may seem unfair, it can actually work to your advantage. The reason — you're entitled to a half of a month's depreciation no matter when during the month you place your property in service, even if it's September 30.

TIP

If you fail to claim a depreciation deduction one year, you may not take it in a subsequent year. But you still have an opportunity to claim the deduction. You may file an amended return for the year you failed to claim your depreciation deduction assuming that year is still open under the statute (generally, 3 years after the date your return is filed).

TIP

You should file Form 4562, "Depreciation and Amortization," to claim your depreciation deductions.

Mortgage interest

You are entitled to deduct mortgage interest on rental real estate. As with other expenses, you claim this deduction on Schedule E of your Form 1040.

Operating expenses

The rules allow a deduction on Schedule E, Form 1040, for a whole host of expenses associated with the operation of a rental property; for example:

- cleaning,
- utilities,
- fire insurance, and
- liability insurance.

You may also deduct any supplies — a receipt book, for example — normally deductible for profit-oriented activities.

TIP

Travel is also 100 percent deductible on Schedule E, as long as the trip is strictly for real estate business. For example, assume you own a house on the Florida coast that you rent, and you head south to inspect and make repairs to your rental property. These expenses — the cost of your airplane ticket to Florida, plus your local transportation expenses — are deductible.

What if you travel to Florida, spend one day attending to your rental real estate business, then five days vacationing? You're not entitled to write off the cost of your plane ticket.

TIP

> You may deduct expenses, even if your property isn't rented for a period of time; however, the property must be available for rent during the period. The IRS will not disallow your deductions simply because your property is hard to rent.

Property taxes

State and local property taxes may be deducted on Schedule E, Form 1040, but you may write off *only* those real estate taxes you actually pay. For example, assume you and your spouse jointly own a small apartment building but file separate returns. Each of you may deduct only the taxes that you individually pay.

The one exception to this rule are taxpayers in community property states — such as Arizona, California, Idaho, Louisiana, Nevada, New Mexico, Texas, and Washington. The tax law considers that taxes paid from community funds are on a fifty-fifty basis.

Also, no deduction is allowed for real estate taxes placed in escrow — in the care of a third party — until they are actually paid out of the escrow account.

Accordingly, if your monthly mortgage payment includes an amount placed in escrow for property taxes, you may not write off those escrow payments. You may deduct only the amount of the tax that the lender actually paid to the taxing authority, such as a city or county.

TIP

> Most lenders pay taxes out of escrow accounts on the tax due date. However, if the due date is shortly after the end of the calendar year, you may want to ask your lender to speed up the payment so that you may claim the deduction a year earlier. But make sure the assessment date (often called the lien date) falls within the earlier year; otherwise, the law will not allow you to accelerate the deduction into an earlier year.

TIP

> If rental property is purchased or sold during the tax year, the seller and purchaser must divide the property taxes for the year of sale. The taxes that may be deducted are based on the number of days each party owned the property.
>
> For example, if you are the seller, you pay and deduct the taxes up to the date of the sale. The buyer pays and deducts the taxes after the sale.

Repairs and improvements

A current deduction is allowed for the cost of repairs but not the cost of improvements. The cost of improvements are capitalized and may be depreciated over their useful lives. Accordingly, a determination must be made as to whether an expenditure is a repair or an improvement.

A repair is an expenditure that keeps the property in good working order and doesn't add to its value or substantially prolong its life. Plastering and painting qualify as repairs, as well as fixing gutters and floors, repairing leaks, and replacing broken windows.

An improvement adds to the value of your property, prolongs its useful life, or adapts it to new uses. Adding a room is an example, as are putting up a fence, installing new plumbing or wiring, or replacing the roof.

Salaries and wages

Amounts paid to individuals to help with the upkeep of the rental property are 100 percent deductible on Schedule E, Form 1040.

TIP

An owner of rental property might consider hiring his/her children to perform the duties associated with the upkeep of the rental property. The amount paid to them is tax deductible. Furthermore, they presumably will pay taxes on the income at a rate that's lower than the owner's rate.

EXAMPLE

You are in the 31 percent tax bracket and own a small apartment building. You pay your son John $3,500 to tend to the yard. This is his only income for the year and he will pay no tax on it because his earnings of $3,500 are less than the standard deduction.

You, in turn, will receive a tax deduction for the $3,500 of salary realizing a tax benefit of $1,085 or 31 percent of the amount paid. Thus, you have saved $1,085 in taxes. (This example doesn't take into account state taxes, the impact of a possible itemized deduction disallowance, or the personal exemption phaseout.)

CAUTION

If you do hire your children to help with the upkeep of your rental property, it's important not only that you keep records of the hours they work and the wages you pay them, but that you are also able to demonstrate they performed legitimate services.

On audit, the IRS is likely to cast a critical eye on your employment arrangements with your children and may disallow deductions unless you have complete records and can demonstrate that the arrangement was bona-fide.

TIP

If your children are under age 18, neither you as their employer, nor the kids as your employees, will owe social security taxes — an added benefit.

Rehabilitation tax credit

The rehabilitation tax credit is intended to encourage the preservation of historic buildings. The credit totals 10 percent of the amount spent to fix up (rehabilitate) a building that was built before 1936.

In addition, the credit increases to 20 percent of the amount spent rehabilitating — but not purchasing — what's known as a certified historic structure (CHS). A local historical society or an office of the U.S. Department of the Interior can provide the guidelines on certified historic structures.

EXAMPLE

You buy a 100-year-old cookie factory, and the building is a CHS. You spend $50,000 converting it into offices to house your law firm. You may be entitled to a 20 percent credit, or $10,000, so long as certain rules are followed.

Congress adopted the credit to encourage people to preserve older buildings, not destroy them. Accordingly, to qualify for the rehabilitation credit of a building (not a CHS) the following tests must be met:

- at least 50 percent of the building's external walls must be maintained as external walls.
- At least 75 percent of the existing external walls must be preserved either as internal or external walls, and
- at least 75 percent of the existing internal structural framework is retained in place.

The tax law specifically exempts a CHS — such as the cookie factory — from the external and internal wall retention requirements. However, as a practical matter, the government will likely not certify a structure as a CHS unless at least 75 percent of the existing external walls are maintained as internal or external walls.

The credit is available only if the amount spent rehabilitating the building exceeds $5,000 or the "adjusted basis" of the building, whichever is greater.

The adjusted basis is generally the amount paid for the structure minus any deductions taken for depreciation.

EXAMPLE

You paid $100,000 for a building (a non-CHS) which was originally built in 1902 and previously claimed $20,000 in depreciation before you decided to rehabilitate it. Your adjusted basis in the building is $80,000, and accordingly you must spend at least that amount to renovate the structure, or you're entitled to no credit.

Finally, the depreciable basis of the property must be reduced by the amount of the credit taken.

EXAMPLE

Using the facts in the preceding example, you spend $180,000 fixing the building up. Since the building isn't a CHS, you may take a credit of $18,000 (10 percent of $180,000). But you have to figure your future depreciation deductions on an adjusted basis of $242,000 — or, $80,000 plus $180,000 minus your credit of $18,000.

CAUTION

You must incur your rehabilitation expenses within a 24 month period before you qualify for the credit. This 24 months becomes 60 months in the case of rehabilitation projects where the work is performed in stages.

Low-income housing credit

The low-income housing credit constitutes one of the few tax breaks that survived tax reform in 1986. The credit expired on June 30, 1992 but was permanently reinstated by the 1993 Tax Act with certain modifications to the credit eligibility rules.

The amount of the credit depends on the type of housing involved in the project and when the building or buildings are placed in service.

- A higher credit is available if you construct new housing or substantially rehabilitate an existing structure.

- A lower credit is available for the purchase of existing housing that is rehabilitated and for new housing constructed with the help of federal subsidies.

To qualify for the credits among other requirements, the housing must remain as low-income rental property for 15 years. If it doesn't, some of the tax benefits previously received must be recaptured.

The tenants must also meet stringent requirements — for example, their incomes must not exceed preset limits and the occupants must not be transients (i.e., you do not get the credit for dormitories, nursing homes, hospitals and similar facilities).

The rate of credit for both categories of property is computed by the Treasury Department and published in the Internal Revenue Bulletin. Your tax adviser or local IRS office will help you determine which credit applies in your situation and which percentages to use when you calculate the credit.

The credit is computed by multiplying the credit percentage in effect for the month the property is placed in service by the "qualified basis" of the property. The qualified basis is usually the cost of the building, plus any improvements or additions made before the end of the year in which the structure is placed in service.

Once computed, one-tenth of the credit may be utilized each year for 10 years.

CAUTION

The rules require your state or local housing credit agency to approve the amount of the credit you claim on your tax return.

The rules mandate that the agency fill out and return to you Form 8609, Low-Income Housing Credit Allocation Certification, specifying the appropriate rate of the credit and your maximum qualified basis. You attach Form 8609 to your income-tax return when you claim the housing credit.

CAUTION

Your qualified basis is reduced if your entire building isn't used as low-income housing. To determine the reduced basis, multiply the total basis by the smaller of these two fractions: The percentage of low-income units in the building to total residential rental units (whether occupied or not) or the percentage of floor space of low-income units to total available rental floor space.

CAUTION

As part of the 1990 Tax Act, the IRS allowed individuals to elect to increase the credit they claimed during 1990 by up to 50 percent of the otherwise allowable credit. If you made this election in 1990, you must reduce the credit you take in future years by the amount you accelerated it in 1990. For example, if you elected to claim an additional $700 of low income housing credit in your 1990 return on low income property that has seven years of remaining credit eligibility after 1990 you must reduce the allowable credit in each of the subsequent seven years by $100 per year.

TIP

The credit percentages you use to calculate the credit change each month. So you may want to lock in your percentage before the month in which you place the property in service, especially if you expect the rates to drop.

To do this, you may elect to the use the credit percentage in effect for the month in which you and the housing credit agency agree to your percentage rate and basis. *Or*, if you're financing your project with tax-exempt bonds, you may elect to use the percentage in effect for the month in which the bonds were issued.

In both cases, you must file the election with the housing-credit agency by the fifth day of the following month.

TIP

If the credit exceeds your tax in any year, you may carry back the excess three years — but not to a year ending before 1988 — or carry it forward 15 years.

How to take the credits on your tax return

Each year, you may offset the tax on your passive income and no more than $25,000 of your ordinary income (i.e., wages or interest), with the rehabilitation credit or low-income housing credit. You are not required to actively participate in managing the property. For example, you could be a limited partner.

Before we see how this $25,000 limit works, we need to give a quick definition. A deduction reduces your taxes by the amount of your marginal tax rate. If you're in the 31 percent bracket, for example, a deduction of $10,000 cuts your taxes by $3,100. But a credit slashes the taxes you pay dollar-for-dollar; that is, a tax credit of $10,000 reduces your tax bill by $10,000. Now, let's return to the $25,000 ceiling.

Under the law you may claim up to the rehabilitation or low-income housing "tax-credit equivalent" of a $25,000 deduction without being an active participant in the venture. You may not take up to $25,000 off your tax bill.

What you may do is take a credit that reduces the taxes you owe by the same amount as a $25,000 tax deduction would. So if your marginal rate is 31 percent, the credit equivalent of a $25,000 deduction comes to $7,750 ($25,000 times 31 percent).

There's one other important rule you should know about if you invest in older structures or low-income housing. The $25,000 credit equivalent phases out as your income rises, except in the case of low-income housing acquired after 1989.

The $25,000 credit equivalent does not phase out until your adjusted gross income tops $200,000.

For adjusted gross income in excess of this amount you must reduce the $25,000 by 50 percent of the amount by which your AGI exceeds $200,000. You must then convert this amount to a credit equivalent. As a result, you get no benefit from the $25,000 credit equivalent once your AGI reaches $250,000.

Finally, it's important to realize that both the rehabilitation and low-income housing credits are classified as general business credits. You may therefore claim no more credit than $25,000 plus 75 percent of any tax you owe over $25,000 in general business credits. Moreover, if you are subject to alternative minimum tax (AMT) or near it, additional limitations on the amount of general business credit you may claim may be imposed.

CAUTION

Assume you own some rental property that you actively participate in managing. Now you're thinking about investing as a limited partner in a rehab deal. You may deduct from your ordinary income no more than a total of $25,000 a year from any combination of rental real estate losses and credit equivalents.

EXAMPLE

You report a $25,000 loss from an apartment building you manage yourself. In addition, you incur a loss of $5,000 from an oil and gas limited partnership, but you record $15,000 of income from a research and development limited partnership. The rules require you to first total all your losses from rental properties in which you actively participate; in your case, the total comes to $25,000.

First, you add up any profits from any such rental activities, and subtract your losses from your profits. Since you post no profits, you're left with a $25,000 loss.

Next, you must add up your income from passive investments — $15,000 in your case. You must then subtract your losses from passive activities, which is $5,000. The result — $10,000 — is your net passive income.

Then, you subtract your $25,000 of rental losses from your $10,000 of passive income and $15,000 is the amount you may deduct on your return as a rental loss.

Remember, you may only deduct rental losses up to $25,000. Therefore, if you also invest in a rehabilitation partnership, you may write off as much as $10,000 in credit equivalents.

If you're in the situation described in the previous example, but have exhausted the $25,000 limit and still have losses and credit equivalents left, you may carry these losses and credit equivalents forward for use in future years. But, even then, you're subject to all the limits we described earlier, including the $25,000 ceiling on rental losses.

12

Maximizing The Tax Advantages of Owning A Vacation Home

- When does your second home qualify as a vacation home, rental property, or some combination of the two?
- Why is it important to keep track of the personal use of your vacation home?
- How does the tax treatment of a vacation home differ from the tax treatment of rental property?

The tax treatment of a second home varies with how it is used. As far as the IRS is concerned, a second home is either a vacation home used exclusively by the owner, rental property, or some combination of the two. The classification determines how the home is treated for tax purposes.

The details of how a second residence is taxed are covered in this section.

A *vacation home* that is used 100 percent of the time as a second residence gets the same tax treatment as your primary residence. This is true even if the only nonpersonal use of the property is when it is rented to others (but for no more than 14 days a year). Mortgage interest and property taxes may be deducted; however, other expenses such as repairs may not be deducted.

The IRS is quite liberal when it comes to defining a vacation home. It does not much matter if you have an A-frame in the woods or a townhouse in the city.

Any dwelling unit, even a boat or house trailer, that contains basic living accommodations — kitchen, bathroom, and sleeping space — qualifies as a vacation home.

CAUTION

The $25,000 passive activity rental exception only applies to real estate; a boat is not real estate, even if you do use it as a vacation home. (See Chapter 9 for more information on these rules.)

TIP

If you rent out your home for less than 15 days a year, the rental income you collect is totally tax free. The IRS does not require you to pay tax on this income — a nice benefit.

Rental property differs from a vacation home. You must recognize income generated from renting the property and deductions are allowed for most of the expenses incurred in generating that income. You may also depreciate the property.

Combination property is treated differently than rental property. Its treatment depends on how much rental use and how much personal use your vacation property gets.

CAUTION

Just one day — one way or the other — often can make a big difference in your tax bill.

PERSONAL USE VS. RENTAL PROPERTY

As rental property has been discussed in a previous chapter, the rules governing vacation homes used as combination property are covered here.

Defining the difference

For tax purposes, the differences between a personal vacation home and rental property are great and accordingly, the tax code is precise about the applicable definitions.

These distinctions are important to those who intend to rent their second home and take advantage of the tax deductions that renting brings.

A second home may be classified as rental property as long as it is not used for personal purposes for more than 14 days in the year or for more than 10 percent of the total number of days that it's rented at fair market value, whichever is greater.

Accordingly, if you rent your second home at the going rate for 300 days, you could use it yourself for as many as 30 days, and it would still qualify as rental property.

CAUTION

If you occupy the home in the example above for 31 days you may still claim a deduction for mortgage interest and taxes allocable to your personal use of the home, but as you will see in the following discussion, you're limited on the deductions you may take for mortgage interest and taxes allocable to rental use, operating expenses and depreciation. So one day can make a big difference, tax-wise.

The IRS is strict about what is considered personal use. It considers the home used for personal purposes if on any part of any day the vacation home is occupied by the taxpayer or any of the following people:

- A person who has an equity stake in the property;
- A spouse or blood relative (meaning parents, children, siblings, and grandparents);
- A person with whom the taxpayer has a barter arrangement that allows the taxpayer to use another dwelling in exchange for the use of the taxpayer's dwelling; or
- A person to whom the vacation home isn't rented at "fair market value" — which, according to the law, means the going rate for similar homes in the area.

Even if a relative or someone with an equity interest in the property is charged a fair market value rent for use of the property, the IRS still considers this use personal.

EXAMPLE

You own a vacation home in Montana and rent it to your brother for the going rate, $1,500 for 10 days.

In addition, as part of a barter agreement, you allow your friend to occupy your vacation home for 11 days. In exchange, you use his home in Florida for 8 days.

Finally, you rent your vacation home to your spouse's boss for 10 days and charge her only half the fair market value rental.

By the IRS rules, all 31 days count as personal use.

What constitutes a day? When you're counting, do it by the 24-hour period the way hotels do.

Suppose you occupy your vacation home from Saturday afternoon through the following Saturday morning. In the eyes of the IRS, you've used your house for 7 days, even though you were actually on the premises for part of 8 calendar days.

The law does make one exception to the rule on renting to relatives. If you rent your property at fair market value to a relative who uses the house as a principal residence — a condo for your parents, for instance, the IRS doesn't consider this use personal.

TIP

In a Tax Court case, a taxpayer reduced by 20 percent the fair market value rent he charged his parents for a home they used as their principal residence. The court ruled the rent was fair because it reflected the amount the man saved in maintenance and management fees by renting to such trustworthy tenants. Therefore, the rental did not qualify as personal use.

CAUTION

The IRS has held that donating a week's use of a vacation home to a charity auction counted as personal use of the home by the home's owner.

The reason? The owner didn't charge the bidder at the auction — the renter — a fair rent. Instead, the bidder paid the rental to the charity.

In addition, the owner could not claim a deduction for a charitable contribution because a gift of the right to use property isn't deductible.

TIP

Plan wisely if you want to donate use of your vacation home to a charity auction. Rent your home out for a week at its fair market value, then donate the rental income to charity. That way, you get a deduction for your contribution and avoid wasting personal use days.

Maintenance and repair visits

Vacation homes require repairs and maintenance. If you stay at the house while doing the repairs, the IRS does not count these days as personal use if your "principal purpose" in staying there is to make repairs or perform maintenance chores.

EXAMPLE

You own a ski house that you rent during the winter. You and your spouse arrive at the house late Thursday evening to prepare the house for the rental season. Assume you work on the house all day Friday and Saturday. Your spouse helps for a few hours each day but spends most of the time catching up on paperwork. By Saturday evening all your work is done. You spend the rest of the evening relaxing, then head home shortly before noon on Sunday.

Since the principal purpose of your trip was for maintenance, none of these days count as personal days. They're all maintenance days.

CAUTION

If your tax return is audited, the IRS may ask you to prove that the principal purpose of your visit was to make repairs and perform maintenance. An auditor may look at how often you did chores, the amount of time you spent performing repairs and maintenance, and whether friends accompanied you.

If, for example, you spend most of your time at your home doing maintenance — but always bring along a few companions — your activities might be considered personal and the IRS may count those days as personal use days.

As a result, you could lose your deductions.

TIP

Maintain a log of your repair and maintenance days. Record when you arrive, how much time you spend on various tasks, and what kind of work you perform to prove how you spent your time.

Rental property

If a vacation home is maintained strictly as rental property, the same rules that apply to rental real estate apply to the vacation home. (See Chapter 11 for a discussion of these rules.)

Combination property

Combination property can be divided into two categories. With the first, personal use of a vacation home is within the 14-day or 10 percent limits previously discussed and most of the deductions applicable for rental property are available.

If use of the property falls into this category, the property is not considered a personal residence. Rather, it is considered to be rental property and the rules do not allow a deduction for any interest or other expenses allocated to your personal use. The interest is personal interest, the same as credit card interest, which is not deductible.

The property taxes allocated to the personal use are deductible on Schedule A. All remaining expenses allocable to personal use are generally nondeductible personal expenditures. However, depending on the number of days you actually rent the property, the expenses allocated to personal use could be insignificant. Your expenses allocable to rental days will be deductible as rental expense.

With the second type of combination property, your personal use exceeds the 14 day or 10 percent limit. As a result, the tax treatment of the property is substantially different.

The portion of interest, taxes, and other expenses allocated to rental use are only deductible to the extent of rental income. In other words, if your second home falls into this category and you incur a loss from renting the house, you may not deduct that loss currently from your other taxable income.

Assuming this type of property qualifies as a second residence, mortgage interest allocable to personal use may be deducted as an itemized deduction on your Form 1040. Similarly, you may deduct the personal portion of the property taxes.

The rules require you to deduct your "rental" expenses in a specified order.

- First, you write off advertising and commission charges,
- then property taxes and mortgage interest,
- then operating expenses, and
- finally, depreciation.

This ordering of expenses requires the deduction of property taxes and mortgage interest that you could write off in any case before deducting operating expenses. However, only if, and to the extent that, rental income is in excess of these expenses may you write off your other operating expenses.

If you have adequate rental income and the home qualifies as a second residence, your total interest and taxes are deductible either against, and to the extent of, rental income, or as personal interest and taxes claimed on Schedule A.

TIP

The rules allow you to carry forward to future tax years any expenses you aren't able to deduct currently — subject to all the limits described above.

CAUTION

If you own a third home and it qualifies as combination property — and your personal use is more than 14 days or 10 percent of the total days it's rented — different rules apply to the interest expense (all other expenses are treated the same as in the case of a second residence).

The portion of mortgage interest allocated to personal use is not deductible as mortgage interest because no more than two homes may be considered as personal residences for the purpose of deducting interest.

Accordingly, the interest allocated to personal use is treated as personal interest and is not deductible. Interest allocated to the rental use is deductible to the extent of rental income less advertising, commission charges, and taxes.

If, however, personal use of the third home is within the 14 days or 10 percent of the total rental days, the treatment of interest expense and all other expenses is identical to the discussion of the first category of combination property as applied to the second home.

Allocation of expenses

Regardless of which category the vacation home falls into, the rules require an allocation of expenses to personal and rental use.

This is true even if the home is used for personal purposes just one day of the year — New Year's Day, say, or the Fourth of July. One day's worth of the vacation home's total expenses must be allocated to personal use. There are no exceptions to this rule.

The allocation formula used to allocate expenses to rental use is the proportion of rental days to total use days. This ratio is then applied to the total expenses incurred (including property taxes and mortgage interest) for the year to determine the amount allocated to rental use. The same methodology is used to allocate expenses to personal use; in this case the numerator of the fraction is personal days. Note that repair and maintenance days and days the property is not used at all (i.e., vacant) are not considered.

Following is an example illustrating the use of this formula. The two scenarios also illustrate the difference just one additional day of personal use can make in the tax cost of a vacation home.

THE FACTS

- Your principal residence is in Massachusetts and you also own a vacation home in Arizona which you actively participate in managing.
- You take out a mortgage to buy the house in Arizona.
- Your interest totals $4,000; taxes, $2,000; operating expenses, $2,000; and depreciation, $5,000.
- Your rental income for the current year adds up to $7,500, after commissions for the year.
- Your adjusted gross income is $100,000 not counting the effect of your Arizona house.

Scenario 1: You rent your Arizona house at a fair market value for 126 days, use it for family vacations for 14 days, and spend four days there making repairs and performing maintenance.

By applying the rules, you would determine that you used the house for a total of 140 days (126 rental and 14 personal). The four days you spent on repair and maintenance aren't included in your total use days.

As a result, you allocate 90 percent — that is, 126 divided by 140 — of the costs associated with the house to rental use.

The numbers calculate as follows:

- Total rental income — $7,500
- 90 percent of taxes — $1,800
- 90 percent of mortgage interest — $3,600
- 90 percent of operating expenses — $1,800
- 90 percent of depreciation — $4,500

The result: a rental loss of $4,200 which is fully deductible under the passive loss rules, as your adjusted gross income is $100,000. For more on passive losses, see Chapter 9.

You may also deduct the other 10 percent of your property taxes, or $200, as an itemized deduction on Schedule A of your Form 1040.

However, the remaining interest — the part allocated to personal use — is classified as personal interest. Personal interest is not deductible. Thus, in total, you have deductions against your normal taxable income of $4,400 — $4,200 plus $200.

Scenario 2: In this case, you increase your use of the house by just one day, bringing your personal use to 15 days for the year, but all the other facts are the same.

Since 15 days exceeds the maximum 14-day limit and is more than 10 percent of the total rental days (126 days), your vacation home is now classified as a residence.

Therefore, your deductions for costs allocated to rental use — that is, 126 divided by 141, or 89 percent — may not exceed the rental income you received. And you must write off expenses allocated to rental use in the following order:

- Commissions and advertising
- Property taxes and mortgage interest
- Operating expenses
- Depreciation

On the plus side, the IRS counts the portion of mortgage interest you allocate to the personal use of your home as deductible — just like the interest expense on your principal residence. You may deduct this amount on your personal return.

Here's how the numbers work out:

- Total rental income — $7,500
- 89 percent of taxes and interest — $5,340
- 89 percent of operating expenses — $1,780 (not limited since the $7,500 rental income exceeds the interest and taxes by $2,160)
- 89 percent of depreciation — potentially $4,450, but limited to just $380, since that is the amount by which rental income ($7,500) tops interest, taxes, and operating expenses ($7,120)

The result: You incurred a rental loss of $4,070, but you may not claim it currently. As the result of exceeding the 14 day or 10 percent personal use limit, your deductible expenses may not exceed your rental income. You may still deduct the remaining 11 percent of property taxes and interest — or $660 — on your Form 1040.

These examples illustrate that using your house more than the maximum days allowed can cause your taxes to rise sharply. That extra day's use in our example costs you $3,740 in deductions (the difference between the $4,400 in deductions in our first example and the $660 in the second).

Remember, however, the rules allow you to carry forward amounts you may not deduct currently — in this case, $4,070 — to future tax years.

There is an alternative method for allocating taxes and mortgage interest — approved by the courts, but not the IRS — that may be used.

This method reduces the amount of interest and taxes allocated to the rental activity, allowing room to use more of your other expenses as deductions against rental income. In turn, it increases the amount of interest and taxes allocable to personal use, resulting in a larger itemized deduction.

Under this alternative method, the number of rental days is divided by the total number of days in the year. The resulting percentage is used to determine the portion of mortgage interest and property taxes that you deduct from your rental income.

The percentage calculated under this alternative method is usually smaller than under the IRS promulgated method because the IRS method requires that the number of rental days be divided by the number of days the property was actually in use. In turn, the alternative method usually results in greater savings.

However, to be certain, both calculations should be performed and the results compared.

EXAMPLE

The facts are the same as in the second scenario above.

Allocating interest and taxes to your rental activity using the alternative method results in the following amounts:

• Gross rental income — $7,500

• Taxes and interest — $2,071 (allocated based on the ratio of rental days to total days in the year — that is, 126 divided by 365, times $6,000)

• Limit on other deductions — $5,429 ($7,500 minus $2,071)

• Operating expenses — $1,780 (89 percent times $2,000)

• Depreciation — limited to the lesser of $4,450 (89 percent times $5,000) or $3,649 ($5,429 minus $1,780)

• Rental income or loss — zero

• Remaining taxes and interest deductible as itemized deductions — 239/365 times $6,000, or $3,929

In this example, the alternative method works better for you. It gives you $3,929 in tax and interest deductions compared to $660 using the other method.

CAUTION

Since the alterative method is approved by the courts, not the IRS, you may be more likely to face questions upon an audit if you use it.

13

TAX TIPS FOR
MUTUAL FUND
INVESTORS

■ What types of income does a mutual fund produce and what are the tax consequences?

■ If I sell my mutual fund shares, how can I plan to save taxes?

■ What are REITs and REMICs and what tax rules apply to them?

Mutual funds are among the most popular investment vehicles around today. You get expert management of your money by people who devote their full time and attention to the task. You also get diversification and convenience.

What do you need to know — tax-wise, at least — when it comes to investing in mutual funds? That's what this chapter is all about.

BASIC CONCEPTS

Mutual funds are investment companies that raise money from shareholders and invest it in a wide range of securities — domestic and foreign stocks and bonds, government securities, and so on.

Mutual funds are either open-ended or closed-ended. What's the difference between the two? Open-ended funds have an unlimited number of shares and investors generally purchase their shares directly from the fund sponsor or securities broker. The company constantly — daily — sells new shares to investors and redeems (i.e., meaning purchases from shareholders) outstanding ones. So the amount of money managed by the fund is always changing.

Closed-ended funds, on the other hand, issue a fixed number of shares, which usually are not redeemed by the company, or if so, are redeemed only at certain times (e.g., every 3, 6, 12, or 24 months). Investors generally trade them just like they do any other stock — on the New York or American Stock Exchanges or over the counter.

With closed-ended mutual funds, the amount of money under management is relatively fixed because it's not affected by sales and redemptions of shares as much as open-ended funds are affected.

Open-ended funds are the most common type of mutual fund. The tax rules for both types of funds are the same.

Most mutual funds are organized as special kinds of corporations — regulated investment companies. Unlike regular corporations, a regulated investment company, or RIC, doesn't pay taxes on income that it distributes to shareholders.

To receive this preferential tax treatment, however, a fund must meet many stringent requirements. For one, it must distribute practically all its income each year. In this regard, the tax law generally treats mutual funds much as it does partnerships and other so-called pass-through entities. The shareholders, rather than the mutual fund, generally pay taxes on any income the fund generates.

Mutual funds are designed to free you from the responsibility of managing your portfolio on a day-to-day basis and provide you with management having the experience and expertise to manage your investment. When you buy shares in a mutual fund you in effect "hire" an investment expert to allow you to benefit from the expert's wisdom in a particular area.

TYPES OF MUTUAL FUNDS

Different mutual funds reflect different styles of investing as well as different investment vehicles. There is a tax component to the return on each investment, including even tax-free investments. There are also many types of portfolio assets, all having different economic and tax advantages or disadvantages.

Since mutual funds may invest in many different types of securities, investors may choose from among many different types of funds dedicated to particular portfolio goals. For example, investors may choose to pursue interest exempt from federal, state or local taxation. Or, maybe only interest that is exempt from state and local taxation rather than federal taxation is desired. United States or municipal bond funds offer these opportunities.

Alternatively, corporate bond or stock funds may provide current income or long-term growth opportunities. Here are some of the broad categories of mutual funds available to investors.

Tax Exempt Funds

Generally, tax exempt mutual funds will pay you federal tax exempt income. But, you may still have to pay federal tax when the fund sells portfolio assets (bonds), or when you sell your shares in the funds. Also, tax exempt funds often have some taxable investments.

Funds designed not only to be tax-free for federal purposes but also tax-free in the state where you live are known as "double tax-exempt." Since some municipalities also have income taxes, when these municipalities also allow the interest on their bonds to be exempt, investments can even be "triple tax-exempt."

By purchasing shares in tax exempt mutual funds, you can avoid state and federal taxes without buying the bonds directly. It also usually enables you to sell more quickly and perhaps at better prices.

TIP

If you live in a state that taxes investment income or has an intangibles tax (i.e., Florida or North Carolina — as well as others), find out which bonds are issued from within your home state and are exempt from these taxes. Then find a fund that has a significant portion of its portfolio invested in such bonds and find out whether the state will respect the pass-through of the exemption for tax purposes.

The mutual fund prospectus should tell you all you need to know. You can also call the mutual fund for this information. You should balance the risk of holding one state or city's bonds (lack of diversification) against the additional tax savings.

Some tax-free funds are formed as partnerships rather than corporations so that it is more likely the fund's tax-free interest will flow through to all of its investors. For the most part, the only difference between a fund organized as a regulated investment company and a partnership is the nature of the reporting provided to its investors.

TIP

Some state and local tax-free bonds — called private activity bonds — are issued to assist corporations building facilities in a particular area. Although free from regular tax, certain of such bonds issued after August 7, 1986 are subject to the alternative minimum tax (AMT) (see Chapter 8 for more information about AMT). For investors not subject to AMT, it may be possible to enjoy the higher yield of these private activity bonds (a higher interest rate compensates for the potential AMT liability).

Money-market Funds

The most popular type of mutual fund during the early 1980s was the money-market fund. Many people may not think of it as a mutual fund since it always sells for $1.00 per share and, therefore, is treated like cash. It is, however, a mutual fund in which the value of the portfolio is always matched with the number of shares outstanding so that the share value equals $1.00. You will thus not likely ever make or lose money buying and selling money-market shares.

Therefore, such funds should be used to temporarily invest cash you may need in the near future. Since the return on such funds usually barely matches or falls just short of inflation, they are not attractive as long-term investment.

U.S. Government Funds

A U.S. government bond fund is made up almost entirely of U.S. bonds and notes and is generally tax-exempt for federal and state purposes (e.g., double tax exempt). Depending on portfolio and trading strategies, some of these funds have almost no risk as to principal and little risk as to return (although share values do fluctuate inversely with interest rates). Since the underlying assets are well known and are similar, the largest difference between competing funds is the expenses charged by the fund.

Many investment advisers recommend holding U.S. government bonds directly for better investment returns. However, if you want check writing, small dollar amount withdrawals or additions to holdings, a fund can accommodate you much easier than owning the bonds directly.

Corporate Bond Funds

Corporate bond funds are fully taxable by both federal and state jurisdictions, but they usually provide higher returns. They also carry more risk depending on the issuer. Investors should always carefully evaluate these funds. As with any bond, the fund's value tends to move in the opposite direction of prevailing interest rates.

These funds usually invest in high grade corporate issues. However, some bonds funds invest in "high-yield" issues of lower investment quality whose value swings with the fortunes of the corporate bond issuers as well as interest rates. Often, bonds perform better in a depressed economy. Corporate bond funds also offer some counterbalance to stocks in a portfolio.

Diversified Stock or Index Funds

If you want to enjoy the historically higher rates of return of the stock market over other forms of passive investment, consider a diversified stock fund or index fund. These funds emphasize long term growth of capital and relative safety of principal.

Depending on the particular market conditions and the fund manager, these funds may balance current income and portfolio turnover of investments with long-term holdings. However, you must recognize that stock funds may fluctuate greatly in value over time, and your stock fund's value may be depressed when you need to sell it.

As with all equity funds, ask about unrealized gains before you buy shares. If a portfolio has a large net unrealized gain (portfolio stocks that have greatly appreciated), then as an investor, you could face a large tax bill when these gains are realized. The situation is very similar to buying a fund immediately before a distribution is made (discussed below).

Balanced Funds

A balanced fund will try to protect principal. Such funds mix bonds and stocks together to compensate for the fact that at any particular point in time, either bonds or stocks will likely provide better current income returns for a reasonably short time horizon. A balanced fund generally holds corporate (taxable) bonds, possibly some U.S. government bonds and stocks.

Foreign Funds

Some funds are set up to invest in foreign securities (i.e., international funds, global funds, regional funds, and single country funds). Such funds have a wide variety of geographic strategies, target securities, trading and risk management goals and strategies.

Your choice of such funds and the amount of your portfolio depends on your risk tolerance and willingness to invest in the different economies of the world. In addition, for tax purposes, since funds may pass through foreign taxes paid by the fund you are entitled to either deduct the foreign taxes paid or claim a credit for the foreign taxes on Form 1116.

TIP

Its generally better to claim the foreign taxes as a credit since a credit reduces your tax liability dollar for dollar. A deduction, meanwhile, simply reduces the amount of your income subject to tax.

CHARACTER OF INCOME

With all of the different types of investments a fund can invest in, there are many types of income you could receive. Generally, for funds not organized as partnerships, 50 percent or more of the fund assets must be invested in a particular type of security if its income is to "pass through" to its investors and retain its character.

For example, 50 percent or more of the assets in a tax-exempt bond fund must be invested in tax-free investments for tax-exempt interest to be passed through to shareholders. Similarly, foreign funds must have 50 percent or more of their assets invested in foreign securities to allow for pass-through of foreign taxes. The fund prospectus should provide the information you need to decide whether a particular fund's investment goals meet your investment goals.

RETURN ON INVESTMENT

Investors will realize a gain or loss from mutual fund investments from two sources — amounts passed out by the fund and the direct investment in the mutual fund stock itself. Gains or losses are computed from the direct investment in mutual fund stock — when the mutual fund shares are sold — much the same way as for other stocks.

BASIS FOR DETERMINING GAINS AND LOSSES

An investor must know his or her basis to determine the gain or loss. The amount paid when mutual fund shares are first bought is the initial basis. This includes not only the listed price of the shares but also other costs of acquisition such as commissions or load fees. If a dividend reinvestment program is elected (discussed later) the basis will also be affected.

The general rules for figuring the basis of capital assets discussed in Chapter 4 apply to your mutual fund shares. But the record keeping for the basis in your mutual fund shares may be more complicated than with other investments.

The reason? Often mutual fund investing results in more ongoing transactions that affect your basis. For example, dividend reinvestment, undistributed capital gains, periodic redemptions or sales, and nontaxable distributions (topics that are all covered later in this chapter) all affect your basis.

You increase your basis for:

- Any undistributed capital gains allocated to you, and
- Dividend reinvestments.

You reduce the basis by:

- Any so-called "nontaxable distributions" which are a return of capital (discussed below), and

- Any redemptions or sales.

As we saw in the Chapter 4, an increase in basis can either decrease your capital gain or increase your capital loss when you subsequently sell the mutual fund stock.

PURCHASE PRICE

How do mutual funds calculate the price you pay for their shares and the amount you receive when you sell those shares? If you look at your newspaper's listing of open-ended mutual funds, you will see listed under the price the letters NAV, which stand for net asset value per share.

Net asset value per share is calculated by subtracting a fund's total liabilities from the market value of its total assets, then dividing the result by the number of shares outstanding.

No-load open-ended funds usually sell or redeem (purchase back from investors) their shares at NAV less any applicable redemption fees or deferred sales charges. By contrast, load open-ended funds impose a charge above NAV when they sell (i.e., investors purchase) their shares. The "loaded" price is usually shown under the appropriate column in the newspaper listing (loads are discussed later in this chapter).

Closed-ended funds usually sell for an amount that is higher (that is, they carry a premium) or lower (they sell at a discount) than their NAV. It all depends on what the market thinks of the stock. In other words, the stock price of closed-ended companies — like the stock price of other companies — is determined by supply and demand.

REINVESTED DIVIDENDS

Many people like to have their mutual fund automatically reinvest dividends (including capital gains distributions) in additional shares of the fund. How does the tax law treat reinvestment?

Investors must report the amount of the reinvested dividends as dividend income. Since investors have "paid" for the shares by reporting the income, they are permitted to increase their basis. This adds to the original basis the value of the shares acquired with reinvested dividends.

EXAMPLE

You invest $10,000 in a mutual fund and elect to have your dividends reinvested in January. In December 199A, the fund pays you a taxable dividend of $1,000, but you receive no cash. Instead, you receive additional shares valued at $1,000.

When you file your 199A tax return, you are required to report $1,000 of dividend income which is the value of the shares you received. What is your basis in the shares? It is your old basis of $10,000 plus $1,000.

TIP

Remember, before you buy, read the prospectus so you know the timing of the fund's distributions. Most mutual funds declare regular dividend distributions at least annually and sometimes more frequently. You're entitled to receive dividends only if you're a shareholder as of the record date.

You may not want to buy into a fund just before a distribution. The reason? You may owe taxes on income that does not represent an actual profit to you.

Since you usually purchase mutual fund shares based on the net asset value (NAV) of the fund, the NAV is higher just before the distribution than just after the distribution. So, you pay a higher price.

When the fund makes its distribution, you recognize taxable income, but receive no cash because of your desire to have your dividends reinvested. And the overall value of your shares hasn't changed.

EXAMPLE

You invest $10,000 in a mutual fund. The next day the fund pays a $500 dividend on your shares. Now, you must recognize $500 of taxable income on your tax return. The value of your original shares falls to $9,500, because the NAV changes to reflect the amount of the dividend. However, you acquire additional shares that represent $500 of NAV with your reinvested dividend, so the value of your investment returns to $10,000. What's the net result?

You pay $10,000 for your mutual fund investment and it's worth $10,000 based on NAV. Your basis is $10,500 (your $10,000 original investment plus the $500 reinvested), but now you have $500 of income to report.

Had you waited until after the fund paid the dividend to make your $10,000 investment, you'd have had mutual fund shares worth $10,000, but would not have had the $500 of dividend income to report. However, your basis in this case would have been $10,000, not $10,500.

If your dividends are not being reinvested you get the same result by receiving the $500 dividend in cash and then purchasing additional shares of the mutual fund worth $500.

TIP

If you are the type of investor who likes to receive a regular check from your mutual fund, you may want to purchase shares in the fund, reinvest your dividends then ask the fund to redeem a set dollar amount periodically. You might choose monthly redemptions to coincide with other income and expenses or, perhaps, to assist in budgeting.

As with other reinvested dividends, the dividend income is currently taxable. As noted, the amount reinvested increases the basis in the fund. In this way, investors may receive level payments from your mutual fund investment similar to a fixed-income vehicle.

CAUTION

A desire to receive periodic payments results in the fund's selling some of the shares, which may generate a taxable capital gain or loss to you.

CAPITAL GAINS DISTRIBUTIONS

You're subject to tax on net long-term gains your mutual fund earns and distributes (passes through) to you. Say the manager of your mutual fund sells some bonds at a profit and distributes this long-term capital gain to you and other shareholders. These capital gains are taxable to you. See Chapter 3 for a discussion on the taxation of short-term capital gains your mutual fund generates.

You report this amount as a long-term gain regardless of how long you've owned shares in the fund. (You'll find this amount listed on your Form 1099-DIV.)

CAUTION

If you reported a pass-through capital gain on RIC stock (most mutual funds are RICs) you held for six months or less and also sold the RIC stock for a loss, you must report this loss as a long-term capital loss to the extent of any capital gain distributions.

This is required since any pass-through capital gain distribution the RIC reports to you is treated as long-term, even if you held the RIC stock for less than the required holding period. However, this special rule does not apply when you have a periodic redemption plan in place.

A similar rule disallows any loss on the sale of mutual fund shares if the fund was held for less than six months and is a tax-exempt fund. You cannot deduct a loss on the disposal of the shares up to the amount of a tax-exempt dividend paid on the mutual fund shares.

EXAMPLE

You bought tax-exempt mutual fund shares for $40,000 and received a $500 dividend. However, before the shares were held for six months you sold them for $39,000. Thus, $500 of the $1,000 loss on this sale would be disallowed.

Now assume the fund had been a fund other than a tax-exempt fund, for example an equity fund, and the $500 was a capital gain distribution (considered long-term regardless of how long the investor held the share). In this case, the loss would be allowed but $500 of it would be considered long-term. This matches the loss with the character of the capital gain distribution received.

TIP

When you're considering investing in a mutual fund, read the prospectus regarding the amount of unrealized appreciation in that fund.

Unrealized appreciation is the amount the securities in the fund have appreciated over the amount the fund paid for them. If a fund has significant unrealized appreciation, you may get back a portion of your original investment as a long-term capital gain distribution — something you may not want to happen.

EXAMPLE

You invest $10,000 in a fund. Assume that $2,000 of the $10,000 is the value of the fund's stocks above their original cost to the fund — in other words, unrealized appreciation. As the fund manager sells these stocks, capital gains are triggered. If these capital gains are distributed to you (which is usually the case), you must pay tax on them.

Assuming the fund earns no other income, if the fund manager sells all the stocks that have appreciated and distributes the capital gains, you end up with an investment worth $8,000 with a tax cost of $10,000 and cash of $2,000, less federal and state capital gains tax.

Even if you reinvested these dividends in the fund so you end up with $10,000 in the fund — your desired result — you still have $2,000 of capital gains income and a $12,000 basis in the fund. This result is similar to the discussion under "Reinvested dividends."

However, a mutual fund may also have capital loss carryforwards or unrealized losses. These carryforwards or losses may prove advantageous because they may reduce the amount of capital gain income you're required to report.

CAUTION

After making certain calculations, your mutual fund may determine that a portion of the distributions you received during the year is actually a return of part of your investment. A return of capital distribution such as this (also known as a "tax-free dividend" or "nontaxable distribution") usually does not represent taxable income. Instead, these distributions reduce the basis of the shares you hold.

However, say the nontaxable distribution exceeds your basis. In this case, the excess results in a taxable capital gain. Whether the gain is long-term or short-term depends on how long you've held shares in the fund.

RETAINED CAPITAL GAINS

Sometimes a mutual fund retains — rather than distributes to investors — its long-term capital gains. The bad news is, the law requires you to report as long-term capital gains income your portion of that amount even if the fund doesn't actually hand the money over to you. It also doesn't matter how long you've owned the shares.

However, if the fund paid taxes on the gains it retained, you're entitled to a tax credit for the amount of tax paid on your share of the income.

Your fund will send you Form 2439, "Notice to Shareholder of Undistributed Long-Term Capital Gains," listing the amount of the long-term capital gain you must report and the tax paid by the fund on that amount. You may claim a credit for that tax on your Form 1040.

How? Enter the amount of tax eligible for the credit on your Form 1040, similar to wage withholding. Then attach Copy B of your Form 2439 to your return.

You also increase your basis in your mutual fund investment by the difference between the amount of undistributed gains you report and the amount of tax the fund paid for you.

What all this means is that you're in essentially the same tax and economic positions as if you'd actually received the capital gain, paid tax on it, and then reinvested the difference in the fund.

CAUTION

Capital gains your mutual fund retains and reports to you on Form 2439 aren't recorded on your Form 1099-DIV. They are in addition to those listed on your 1099-DIV.

CAUTION

Make sure you keep Copy C of your Form 2439. That way, if you're audited — either in the current year or in the year you sell your mutual fund shares — you can substantiate amounts claimed on your return, including increases in the basis of your mutual fund stock.

INCOME AND EXPENSE REPORTING

Funds report income to the investors on a calendar year basis because most investors file their tax returns based on a calendar year. However, the fund itself may have any year end it chooses.

Also, the accounting for certain investments, income and expenses of the fund may be different for the "books" of the fund than for tax purposes. Therefore, the income reported on either Form 1099-DIV (for funds organized as corporations) or Form K-1, Partner's Share of Income, Credits, Deductions, Etc. (for those organized as partnerships) may not agree with the financial statements issued by the fund.

Some funds are deemed to have paid their dividends in October, November or December, even though you did not receive the dividends until January. These amounts are taxable to you in the year the dividends are deemed paid.

Miscellaneous itemized deductions

Your mutual fund incurs expenses in managing and investing your money. But since the fund subtracts its expenses from its net income before it distributes this income to you, these expenses aren't subject to the two percent of AGI floor on miscellaneous itemized deductions. (See Chapter 7 for more on miscellaneous itemized deductions.)

Sales commissions and loads

Sales commissions and loads (money paid to buy shares) are capital costs, not expenses. You cannot write these costs off in the year paid. Instead, they are included in the computation of basis when it comes time to calculate the gain or loss and reduce the taxable gain or increase the taxable loss.

You may want to look at "no-load" or "low-load" funds. Why? So-called load funds impose a sales charge of up to 8.5 percent of the amount you pay for your fund shares to cover the cost of marketing their shares through sales representatives or brokers. They usually set sliding scales under which this percentage charge gradually decreases as the size of your investment increases.

No-load funds pay no sales representative or brokers. All of the money you invest in no-load funds goes to work for you. A newer breed of mutual fund, called a low-load fund, carries a smaller sales charge of perhaps 2 to 4 percent.

CAUTION

The tax law limits the adjustment you can make in your basis for load charges in certain cases.

For example, suppose you purchase shares in a mutual fund, sell the shares soon after you buy them, and, in the process, incur load charges.

If the investment company allows you to reinvest the proceeds in another of its funds at a waived or reduced load charge, you may not take into account the load you paid on the first shares in figuring your gain or loss (the load charges are added to the basis of the new shares purchased).

However, the law only applies when you sell or exchange the first shares within 90 days of when you acquired them.

IDENTIFICATION OF SHARES SOLD

If you maintain adequate records and you liquidate your entire investment in one transaction, the determination of the basis is relatively simple. You simply determine basis by following the rules discussed previously in this chapter and in Chapter 4.

But what happens if you sell only a portion of the shares you hold? Determination of the basis of individual shares may be quite difficult, particularly if you've had any combination of nontaxable distributions, undistributed capital gains, reinvested dividends and past sales.

As with other investments, the general rules of share identification apply. If you can specifically identify the shares sold, you can use the basis of those shares to determine the amount of the gain or loss.

To accomplish the specific identification of shares within a mutual fund, you must have the cooperation of the fund's transfer agent to identify each share. This involves additional work for the transfer agent as he or she must record the purchase and sale of individual shares within the mutual fund and then report this information to you.

Sometimes, particularly, with certain no-load funds, the transfer agent will not identify the shares for you. In a situation such as this, you must use one of the other techniques for share identification.

TIP

You will usually want to identify as the shares sold those shares with the highest basis. This way, your gain on the sale will be minimized.

TIP

If you already have a net capital loss for the current year, you may want to sell the shares with the lowest basis thereby increasing potential gain from the transaction. Doing this will enable you to offset the capital loss carried forward against the capital gain to reduce or eliminate tax on the gain in the current year.

Like sales of other stocks, if you can't specifically identify the shares you sell, the general rule is that you use the first-in, first-out (FIFO) approach i.e., the first ones bought are the first ones sold.

If specific identification of shares is impracticable and the FIFO method would result in large capital gains, there are two averaging methods for determination of the basis of shares sold. Only mutual fund shareholders may use these averaging methods.

The two methods are called the single-category method and the double-category method. Under both these methods, you use the average basis of the shares you hold when you sell to determine the cost basis of the shares sold to be used for the calculation of gain or loss.

CAUTION

To use either method, you must maintain your shares in the custody of an agent or custodian in an account maintained for the acquisition or redemption of shares of the mutual fund.

Single-category Method

If you elect the single-category method, all the shares you own in a given mutual fund are grouped into one category, and the average basis per share is calculated. Your average basis per share is determined by taking your total basis of all shares of that fund at the time of the sale and dividing that amount by the total number of shares you hold at that time.

The determination of whether the gain or loss is long-term or short-term is based upon the FIFO method. Thus, the shares you sell to other investors will always be considered to be the ones you have held the longest.

Double-category Method

The double-category method, as the name implies, divides your holdings at the time of sale into two categories — those shares held for more than 1 year and those shares held 1 year or less. So your shares are divided into long-term and short-term categories. You then determine the average basis for the shares in each category in the same manner as you do for the single-category method.

When using the double-category method, you specify to the transfer agent the category from which the shares will be sold. The shares will be deemed to have been sold from this category without regard to any stock certificates actually delivered.

For this method to work, you must receive, within a reasonable period of time after the sale, a written confirmation of your specification from the custodian or agent. If you do not receive a confirmation or if you do not make a specification, the FIFO method will be assumed. That is, you will be deemed to have sold the shares from the long-term category first.

TIP

The double-category may present savings opportunities over the single-category method because of the flexibility to use the basis which allows the smaller current tax bill.

In practice, however, the double-category method may be more difficult to work with. You must determine whether the preferential tax treatment of long-term capital gains is significant enough to justify the extra burden from this method.

CAUTION

Once you elect either of the averaging methods for a fund, you must continue to use that method with respect to all sales from that fund until you have completely liquidated your interest.

EXCHANGING MUTUAL FUNDS

The exchange of one mutual fund for another is usually treated as a taxable sale. If you do exchange shares in one mutual fund for shares in another mutual fund, add any service charge or fee paid in connection with the exchange to the basis of the new shares.

If, however, the mutual fund deducts the service charge from your proceeds rather than requiring separate payment, use the net proceeds when you calculate the gain on your old shares rather than adding the charge to the basis of your new shares.

Sometimes one fund may merge with another fund. If the merger qualifies for tax purposes as a "tax-free" merger, the investors in the fund going out of existence will surrender their shares and receive shares in the surviving or new fund in exchange.

Generally, the new shares you receive will take the basis of the shares you surrendered. There will likely not be any taxable income to be recognized in this type of exchange. However, since these types of transactions are relatively rare, be sure you read all of the material related to the exchange provided to you by the fund, or consult your tax adviser.

REAL ESTATE INVESTMENT TRUSTS (REITs)

If you do not want to invest in real estate directly or through partnerships, you can buy shares in a REIT. You can think of a REIT as a mutual fund with real estate or mortgages as a portfolio (at least 75 percent of its assets) rather than stocks or bonds.

As an investment, the reporting is very similar to a conventional mutual fund in that you will receive the same reporting paperwork (i.e., a Form 1099-DIV) after year end which will enable you or your accountant to prepare your tax return.

There are a few twists to tax reporting on the ownership of REITs. Similar to RICs, if you reported a pass-through capital gain on REIT stock that you held for six months or less and also sold the REIT stock for a loss, you must report the loss as a long-term capital loss to the extent of the capital gain distribution.

This is required since any pass-through capital gain distribution the REIT reports to you is treated as long-term, even if you held the REIT stock for less than the required holding period. However, this special rule does not apply when you have a periodic redemption plan in place.

Your REIT will mail you a 1099-DIV listing this amount soon after the close of the tax year.

REAL ESTATE MORTGAGE INVESTMENT CONDUITS (REMICs)

Another way to add real estate related assets to your portfolio is to invest in mortgages by owning an interest in a REMIC. Investment professionals take pools of mortgages and create interests that reflect the economics of mortgages cut into many pieces (branches) and then sell securities designed to perform as these pieces would perform depending on what actually happens to interest rates, defaults, prepayments, etc.

For instance, certain of these pieces are called "regular interests" and behave mostly like debt. Therefore, the regular interests are treated like debt for federal tax purposes. The "residual interests" which behave more like an equity interest in the pool are treated similar to a partnership interest. Generally, REMICs only produce portfolio income and only regular interest holders of single-class REMICs can deduct expenses allocated to the investors.

Investing in REITs and/or REMICs is a complicated matter. Consult your tax adviser for details on the tax aspects of investing in these products.

14

Investing In Life Insurance Or Annuities

- Should you invest in life insurance?
- Are there advantages to using insurance for investment purposes?
- What are the different types of insurance policies?
- How can you use annuities as a tax-deferred long-term investment?

Many of us overlook the investment value of life insurance. Although that's not to argue that everyone ought to invest in it and certainly not to say all life insurance is an investment. However, you should take the time to explore the possibilities.

Defining Life Insurance

A life insurance policy is a contract payable at the death of the person who's insured. An endowment policy, on the other hand, is life insurance that's payable either at the death of the person who's insured or at a specified time during that person's life.

Death benefits

A death benefit is the amount an insurance company will pay upon the death of the insured while a policy is in force.

In most cases, the death benefit equals the face value of the policy. If you take out a $500,000 policy on your life and subsequently die, your insurance carrier will pay $500,000 to your beneficiaries — the people you designate to receive your death benefit.

Death benefits paid in a lump sum are generally not taxed as income to the beneficiary; however, the tax law carves out an exception to this rule in the case of a beneficiary who acquired a policy in exchange for payment.

EXAMPLE

You accept as payment for an amount owed to you an insurance policy covering the life of another person. If you continue to make premium payments and ultimately receive the death benefit, some of the proceeds received may be taxable to you.

Under the rules, you may exclude from your income only the amount of your basis in the contract — that is, the fair market value of the policy on the date it was transferred to you plus any premium payments you made on the contract. Usually, the transfer of a policy by gift isn't subject to this exception and proceeds are free from federal income taxes.

Death benefits may also escape federal estate taxes if the spouse is the beneficiary and he or she is a United States citizen. This is because a person may leave his or her entire estate — no matter how large — to a spouse tax free, due to a device known as the unlimited marital deduction.

Life insurance proceeds may still escape federal estate taxes even if the spouse is not the beneficiary. Under another provision of the tax law known as the unified credit, estates and accumulated gifts of U.S. citizens with a total value of $600,000 or less aren't subject to estate taxes.

The rules require the proceeds from life insurance policies that you hold in your name be added to the value of your estate upon death. This amount may cause the estate to be valued at more than the $600,000 threshold for estate taxes.

If you think your estate may be valued at more than $600,000 with the addition of your life insurance proceeds, you may want to talk to your tax adviser about changing the ownership of your life insurance policy. He or she will help you with this complicated procedure.

Although life insurance proceeds paid in a lump sum are not taxable as income to the person who receives them, it's a different story if the benefits are paid over time.

This is because the insurance company invests the proceeds from the policy. A portion of the dollars the beneficiary receives is principal, meaning death benefits, and a portion is investment income such as interest, dividends, etc.

The death benefits the beneficiary receives are not taxable, but the investment income on those benefits is subject to ordinary income taxes.

If your spouse died before October 23, 1986, and you receive insurance death benefits in installments, the rules treat you favorably by allowing you to exclude from taxation up to $1,000 a year of the interest included in those installment payments.

Example

Your husband passed away in June 1986, and you opt to receive the proceeds of his $75,000 life insurance policy in 10 annual installments of $11,250. Principal payments add up to $7,500 a year, while interest on the installments comes to $3,750. You should be paying taxes on only $2,750 of your interest income — that is, your interest payments of $3,750 minus the $1,000 annual exclusion.

What if your spouse died after October 22, 1986? Unfair as it seems, you're not entitled to claim the $1,000 annual interest exclusion.

Caution

Almost every new tax law that's introduced in Congress takes aim at the interest, dividends, and so on that accumulate tax-deferred in life insurance policies.

Keep your eye on Congress and the President. Chances are, the rules governing the tax treatment of investing through life insurance policies will change sooner or later. But there's no way to know if existing policies will retain their current tax treatment. So if you've invested in life insurance make your tax adviser aware of your interest in this area.

Term Insurance

Term life insurance is what life insurance agents refer to as "no-frills" insurance. It provides coverage for a fixed period, usually a year. All your premiums go to pay for your current coverage. In other words, term insurance includes no investment portion.

Tip

Many professional organizations offer term insurance at preferential rates to their members.

Caution

The cost of term insurance — or any other life insurance policy for that matter — isn't deductible on your personal return. That's because, in the eyes of the IRS, life insurance is a personal expense.

CAUTION

The IRS requires your employer to report as income (to you) the cost of life insurance it provides for you unless the insurance is provided under a group-term policy. But even under group-term plans, the benefit is tax free only up to the first $50,000 of coverage.

Amounts your company pays for additional coverage is compensation to you. The cost of additional insurance that's reported as income to you isn't what the company actually pays. Rather, it's an amount based on an IRS table of "average" or "uniform" premiums. Here's the table.

Employee's age:	Reported as taxable income: per month for each $1,000 of protection:
Under 30	8¢
30 – 34	9¢
35 – 39	11¢
40 – 44	17¢
45 – 49	29¢
50 – 54	48¢
55 – 59	75¢
60 – 64	$1.17
65 – 69	$2.10
70 and older	$3.76

WHOLE LIFE INSURANCE

Whole life insurance is simply term insurance with a built-in investment feature. It works like this: You pay your insurance company or carrier premiums. Then, the company takes a chunk of your premium to pay for the insurance portion of the policy. The remainder of your premium, with the exception of some insurance company administrative expenses, is invested by the insurance company on your behalf.

Here's where the tax law gives you a break. It doesn't tax the interest and other earnings that accumulate on your deposit until those amounts are withdrawn. This deferral is the primary tax reason to use a life insurance policy as an investment.

TIP

In most cases, the IRS doesn't treat as taxable income amounts you borrow from your life insurance policy. (We cover the exceptions to this rule later in this chapter.) The interest you pay on these loans may be deductible based on how you use the proceeds.

If for example you borrow $4,000 on your policy and use the money to purchase $4,000 worth of stock, the interest is classified as investment interest and may be deductible under the investment interest expense rules. (See Chapter 6 for the details.)

CAUTION

The interest on the money borrowed to pay your insurance premiums is treated not as investment interest but as personal interest. Personal interest is not deductible.

Also, if you borrow any portion of four or more of the first seven annual premium payments, the interest paid on the amounts borrowed is probably not deductible.

CAUTION

You cancel your life insurance policy and receive what is known as its surrender or cash value. Except in the case of modified endowment contracts and life insurance policies issued by financially troubled companies, amounts received from surrender of a life insurance policy are first treated as a recovery of your premiums, then as ordinary income after your investment is completely recovered. However, if the amount you receive on complete surrender is less than your investment, you're not allowed to deduct the loss. Such amount is considered a personal expense of insurance protection.

TIP

If your insurance policy was issued by a company now considered "financially troubled" under the tax rules, the IRS provides a limited exception to the rule discussed above. You may elect to receive nonrecognition treatment for any cash withdrawn and reinvested in another policy provided certain conditions are met. (See your tax adviser if you think this may apply.)

Because the surrender of a policy may cause an income tax payment to be due, a policyholder should choose whether it's more advantageous to borrow from the policy or surrender it.

TIP

Dividends from your insurance policy are partly a return of the premiums you've paid. The IRS says you don't need to include these dividends in your income until they add up to more than all the premiums you've paid under the policy.

Assume you have a life insurance policy. The policy credits dividends to you annually and you can choose to withdraw them whenever you like, apply them to your premium payments, or leave them on deposit to earn interest.

You decide to leave the dividends your policy earns on deposit with the insurance company. The interest you earn on these deposits is taxable to you when it's credited to your account.

For some policies, however, the insurance company restricts your ability to receive the interest that it credits on your deposits. In this case, the interest becomes taxable in the year that the restriction no longer applies.

TIP

The Form 1099-INT mailed to you by your insurance carrier lists the interest earned on insurance dividends that were paid in past years and are now accumulating in a savings account. You should ask what rate of interest you're earning; you may want to withdraw your money and invest it elsewhere.

Universal life insurance

Universal life — a variation on whole life — is one of the more popular types of policies. With universal life, the investment portion of your premium goes into money-market funds that yield current interest rates.

Also, unlike the cash value of a traditional whole life policy, a universal life policy's cash value grows at a variable rate. The rate varies with the money markets, but most insurance companies will notify you annually of the interest rate your policy will earn in the coming year.

One selling point of universal life policies is that they offer life insurance protection along with a competitive yield on the savings portion of the policy.

Another advantage of universal life over traditional whole life is that you may vary your annual death benefit and your annual premium. Whole life premiums are usually fixed, but with universal life you may decide, within limits, what you can afford to pay in premiums each year.

In leaner years, you may skip paying the premium altogether. When you skip payments, the carrier simply deducts the cost of maintaining the life insurance portion of your plan plus administrative expenses from the accumulated cash value.

In good years — financially speaking — you may decide to put more money in the policy and get a faster buildup of your cash value.

CAUTION

If your premium payments for a universal life policy — or any other life insurance plan — top limits outlined in the law, the policy may be classified as a modified endowment contract which has adverse tax consequences.

ENDOWMENT CONTRACTS

An endowment contract is a life insurance policy payable either:

- at the death of the policyholder, or
- at a specified time during the life of the policyholder.

Life insurance proceeds under an endowment contract are generally payable over a fixed period of time. If the taxpayer makes an election within 60 days of receiving the right to receive payments under the endowment contract (i.e., when it is paid up), the amounts received under the contract are generally taxed as an annuity (discussed later in this chapter).

CAUTION

Failure to make the election or making it outside of the 60 day period will result in a taxable event for the policyholder. The conversion into an annuity will be treated as if the policyholder received a lump sum from the endowment contract and reinvested it in an annuity contract. The excess of that lump sum over the cost of the endowment contract would then be a taxable gain in the year the conversion occurs. Any taxable gain is added to the basis of the annuity.

MODIFIED ENDOWMENT CONTRACTS

With a modified endowment policy, the law assumes that the first dollars you borrow or withdraw are your accumulated earnings. And these dollars are subject to income taxes.

Also, if you're under the age of 59 ½ the IRS may assess you a 10 percent penalty on the amount of earnings you borrow from such a plan.

If your policy is classified as a modified endowment plan but you don't borrow or withdraw any of your dollars, then the plan is basically treated like an annuity.

The amounts you contribute to your policy continue to accumulate tax-deferred until you withdraw them or assign or pledge the policy as collateral for a loan. When you assign or pledge a policy, the amount is treated as a distribution to you for tax purposes.

The modified endowment rules apply only to policies entered into or materially changed on or after June 21, 1988. The law exempts from this rule cash from an assignment or pledge of policies with death benefits of $25,000 or less used to purchase burial expenses or in connection with prearranged funeral expenses.

TIP

> If you want to avoid the tax trap of the modified endowment policy rules, see your tax adviser before you boost your premium payments. With the help of your insurance agent, he or she will be able to tell you if your policy or plan will be reclassified as a modified endowment policy.

VARIABLE LIFE INSURANCE

As with traditional whole life, a portion of the variable life premium goes to cover the cost of insurance and the rest is invested. But while whole life premiums are usually invested in long-term bonds and mortgages, such as Ginnie Maes, and universal life premiums usually go into money-market funds, variable life premiums are invested according to your wishes as the policyholder.

The carrier will invest your premiums in an array of investment vehicles, ranging from mutual funds to fixed-income instruments. Carriers manage the specific funds in which your money is invested. So, you can't choose an investment that's not in your carrier's portfolio.

Several times a year, you may — as the terms of your insurance policy allow — switch among investment vehicles without penalty. It's up to you, for instance, to decide when to move funds in or out of a stock or bond mutual fund; thus, you're the one making the calls on market fluctuations.

If you're comfortable with investment decisions, variable life offers a hands-on alternative to whole life policies while also meeting your basic insurance needs. On the down side, the cash value of variable life policies is uncertain. The cost of the insurance portion of the policy, though, never falls below a certain floor.

CAUTION

> Keep in mind that variable life is expensive. The sales commission and service fees cut considerably into the amount available for investment.

Like whole life policies and universal life, variable life policies may not be for those concerned with short-term insurance needs. Rather, variable life is better used by those who can predict their future insurance needs with reasonable certainty.

FLEXIBLE-PREMIUM VARIABLE LIFE INSURANCE

These plans combine features of universal and variable life. As with universal life, you may change the premiums and death benefits.

However, as with variable life policies, you specify how you want the savings portion of the policy invested. With most policies, you may also shift your money from one investment vehicle to another during the year although the insurance carrier may charge you a fee to make the switch.

SINGLE-PREMIUM INSURANCE

With a single-premium life insurance policy, an individual puts up a large sum — usually no less than $5,000 — to pay for death benefits, and he or she earns a competitive tax-deferred interest rate.

Cash may be obtained from the policy at any time through a policy loan that generally charges interest of about four to six percent. Insurance companies offer attractive interest rates, and they may offer guarantees to hold a steady rate over three to five years if you direct them to.

Be aware that the insurance company may impose a back-end load; in other words, they may charge you a percentage of your account when you take your money out.

For instance, one carrier's early cancellation penalty may be seven percent of premiums in the first or second year and drop by one percent a year after that time. In other words, you must keep your money in the policy for nine years before you withdraw it without an insurance company penalty.

CAUTION

Any single-premium policy you enter into or materially change after June 21, 1988, falls into the category of a modified endowment policy. So, you may want to think twice before you use such a policy for investment purposes.

CAUTION

Make sure the company offering this type of policy is sound. Single-premium and other investment-oriented policies often attract a fickle pool of policyholders, quick to bail out with changes in market conditions. So a large run on a particular type of policy may seriously undermine a financially weaker insurance company's ability to return your money.

One good source of information to check out the financial stability of your insurance carrier is A.M. Best. It publishes a directory, available in most libraries, of insurance carriers and rates them according to their financial strength.

CAUTION

Interest you pay on money borrowed to purchase a single-premium life insurance policy isn't deductible. Furthermore, any contract where substantially all of the premiums are paid within the first four policy years is classified as a single-premium contract for this purpose.

Borrowing from a single-premium contract to make other investments, such as the purchase of corporate stock, is classified as interest incurred to carry the contract and is therefore not deductible, even under the investment interest rules.

"LIVING" BENEFITS

In recent years, insurance companies have developed insurance contracts that provide both death and "living" benefits designed to help policyholders cope with rising medical costs, particularly in later years. These contracts may provide for accelerated death benefit payments for terminally ill people who may incur substantial medical and living expenses prior to death.

Generally, the accelerated death benefit is equal to all or a portion of the normal death benefit discounted for the remaining life expectancy (usually 12 months or less) of the insured. The payment of a benefit is conditioned upon the surrender of all or a portion of the policyholder's rights under the life insurance contract.

Another living benefit some life insurance contracts are providing is accident and health benefits for a "specified risk" — for example, a condition requiring long-term stay in a nursing home or certain dread diseases. This "morbidity" benefit is usually a specified amount determined by reference to all or a portion of the death benefit otherwise payable. As with accelerated death benefits, the payment of a morbidity benefit is conditioned upon the surrender of all or a portion of the policyholder's rights under the life insurance contract.

CAUTION

The IRS has issued proposed regulations setting forth the rules that would provide insurers with the standards needed to design and market insurance contracts providing both death benefits and medical benefits without losing the tax benefits ordinarily accorded life insurance. Consult with your tax adviser before entering into an insurance contract which provides for these types of benefits.

ANNUITIES

An annuity is a contract sold by an insurance company promising to make installment payments to a person commencing at some future date, usually at retirement.

Annuities come in two forms — fixed and variable. With a fixed annuity, the amount received is paid out in regular equal installments. The purchaser decides how frequently he or she wants to receive payments. For example, you may decide to receive payments monthly or quarterly. Or you may opt for annual payments.

With a variable annuity, the amount received fluctuates with the type of account. This is because the purchaser decides how the dollars set aside are invested, so the amount received depends on the value of his or her underlying portfolio.

Annuity payments are made either over a fixed period — 20 years, for example — or over an indefinite period such as the remainder of a person's life. The terms are spelled out in the annuity contract.

Some annuities — so-called joint and survivor annuities — continue to make payments to a beneficiary after the death of the primary "annuitants".

Thus, joint and survivor annuities are annuities that make regular payments over the primary annuitant's (investor's) life and the life of his or her spouse. So if the investor dies, his or her spouse continues to receive annuity payments although the amount of the payments may change.

Annuities are available from a variety of sources such as insurance companies, financial planners, banks, and brokerage firms.

An annuity generally allows investment dollars to grow fast. Millions of annuity policies are in force nationwide.

One way to think of an annuity is as the opposite of a life insurance policy. A life insurance policy pays after you die, an annuity while you're alive. Although annuities come in a variety of types, there are two primary types of annuities:

- an immediate annuity, and
- a deferred annuity.

With an immediate annuity, you usually begin receiving benefits 30 to 90 days after you purchase your contract. Your purchase is usually in a lump sum.

A deferred annuity, on the other hand, pays you benefits starting at some future date, usually at retirement. You buy your annuity contract either by paying a lump sum, making installment payments, or through some combination of the two.

CAUTION

Interest on loans taken out to buy investment annuities will generally be classified as investment interest. Although classification as investment interest is certainly better than classification as personal interest, investment interest is only deductible to the extent of your net investment income.

Also, interest on loans to purchase single-premium annuities isn't deductible at all. In fact, the same interest deductibility rules that apply to single-premium life insurance policies, which we discussed earlier, apply to single-premium annuities.

With an annuity, the interest, dividends, and capital gains you earn accumulate tax-deferred until they're paid to you under the terms of your annuity.

Annuities are long-term investments because restrictions apply to amounts you can take out. For example, the law imposes a 10 percent penalty on certain taxable amounts you withdraw from annuities before you reach age 59 ½.

These amounts (interest, dividends, etc.) are all taxable except for those:

- made on or after the death of the annuityholder;
- made after the annuityholder becomes disabled;
- that are part of a series of substantially equal periodic payments made for the life of the annuityholder or the joint lives of the annuityholder and his or her beneficiary; or
- allocable to investment in the contract before August 14, 1982.

In addition, any amount you receive as a loan against your annuity or the value of an annuity pledged or assigned for a loan is treated as a taxable withdrawal. Also, your insurance company may impose surrender charges if you cash out early.

When you begin receiving your regular annuity payments, part of each payment is taxable, and part is not.

A portion of the dollars you receive is a return of the amount you paid for the contract — your cost basis, sometimes called your investment in the contract — and a portion is investment income such as interest, dividends, and so on. You pay taxes *only* on your investment income.

The taxable amount of each annuity payment is the entire payment you receive minus the portion that's treated as nontaxable.

As with distributions from IRAs, the recovery of your nontaxable cost basis is spread over the payments you expect to receive from the annuity.

For instance, with a fixed annuity, the exclusion ratio is applied to each regular payment to determine the nontaxable amount. The exclusion ratio is the relation of your cost basis in the contract at the date annuity payments begin to your total expected payments from the annuity.

$$\text{Annuity Payment} \quad \times \quad \frac{\text{Cost Basis in the Contract}}{\text{Total Expected Annuity Payments}} \quad = \quad \begin{array}{l}\text{Nontaxable} \\ \text{portion of} \\ \text{payment}\end{array}$$

With a variable annuity, your nondeductible amount is spread evenly over the number of annuity payments you expect to receive. Since most annuities don't call for a fixed number of payments, the IRS has devised actuarial tables of life expectancies to determine the number of payments you can expect.

And, as with IRAs, the taxable portion of your annuity may be subject to a 10 percent penalty for withdrawals prior to age 59½. However, there are exceptions to the penalty that are similar to those that apply to IRAs.

See Chapter 16 for the details on IRA withdrawals.

CAUTION

Some annuities allow you to "partially surrender" — that is, partially cash out — your contract before your regular annuity payments are scheduled to begin. You should know that different rules apply to the money you receive on a partial cash out in determining its taxability. (Any amounts that are taxable to you cannot exceed the total income on the contract).

For annuities where the deposits (i.e., the annuity purchase deposits) are made after August 13, 1982, any partial withdrawal is treated as a return of your investment income first. So any amount withdrawn is fully taxable to the extent of the income accumulated in the contract.

EXAMPLE

You deposited $5,000 in a deferred annuity in January 1985 and until now you've made no withdrawals. The cash value of your account has grown to $7,500. Now, you want to receive a payment of $2,500. Under the rules, the withdrawal is all taxable as income from the contract. None of it is treated as a nontaxable return of your investment. And, as we pointed out earlier, you may also be faced with the 10 percent penalty tax for withdrawals before age 59 ½.

Another rule applies to annuity deposits made before August 14, 1982. In this case, you get to withdraw your deposits first and your investment earnings last. Until the point when you've received the full amount of your deposits, you have no taxable income to report.

As you might expect, the rules are a bit more complicated if you own a contract to which you've made contributions (i.e., deposits) both before and after the August 13, 1982, cutoff. Generally, you get to pull out your pre-August 14, 1982, deposits first. But after that, you pay taxes on up to the full investment income earned in the contract.

TIP

The rules allow you to switch from one annuity contract to another with no tax consequences to you. This switch is known in IRS parlance as a Section 1035 exchange.

If you plan to make a Section 1035 exchange, consult your tax adviser before you make it. That way, you're sure to make the exchange according to the tax rules.

CAUTION

Think twice before you purchase an annuity to fund your child's college education. Why? The amounts you withdraw to pay tuition bills are subject to a 10 percent early-withdrawal penalty if you're younger than age 59½.

Therefore if your child will enter college before you reach age 59 ½, you may want to steer clear of annuities for funding the education.

TIP

Are you thinking about making a nondeductible contribution to an IRA? Consider putting your money into an annuity instead.

Why? With an annuity, you aren't subject to the $2,000 ceiling on IRA contributions. Nor do you have to report the amount you sock away to the IRS. For more information on IRAs, see Chapter 16.

Exchange of policies

If one type of annuity or life insurance policy is exchanged for another, the transaction is not taxable if the policyholder remains the same and no cash or other property is received as a result of the exchange. A summary of the tax consequences of other policy and contract exchanges follows.

Nontaxable exchanges:

Life insurance policy .... > life insurance
.... > endowment contracts
.... > annuity contracts
annuity contracts .... > annuity contracts
endowment contracts .... > endowment contracts
.... > annuity contracts

Taxable exchanges:

annuity contracts .... > endowment contracts
annuity contracts .... > life insurance policy
endowment contracts .... > life insurance policy

With exchanges for endowment contracts, however, the rules say the exchange is tax free only if the new policy provides for regular payments to begin no later than payments would have begun under the old contract.

15

YOUR GUIDE TO EMPLOYER-PROVIDED STOCK OPTIONS

- What are the tax consequences of stock options?
- How the rules affect the use of Incentive Stock Options (ISOs).
- How are stock appreciation rights (SARs) taxed?
- What is restricted stock and how is it taxed?

Stock options, stock appreciation rights and restricted stock are significant employee recruiting and retention tools for businesses. All these instruments let employees share in the success of their employer. And, from the company's perspective, each of them boost employees' incentive to work for that success.

Some companies restrict options to top executives; others spread this benefit down the line. Often, options are a negotiable part of a total compensation package.

Using stock options and stock appreciation rights to your best advantage requires an understanding of the tax rules that govern them. These rules aren't difficult, and in fact, they do provide some flexibility. This flexibility requires you to make choices when you exercise or sell the underlying stock.

This chapter helps you make those choices. We begin with a few words about how options work. (We cover options that aren't employment-related in Chapter 5.)

STOCK OPTION CONSIDERATIONS

When your employer grants you a stock option, you have received the right to purchase a specific number of shares of your company's stock at an option price within a specific period of time. What do we mean by option price? It's the amount you pay for the stock when you exercise your option and, in most cases, is the fair market value of the stock on the date your option was granted. You are not required to buy (i.e., exercise the option) but you may — at your option.

One of the beauties of purchasing optioned stock — which you buy through your company, not through your stockbroker — is the price you pay.

EXAMPLE

As a result of your outstanding performance last year, your boss gave you a bonus — an option on 2,000 shares of company stock. The option price is $12 a share.

Now, a year later, the market price of the stock has increased to $20 a share, and you decide to exercise the options. When you do, you pay $24,000 — that is, $12 times 2,000 shares — for stock that is currently worth $40,000. Not a bad deal.

It becomes even a better deal if your options are incentive stock options (ISOs). Options come in two varieties — ISOs and nonqualified stock options (NQOs). The difference lies mainly in the tax benefits provided by ISOs.

There's no regular tax due on an incentive stock option until you eventually sell or exchange the stock, and then only if you sell or exchange it for more than you paid for it. (You must hold stock acquired by exercising ISOs for a specified period of time if your profits are to be taxed as capital gains. See "Capital gains" in this chapter for the details.)

On the other hand, generally, with NQOs there's an immediate tax bite when you exercise the option, as well as a tax you pay when you sell the stock at a profit.

Let's return to our example.

If you were granted NQOs instead of ISOs, you would have incurred a tax liability when you exercised them. The IRS taxes you on the difference between the option price, $12, and the market price, $20, at the time you exercise the option. So you're taxed on $16,000 when you exercise your NQO, and this income is treated as ordinary income.

If you're able to sell the stock a year later for $30 a share, you're taxed again — this time as capital gains on the difference between $20 and $30. With an ISO, you're taxed just once for regular tax purposes — when you finally sell the stock for $30 a share.

But, with an ISO, the entire amount of your gain — the difference between the $30 a share you receive at the sale and the $12 a share option price that you originally paid — is taxed more favorably as a capital gain. (For more information on capital gains, see Chapters 4 and 5.)

You can see the advantage of the ISO. You pay no regular tax until you actually realize a gain when you sell or exchange your stock, and all of that gain is treated as a capital gain.

With the NQO, on the other hand, you generally pay tax on your paper profit as ordinary income when you exercise the option. That means that you not only must have cash to buy the stock when you exercise an NQO, you also need the money to pay the tax due. (An amount normally must be paid to your employer and remitted as withholding taxes.)

Fortunately, you do get to increase your basis in the stock — that is, the stock's cost to you — by the amount of your reported gain.

The bargain element — the difference between the price at which you buy your stock and the fair market value — on the exercise of ISOs is a preference item when you compute your alternative minimum tax (AMT).

So, timing is an issue. You may not want to exercise an ISO if it will throw you into an AMT situation. (See Chapter 8 for the details on the AMT.)

Which is the better deal? ISOs? NQOs? The answer is: it depends. You may be better off from a tax perspective with ISOs, but ISOs do come with a restrictive set of rules that can make them less desirable for other reasons.

RULES AND RESTRICTIONS

Specific rules and restrictions define an ISO. If a stock option doesn't specifically conform to these rules and restrictions, it is, by definition, an NQO and is automatically treated as such. Even if an option qualifies as an ISO, you may be able to have it qualify as an NQO if its terms give you that option, or, if you violate the rules governing ISOs, your ISO will be treated, tax-wise, as an NQO. So, let's take a look at these specific rules and the restrictions they impose.

Employee status

From the day you receive the ISO until three months before you exercise it, you must be employed by the company (or a related company) granting it. So you may — if your employer's plan allows — exercise the option up to three months after you leave the company, and still obtain the favorable tax benefits.

But, if you leave a company due to permanent and total disability and your employer's plan allows it, the three-month period is extended to one year. Sick leave or any other company-approved leave doesn't count, however.

If you die, your options remain ISOs and go to your beneficiaries — meaning the people you specify as your heirs — and they may, in turn, exercise them.

Option period

You must exercise your ISO within 10 years of the date it's granted. However if you own more than 10 percent of your company's stock, the option period may not exceed five years.

As for your employer, the company must grant ISOs within 10 years of the date the shareholders formally approve the stock option plan or the plan is adopted, whichever is earlier.

Fair market price

The ISO rules require that the option price not be less than the fair market price of the stock on the date the option is granted.

CAUTION

A special rule applies to individuals who own more than 10 percent of a corporation's stock. The option price must at least be equal to 110 percent of the fair market value of the stock on the date the ISO is granted.

$100,000 ceiling

Of all the ISOs granted after 1986, no more than $100,000 worth (valued at the time they're granted) of optioned stock may become exercisable for the first time in any one year. If you violate this rule, the first $100,000 of optioned stock still qualifies as ISOs, but the remainder falls into the category of NQOs.

You calculate the first $100,000 of options that qualify for ISO treatment by adding together your options in the order you receive them.

EXAMPLE

Your company grants you two options that are first exercisable in 199A. You receive the first, which is to purchase 6,000 shares at $10 a share (or $60,000), on January 15. You receive the second — to purchase 7,000 shares at $10 a share, or $70,000 — on July 15. In each case, $10 a share is the fair market value of the optioned stock on the day you receive the options.

The first option of $60,000 qualifies as an ISO. So does $40,000 of the second option. The remainder of the second option ($70,000 minus $40,000, or $30,000) is classified as an NQO.

CAUTION

The $100,000 limit isn't on the value of the options your employer may grant you in a particular year; your company may grant you any amount in options it sees fit. Rather, the limit is on the value of the optioned stock first exercisable by you in any year.

TIP

You determine the value of the optioned stock by multiplying the number of shares in the option by the fair market value of the stock at the time the option is granted.

EXAMPLE

Your employer grants you $300,000 worth of optioned stock in 199A. The entire amount would qualify as ISOs — as long as the option states that you could only exercise $100,000 in 199A, and the second and third $100,000 in 199B and 199C, respectively. You don't have to exercise them, or you could exercise all three in 199C; however, you may not **first** exercise more than $100,000 in any one year.

What if your employer grants you $150,000 worth of optioned stock in 199A, all of which can be exercised in the same year? In this case, you should instruct your employer at the date of exercise to issue you separate stock certificates for $100,000 of the stock, and identify the certificates as an ISO exercise in the stock transfer records.

Otherwise, each share of stock will be treated as two-thirds acquired by an ISO and one-third acquired by the exercise of an NQO. The separate designation will provide you with greater flexibility in recognizing income in future years.

Order of exercise

You must exercise ISOs granted to you in 1986 and earlier in the order in which they were granted. But you may exercise ISOs granted *after* 1986 in any order you like.

EXAMPLE

You hold an option to purchase 2,000 shares of stock at $15 a share, another to buy 1,000 at $10 a share, and still another to purchase 5,000 at $5 each. You received the $15-per-share option in 1985, the $10-per-share option in 1986, and the $5-per-share option in 1987. You may exercise the post-1986 option — the $5-per-share option issued in 1987 — before the other two.

But, you must exercise options issued before 1987 in the order in which they were granted. In other words, you must exercise the 1985 option before you exercise the 1986 option.

Capital gains

You may claim long-term capital gain tax treatment for the entire gain on the sale of stock bought with ISOs *only* if you hold the shares for the later of:

- more than two years from the date the option was granted

- *or* more than one year from the date the shares were actually transferred to you.

Otherwise, a portion of your gain — the difference between the option price and the stock's fair market value when you exercised the option and acquired your stock — is taxed as ordinary income.

EXAMPLE

You receive an option on July 3, 199A. You exercise the option six months later on January 3, 199B. Under the law, to have your entire gain considered long-term, you must hold the shares until after July 3, 199C — that is, two years after the option was granted to you.

If you do not meet the holding period rules, the gain that would have been realized at the time the option was exercised if the option were not an ISO is included as ordinary income in the year of the disqualifying sale. Gain for these purposes is the lesser of:

- the FMV of the stock on the date of the exercise over the option price of the stock

- *or* the amount realized on the sale of the stock over the adjusted basis (usually the option price) of the stock.

Any additional gain would be taxed as capital gain.

Transferability

There are a number of other requirements that must be met to make sure that your options will be treated as ISOs rather than NQOs.

Only you and your heirs may exercise ISOs. But you may not contribute your options to an IRA or other retirement plan. The IRS doesn't want you deferring gains on options even longer than the options themselves permit.

No one else — not even your spouse — may exercise your ISOs during your lifetime, and you may not assign options in a divorce settlement. Therefore, options are often an issue during separation or divorce negotiations. Both sides must devise a formula to compensate for the fact that much of an executive's wealth may consist of nontransferable stock options.

This rule also means that you may not sell your right to exercise an option or use the right as collateral for a loan.

With all the restrictions that apply to them, why might you still prefer ISOs to NQOs? Tax deferral and the lower tax rates are the best reasons. As we pointed out earlier, you report no gain for regular tax purposes until you sell or exchange your ISO stock, and so long as you meet all the holding period requirements, the gain is taxed at the capital gain tax rate.

TIP

This and the fact that you may use company stock you already own to pay for ISO stock, which is another feature of many plans, allow you to use a powerful strategy.

EXAMPLE

You join a young company whose shares are selling for $2. At the time you come on board, you buy 1,000 shares of stock and receive ISOs for 5,000 shares at $2 a share. In five years, the stock price hits $10 and you decide to exercise your option.

You do so by exchanging the 1,000 shares you bought earlier and now selling for $10 a share (for a total of $10,000). In essence, you pay for the 5,000 shares with the 1,000 shares. Now, you own 5,000 shares worth $50,000 at the current market price, but your investment cost just the $2,000 you paid for the initial stock (i.e., which is now worth the $10,000 you need to exercise the option for 5,000 shares at $2 a share.) Since the options are ISOs, this transaction is tax free until you sell the optioned stock.

Let's say that you use this same strategy but, instead of paying with shares you bought, you pay with shares acquired under an ISO. In such case, the same rules apply — but only if you have held the stock for more than two years after your ISOs were granted or more than one year after the shares were transferred to you, whichever is longer.

Otherwise, the shares you exchange no longer qualify for treatment as ISOs — and will be treated as NQOs — because you have made a so-called disqualifying disposition; that is, you have disposed of ISO stock before meeting the holding period requirement. Therefore, you must pay tax on your profit, the appreciation, at ordinary income rates when they are exchanged.

TIP

> The capital gain income that ISOs yield — besides giving you the benefit of the preferential tax rate ceiling on long-term capital gains — may be useful to offset your capital losses. (For the details on capital gains and losses, see Chapters 4 and 5.)

NQOs, however, have their place mainly because you don't have to worry about any of the special rules and regulations affecting ISOs including the limits on when you can exercise your options or sell the stock you have acquired.

STOCK APPRECIATION RIGHTS

At the beginning of the chapter we mentioned stock appreciation rights, SARs for short. With SARs you do not actually buy your company's stock, but yet you profit from the stock's appreciation. The company stock is the yardstick by which you measure appreciation.

EXAMPLE

> Your company gives you a one-year SAR on 5,000 shares of stock when the market price is $2 a share. A year later the stock price has risen to $3. You could get a check for $5,000 (less any withholding tax, of course). Or, your company could give you $2,000 (again, less any income tax withholding) plus 1,000 shares of stock valued at $3 a share. At any rate, your total compensation comes to $5,000.

The gain is taxed at ordinary rates — just like the gain on an NQO. But, unlike stock options, you never have to put up any cash of your own with a SAR. Because you put up no cash with SARs, companies sometimes use them in tandem with ISOs to provide employees with the dollars they need to exercise their ISOs.

EXAMPLE

> Your company grants you a one-year SAR on 5,000 shares of stock. At the end of the year, it yields $1 a share or a total of $5,000. You receive a check for $4,000 after income tax withholding.
>
> Along with your SAR your company grants you an ISO to purchase 2,000 shares of company stock at an exercise price of $2 a share. You use the dollars you receive from your SAR at year end to exercise your option. You're out of pocket only the additional taxes you pay on income from your SAR.

INSIDER RULES

If you're a corporate insider — generally an officer, a director, or a more-than-10-percent shareholder of a public company — take heed. You must conform to special requirements regarding ISOs and NQOs. Among these requirements is the so-called "six-month rule" imposed by the Securities and Exchange Commission (SEC) under which you may have to forfeit to the company profits you realize from the purchase and sale of the company's stock.

Generally, you will be subject to the "six month rule" only if you exercise or otherwise dispose of options within six months of the date the options were *granted* to you. However, most stock option plans don't allow you to exercise or otherwise dispose of your options within six months of the date they were granted, so the new rule generally will not apply.

CAUTION

> If, under your company's stock option plan, you may exercise options within six months of the date of grant and you do so, contact your attorney to determine whether this new rule applies to you.

The SEC rules thus impose restrictions on when an insider may sell his or her company stock. Accordingly, the IRS generally does not require you to recognize your paper gain from the exercise of a NQO — or your AMT income from the exercise of an ISO — until the SEC restrictions on sale no longer apply. In the unusual case where the new six-month rule is applicable which prevents you from selling the stock immediately after you exercise the option, an election is available that allows you to recognize the income as of the exercise date. If the situation is right, and you can benefit from this election — just be sure to make the election within 30 days of the exercise of your option. See your tax adviser for details on how to make the election.

CAUTION

> Insider regulations are quite strict and complex. You need to choose carefully when you exercise and when you sell your stock. If you're an insider, our advice is to ask your tax adviser and attorney to help evaluate your personal situation. Enlist their help as soon as you get an option. This way, you won't unknowingly violate these rules and jeopardize your gain.

RESTRICTED STOCK

Where an employer gives or sells stock to an employee on the condition that the employee must work for the employer for a prescribed period of time, the stock is referred to as restricted stock. If the employee does not meet the length of service requirement set by the employer, the stock is usually sold back to the employer for the amount paid (if any). Often times, the length of service requirement (i.e., vesting) takes place in installments over a period of time. The following example illustrates the tax consequences associated with restricted stock.

EXAMPLE

On May 1, 1993 your employer sells you 1,000 shares of stock, having a market value of $20 per share, for $5 per share. The sale of the stock is subject to the condition that you must continue to work for the company for a period of four years. If your employment terminates for any reason during this period, you are required to sell your shares back to the company for $5 per share.

Until you "vest" in the restricted stock (i.e., the length of service requirement is met), it is not considered to be compensation income for tax purposes. When the stock vests and is no longer restricted, a taxable event occurs. You recognize ordinary income equal to the spread between the value of the stock on the date the stock vests and the amount, if any, you paid for it. Thus, once the stock vests, you must report $15,000 as ordinary income. (Assuming the value of the stock is still $20 per share.)

TIP

An election is available that minimizes the tax consequences of restricted stock. Called a Section 83(b) election (after the section in the tax code), the election allows you to include in income, to be taxed at ordinary income tax rates in the year the restricted stock is issued, the difference between the fair market value (FMV) of the stock on the date the stock is purchased and the cost of the stock. The restricted stock must be received in connection with performing services (i.e., your job) for you to be eligible to make the election.

As a result of this election, when you fully vest and your stock is no longer restricted, you do not incur a taxable event. So if the stock appreciates between the date you purchase it and the date it vests, you do not report the appreciation as ordinary income. When you sell the stock, any gain — including the appreciation when the stock vested — is considered to be a capital gain, potentially resulting in a significant tax savings.

CAUTION

You must make the Section 83(b) election within 30 days of your receipt of the restricted stock. Consult your tax adviser to determine if you can take advantage of this election.

16

RETIREMENT PLANNING BASICS

■ What are the benefits of tax-deferred investing?

■ How can you choose the right retirement plan?

■ What are the different benefits of IRA, SEP, Keogh and 401(k) plans?

A tax-deferred plan is an excellent tool for helping you save taxes and achieve your goal of a comfortable retirement.

You can reduce your current tax bill by investing in a tax-deferred retirement plan. This may be accomplished by deducting — within limits — your contributions to the plan.

Further, the income you earn in the plan — interest, dividends, and so on — escapes taxation until you withdraw it, usually at retirement.

The effect of the tax deduction and the tax-deferred compounding is significant.

EXAMPLE

You're in the 36 percent bracket and you put away $7,000 a year for 25 years in a Keogh, a tax-advantaged retirement plan for someone who's self-employed.

Note that your out-of-pocket cost is actually only $4,480 — your $7,000 contribution minus a tax savings of $2,520 (36 percent times $7,000).

Assume your contributions earn 10 percent annually. At the end of 25 years, when you pull out your money in a lump sum, you pocket — after taxes — $484,654.

On the other hand, if you take the same $4,480 and invest it each year in a plan that isn't tax-advantaged, you won't have as much at the end of 25 years. Even if your investment increased in value at the same rate as your Keogh, 10 percent, you'd end up with $276,741 — that is, $207,913 *less* than in your Keogh. Obviously, a tax-deferred plan is an excellent tool for helping you save taxes and achieve your goal of a comfortable retirement.

There are a number of tax-deferred plans from which you can choose. This chapter explains how these plans work and who is eligible to participate in them. You also may want to refer to *The Price Waterhouse Personal Tax Adviser* for advice on how to put money into these plans and how to take it out.

The goal is to be able to make intelligent choices among the retirement plans available to you.

Here are a few basics you should know:

Contributions are made to these tax-deferred retirement plans *only* if you have earned income — i.e., compensation for services rendered.

This compensation may take the form of wages paid to you as an employee or as income you've earned from running your own business. If your business is managing your investments, this income is classified as investment income, not earned income.

IRAs (INDIVIDUAL RETIREMENT ACCOUNTS)

IRAs are a type of retirement plan you create and contribute to yourself. IRA contributions and deductions are capped at the lesser of $2,000 or 100 percent of your earned income; $2,250 if you and your nonworking spouse file jointly. It used to be that anyone with earned income could contribute to an IRA and take a tax deduction. This is no longer true.

Currently, although anyone with earned income can still contribute to an IRA within the above dollar limits, only those who do not actively participate in an employer's qualified retirement plan, and those whose adjusted gross income (AGI) falls below certain levels may take an IRA deduction.

TIP

When it comes to IRAs, alimony also counts as earned income. Therefore, you may be able to deduct your IRA contribution even if the only income you receive during the year is alimony.

Active participation rules

The quick way to see if you're an active participant in your employer's qualified retirement plan is by looking at your W-2 form. The form provides a box labeled "pension plan" for your employer to check. Obviously, if this box is checked, you are an active participant in your employer's retirement plan. If this box is blank, though, there's more work to do. You will need to familiarize yourself with the active participation rules.

In the case of a *defined-benefit plan* — a plan that will pay you a set amount each year after you retire — you are considered to be an active participant if the rules of the plan say you're eligible to participate.

CAUTION

It doesn't matter whether you actually take part in the defined-benefit plan; it matters only that you are *eligible* to participate.

For example, assume you are eligible to participate in your employer's defined-benefit plan and the rules of the plan state your employer will not make any contributions on your behalf unless you contribute some of your own earnings to the plan.

You will be considered to be an active participant even if you elect *not* to contribute any of your own dollars to the plan. You become an active participant merely because you are eligible to participate.

The rules for a *defined-contribution plan* — a plan that requires your employer to put aside a set amount for you each year — are different. In this case, you are an active participant if — during the year — you, your company, or both of you contribute money to the plan on your behalf. However, you are not an active participant if the only money added on your behalf during the year are earnings from the investments already in the plan.

TIP

The active participation rules are not affected at all by whether you're vested (i.e., whether you have met the minimum length-of-service standards necessary to attain the nonforfeitable right to the amount of money contributed by your employer to the plan).

For example, your company contributes an amount annually on your behalf to its defined-contribution plan and the rules of the plan state that you aren't vested until you've worked at the company for a full three years. In the eyes of the IRS, you are an active participant in the plan even if you aren't vested because you are only a one- or two-year veteran of the company.

You are also considered to be an active participant if you take part in a retirement plan for just a portion of the year.

CAUTION

This rule can lead to unexpected tax consequences.

EXAMPLE

You resign your post at Freeze-Dried Inc. on November 15, 199A to accept a more lucrative position at Meltdown Corp. You're a good employee and give Freeze-Dried a one-month notice. On December 15, 199A, you clean out your desk at Freeze-Dried.

Two weeks later, you report for work at Meltdown. Under the rules of Meltdown's pension plan, you are not eligible to participate in 199B, your first year on the job, although you may take part in 199C.

You decide you can at least make an IRA contribution in 199B and deduct it. This is where the rules get complicated. You are unaware that your former employer's pension plan ends its 199A tax year on January 31, 199B.

So as far as the IRS is concerned, you were eligible and therefore active in that plan for part of 199B. Therefore, the deductibility of your IRA contribution may be limited for 199B.

What counts as a qualified retirement plan when it comes to the active-participation rules? Actually, there are several types of qualified plans. Qualified plans include:

- Qualified pension, profit-sharing, or stock bonus plans such as Keogh plans, 401(k) plans, and simplified employee pension plans (SEPs); and
- Retirement plans for federal, state, or local government employees.

Other plans falling into the category of qualified plans are:

- Tax-sheltered annuities for public school teachers and other employees of charitable organizations; and
- Certain union plans — so-called Section 501(c)(18) plans.

If you participate in any one of them, you are considered an active participant and not allowed to write off your IRA contribution unless your AGI falls below certain levels.

CAUTION

What happens if you're an active participant in an employer-sponsored plan, but your spouse isn't? Unfair as it may seem, you are both subject to the limits if you file jointly. You don't even escape this strict rule if you file separately, because your IRA deduction is phased out beginning with the first $1 of your AGI if you're married and file separately. (We'll explain the phaseout in a moment.) Therefore, when your AGI reaches $10,000, you're entitled to no deduction at all.

You do fall under different rules if you're married, file separately, and live apart from one another for the entire year. Then you are treated as if you're single.

In this case, say it's your spouse who's not covered by a qualified plan. He or she may contribute up to $2,000 to an IRA and deduct the full amount, regardless of

- how much either of you earn, and
- whether you are covered by a qualified plan.

Of course, if you're an active participant in your employer-sponsored retirement plan, you may claim an IRA deduction only if your income falls within the limits set for single people.

Not all is lost, however. You may contribute at least $200 to an IRA and write off the full amount, as long as your calculation shows that your deductible contribution is limited to no less than $10.

TIP

If you own your own business and your spouse helps out occasionally, think about paying your spouse for the work he or she does.

This way, as an employee, your spouse may — subject to the normal deductibility rules (including whether you are an active participant in a qualified plan which includes a Keogh)— put away all or part of his or her earnings in an IRA and deduct the contribution.

EXAMPLE

During the year, you pay your spouse $2,000 for her marketing advice. The $2,000 is her only source of income.

You and your spouse file a joint return and declare AGI of $32,000. You will each be allowed to make a tax-deductible IRA contribution up to $2,000.

You should know, though, that the IRS is fussy about your spouse performing real work and being paid appropriately for it. In other words, your employment arrangement with your spouse must be bona fide.

You should not simply make a deposit in your joint bank account as payment for services. Instead, you should write out a regular payroll check for your spouse. For the same reason, make sure you can prove that your spouse's employment is genuine.

You should also make sure that when you pay your spouse a salary, his or her wages are subject to Social Security taxes of 15.30 percent for 1993. That's 7.65 percent paid by the employee and 7.65 percent paid by you, the employer.

Income requirements

Even if you're an active participant in another qualified plan, as the following chart shows, you are allowed to deduct your IRA contribution if your income falls within certain ranges.

Can You Take an IRA Deduction?

If you are covered by a retirement plan at work, you can take the following amounts as an IRA deduction:

Adjusted Gross Income	Single/ Head of Household	Married Filing Jointly/ Widower	Married Filing Separately
0 – 10,000	full	full	partial
10,000 – 25,000	full	full	none
25,000 – 35,000	partial	full	none
35,000 – 40,000	none	full	none
40,000 – 50,000	none	partial	none
50,000 +	none	none	none

Even if you are an active participant in another qualified plan you're entitled to a partial IRA deduction if your AGI falls within certain levels. For this purpose your AGI is calculated differently. You must use your AGI before you deduct an IRA contribution, but after you claim investment losses and subtract Keogh contributions. It also includes any **taxable** Social Security benefits that you or your spouse receive.

If you're single and your AGI falls between $25,000 and $35,000 or married and your joint AGI is between $40,000 and $50,000 the deduction may be calculated as follows:

First, add up your AGI, then subtract this amount from the ceiling — $35,000 if you're single, or $50,000 if you're married and file jointly. Next divide the result by $10,000. The result is the percentage of the maximum IRA contribution you are allowed to deduct.

EXAMPLE

You are married, file a joint return, and actively participate in your employer-sponsored plan. Your joint AGI totals $44,000, so you subtract $44,000 from the $50,000 ceiling to get $6,000.

Next, you divide $6,000 by $10,000, and the result is 60 percent. Multiply 60 percent times $2,000 ($2,250 if you and your nonworking spouse file jointly). The answer — $1,200 (or $1,350) — is the amount of your IRA contribution you may deduct.

You still may contribute the full $2,000 (or $2,250); however, you won't collect a deduction for that extra $800 (or $900).

KEOGHS

If you are self-employed, consider establishing a Keogh plan to help you achieve a comfortable retirement. Sometimes called HR-10 plans after the number of the House of Representatives tax bill that created them, Keoghs came into existence in 1962. The author of HR-10 was Eugene Keogh, the late congressman from New York. His idea was that self-employed people should have the same opportunity to save for retirement as employees who enjoy the benefits of employer-sponsored pensions.

Keoghs — like other qualified retirement plans — allow you to slash your tax bill while building your retirement savings at a faster pace.

When you put money in a Keogh plan, you deduct your contribution on your tax return (within limits, of course) and your earnings accumulate tax-deferred until withdrawn. Keoghs come in two basic varieties — defined-benefit plans and defined-contribution plans.

With defined-benefit plans, you receive a specified sum every year after you retire. This amount is defined in the plan document. Each year an amount is contributed based on actuarial tables to fund the specified retirement benefit.

In 1993 for example, the ceiling on payouts from this type of plan is generally the lesser of 100 percent of your average annual earnings for the three consecutive years in which you made the most money (not exceeding $235,840 for benefits accruing in years beginning in 1993) or $115,641. These numbers are adjusted annually for inflation.

You are not allowed to contribute more than your current annual income. And you are required to make your retirement plan contributions quarterly — not annually.

With a defined-contribution plan, you put away a specified amount — 10 percent of your earnings, for example — each year until you retire. The contribution is credited to an account in your name. And the amount you receive after you retire is based on two factors — how much was set aside on your behalf, and how well that money was invested.

What if you employ people other than yourself? You are required to include them in your Keogh plan and make contributions on their behalf. So before you set up your plan, you may want to weigh the cost of providing this fringe benefit.

This sounds simple so far, but it gets more complicated.

The second type of Keogh we mentioned, a defined-contribution plan, also comes in two types — profit-sharing plans and money-purchase plans.

With a profit-sharing plan, you may contribute up to 15 percent of your net self-employment income (i.e., gross income minus expenses).

TIP

You may vary the amount you set aside each year based on how well your business performs. In other words, if your business does poorly one year, you are not required to make a contribution.

With a money-purchase plan, you are required to contribute a set amount each year, up to a maximum of 25 percent of your net self-employment income.

With either of these defined-contribution plans, your total contribution may not top $30,000 in any single year.

To make matters more confusing, the rules also require you to subtract your Keogh contribution *and* your deduction for one-half of your *actual* self-employment taxes for the year to calculate your annual net self-employment income.

Here's a simple formula to make this calculation easier.

For profit-sharing plans:

Multiply self-employment income, before you deduct one-half of your self-employment taxes and your Keogh contribution by 12.12 percent, to figure the maximum contribution amount allowed.

For money purchase plans:

Multiply self-employment income by 18.59 percent to figure the maximum contribution allowed.

These percentages apply to self-employment income of less than approximately $58,000. If your self-employment income exceeds this amount, the percentage varies slightly. Contact your tax adviser to determine how much you can contribute.

TIP

Consider pairing plans by combining a money-purchase plan with a profit-sharing plan. That way, you get the best of both worlds.

With a paired program, you may contribute and deduct on your return a full 18.59 percent of your self-employment income — again, before deducting half your self-employment taxes and your Keogh contribution — just as if you had fully funded a money-purchase plan. You're not locked into making a mandatory 18.59 percent contribution each year but your contributions cannot exceed 18.59 percent of self-employment income each year.

How does pairing work? Assume you set up a money-purchase plan that shelters 8 percent of your income. Under the IRS regulations, you must contribute that 8 percent each year.

At the same time, you also establish a profit-sharing plan to which you may contribute, at your discretion, up to an additional 10.59 percent (for a total of 18.59 percent) of your net self-employment income. This part of the contribution is entirely discretionary.

With a paired approach, you can protect from taxation up to $30,000, or 18.59 percent of your income, whichever is less.

A paired program makes sense if you want to put away — and deduct on your tax return — more than 12 percent of your earnings in a retirement plan, but you don't want to tie yourself to saving a hefty percentage of your income each year.

TIP

Fees you receive as a corporate director count as self-employment income even if you're employed full time somewhere else.

SEPs

A SEP, short for a simplified employee pension, is actually a form of an IRA. Instead of setting up a pension plan, your company may contribute to IRAs in the names of each of its employees, and may claim a deduction for the dollars contributed — within limits.

For each employee, the employer contribution limits are 15 percent of compensation or $30,000, whichever is less. If the terms of the SEP allow it, employees may also make contributions toward this limit, but the employee's contribution is limited each year. For example, the most an employee may contribute is $8,994 in 1993. This limit is adjusted annually for inflation.

Self-employed individuals can also take advantage of SEPs. Your earned income (i.e., self-employment income) — instead of compensation — tells how much can be put into your account.

401(k)s

Another tax-saving device is a 401(k) plan — or cash or deferred arrangement. 401(k) plans take their name from the section of the Internal Revenue Code that describes them.

Here's how these great savings plans work.

When you sign up for a 401(k), you authorize your employer to deduct a set amount from your earnings each pay period and put it in an account in your name.

This deferred salary — plus any interest, dividends, and capital gains that accumulate on it — is excluded from current taxation. The IRS doesn't get its share until you withdraw your money, usually at retirement. In this respect, 401(k)s are similar to IRAs.

What separates the two plans is the tax treatment of the money. Your 401(k) contribution doesn't get deducted on your Form 1040. Instead, the money set aside in a 401(k) is treated as tax-deferred compensation; this means it is not even reported as income to you.

EXAMPLE

Your 1993 earned income — salary and bonus, in your case — adds up to $60,000. At the beginning of the year you instructed your employer to subtract $500 a month from your paycheck and deposit the money in a 401(k) plan.

The year comes to a close. When you receive your W-2 form from your employer, you see that it lists your earned income as $54,000, not $60,000. This is because you opted to contribute $500 a month for a total of $6,000 to your 401(k). And the IRS treats the $6,000 as tax-deferred compensation.

The only catch is that the dollars you contribute to a 401(k) are still considered part of your income when it comes to federal Social Security (FICA) taxes. In other words, you pay FICA taxes on the money you contribute to a 401(k), but only to the extent that it and your other earned income falls within the FICA wage base — in 1993, $57,600 for the OASDI (old-age, survivors and disability insurance) portion of FICA and $135,000 for the Medicare HI (hospital insurance) portion of FICA. After 1993, you may have to pay even more FICA taxes on your 401(k) contributions because of the removal of the cap on the HI portion.

Another difference between 401(k)s and IRAs is the amount of money you may set aside. The maximum you may contribute to an IRA annually is $2,000.

There are two caps on 401(k) contributions — one applies to how much you may contribute, another to how much you and your employer may jointly contribute. Both limits are adjusted annually for inflation. When it comes to how much you may contribute to a 401(k), the ceiling for 1993 is $8,994; $9,500 for a tax-sheltered annuity.

A tax-sheltered annuity is a tax-deferred retirement account for teachers, church workers, and employees of other non-profit institutions.

Most annuities are sold by life insurance companies in the form of a contract that guarantees a payment to the owner at some future date, usually at retirement.

When it comes to how much your employer may contribute to your 401(k), the rules are more complicated. Together, the two of you may contribute no more than $30,000 or 25 percent of your after-contribution salary, whichever is less, to a 401(k) and all other defined-contribution plans. The key phrase here is "all other defined-contribution plans."

EXAMPLE

Your salary comes to $100,000 in 1993 and you sock away $8,994 of your salary in a 401(k). How much may your employer contribute?

First, multiply 25 percent times your after-contribution salary — that is, your $100,000 salary minus your $8,994 401(k) contribution or $91,006.

The result is $22,751 (25 percent times $91,006).

Since $22,751 is less than $30,000, $22,751 is the most you and your employer together may contribute to a 401(k) and all other defined-contribution plans.

You've already put away $8,994, so your employer's maximum contribution is just $13,757 ($22,751 minus $8,994).

You may be better off if you put less into your 401(k). This happens because your employer contributes a set percent of your compensation to your 401(k); it doesn't use a matching formula that ties its contribution to the amount you kick in.

EXAMPLE

Continuing our previous example but instead, you reduce your contribution from $8,994 to $5,000. Your after-contribution salary would total $95,000 — your $100,000 salary minus your $5,000 401(k) contribution. And 25 percent of that amount is $23,750.

By cutting your contribution, you've raised the maximum ceiling on the total retirement contribution for the year by $999 (the difference between $23,750 and $22,751). What's more, you've allowed your employer to increase its contribution.

The company may now chip in as much as $18,750 — $23,750 minus your $5,000 contribution. In this case, at least, less is actually more.

Obviously, one reason to participate in a 401(k) is to take advantage of the favorable tax rules. Another is to capture additional dollars from your employer.

Many companies match the amount their employees set aside in these accounts. It is worth contributing to the plan to earn these extra dollars from your employer.

You should also check with your employer to see if your participation in a 401(k) plan affects the level of other benefits you might receive. Here's how it might work.

Sometimes companies tie benefits — contributions to profit-sharing plans, say, or life and disability insurance coverage — to your total earnings. What you collect in these benefits can go up or down depending on whether your 401(k) contribution is included in your compensation.

You should ask your company if it reduces your compensation by the amount you've contributed to a 401(k) or if it adds your contribution back before it calculates the value of your other fringes. Many companies take the latter course, even though the law doesn't require them to do so.

EMPLOYER-SPONSORED RETIREMENT PLANS

These are plans created, and for the most part funded, by the company that employs you. As with Keoghs, employer-sponsored plans come in two flavors: defined-contribution plans and defined-benefit plans.

And, as with all retirement plans, any earnings that accumulate in employer-sponsored plans remain untaxed until you begin withdrawing funds at retirement.

17

INVESTING IN (FINANCING) YOUR CHILD'S EDUCATION

■ What are some worthwhile strategies for financing my children's education?

■ How can I use trusts to shift wealth and save taxes?

■ Are there tax implications if I receive a scholarship or fellowship?

A s astronomical as college costs are today, they will undoubtedly climb even higher in years to come.

For some, this kind of price escalation is not a worry; however, many others have to prepare for financing their children's future education, a process that includes tax planning.

In this chapter, we suggest tax-efficient ways to put money aside for college expenses ahead of time. We also show you how to get the most out of the cash you set aside for college costs, including minimizing the share that goes to the IRS.

PLANNING AHEAD

What is the best way, tax-wise, to finance your child's education? The answer depends in large part on whether the child whose education you are saving for has reached 14 years of age yet.

The tax law makes a distinction between those who have reached age 14 and those who have not. The distinction is a result of Congress' effort to significantly reduce tax benefits of a common tax-savings strategy known as income-shifting. Parents using this popular technique would shift income to their children to be taxed at the child's lower marginal rate.

We first look at the techniques that apply in the case of a child under age 14. The opportunities to minimize the tax bite are fewer before your child reaches 14. But even with the harsher rules, you do have some options when it comes to cutting the tax bite on college savings.

STRATEGIES FOR CHILDREN UNDER AGE 14

Assume you have set aside a few dollars for your child's education, and you want to put them in an investment that pays current income — dividends or interest, say.

Should you make the investment in your name? Or should you make it in your child's name? If your child is under age 14, for tax purposes, it does not matter much. As a result of the so-called "kiddie tax" rules, a child under age 14 pays taxes on his or her unearned income at the higher of the parents' rate or the child's rate. And the parents' rate is almost always higher.

TIP

Whether your child is under or over age 14, you may feel uneasy about shifting property to him or her especially if you have a specific use in mind for the income from it (i.e., college). To make sure your kids don't squander their college money on something foolish, you will probably want to use the Uniform Gifts to Minors Act (UGMA) or the Uniform Transfers to Minors Act (UTMA) to effect the transfer of property.

The use of UGMA or UTMA will allow you to appoint a custodian to manage the property on behalf of your child. The rules of UGMA and UTMA may differ depending on what state you live in so consult your tax adviser to discuss the applicable rules for the transfer of property under these provisions.

The only significant difference is that younger children are not taxed on the first $600 of unearned income, and the next $600 is taxed at their lower 15 percent rate. Given a maximum effective marginal tax rate of say, 45 percent, this small break could yield a tax saving of up to $450 each year.

Keep in mind your effective marginal tax rate could easily be as high as 45 percent — and maybe higher — given the new top statutory rate of 39.6 percent and taking into account state taxes, as well as the effect of the itemized deduction limitation and the phaseout of personal exemptions.

TIP

These savings help, of course, but not to a great degree.

The best tax strategy you can use when putting aside education money for younger children is one that involves tax deferral — delaying the tax until the child reaches 14. After that point, more tax saving is possible.

You can obtain tax deferral by investing in:

* Series EE U.S. savings bonds (see Chapter 2)
* Non-dividend-paying (or low-dividend-paying) growth stocks
* Other appreciating property

One other idea, for parents who are business owners, is to shift some of your income to your under-14-year-old child by putting the child to work. (For details on this strategy, see *The Price Waterhouse Personal Tax Adviser.*)

MINORS' TRUSTS

Minors' trusts allow you to make one or more gifts to a child subject to the usual $10,000 per person per year limit — the annual gift tax exclusion.

This rule means that you and your spouse can add up to $20,000 a year to each of your children's trusts without worrying about a federal gift tax. (Check with your tax adviser for the rules governing gift taxes levied by your state.)

The principal and earnings that accumulate remain in the trust until the trustee — who may be any competent adult (or trust company) you would like — distributes them.

The trust document, which creates the trust, must specify that the trustee has the discretionary power to distribute the property and income for the child's benefit until the child reaches age 21. You are free to specify how and when you want the assets distributed, but unless the trust document grants the trustee the authority to carry out your wishes, the gift tax exclusion does not apply.

CAUTION

It is usually a good idea not to name yourself as trustee. If you do and if you die, the assets of the trust would be included in your taxable estate.

The income earned by the property in the trust is taxed each year but at a partially reduced rate as long as you allow earnings to accumulate within the trust.

The reason is that the trust is taxed, not the recipient. In 1993, the first $1,500 of income in a minor's trust is taxed at only 15 percent; income exceeding $1,500 up to $3,500 is taxed at 28 percent; income exceeding $3,500 up to $5,500 is taxed at 31 percent; income exceeding $5,500 up to $7,500 is taxed at 36 percent; and the rest is taxed at 39.6 percent.

The potential annual tax savings is $845 — that is, the difference between the first $7,500 of trust income being taxed to the trust at rates of between 15 and 36 percent versus being taxed at a potential rate of 39.6 percent to the individual recipient.

Income distributed from the trust, on the other hand, is taxed under the aforementioned "kiddie tax" rules.

CAUTION

Because the higher trust rate of 39.6 percent begins at a relatively low level ($7,500), tax savings by using a trust may not result if the parent's or child's tax rate is lower than 39.6 percent. Consult your tax adviser to see if a minor's trust can benefit you.

Another tax advantage of a minor's trust is that the rules allow you to specify when a child is to receive the dollars in trust. If you want to ensure that a child spends his or her money on college, pick 18 or 21 as the age for distribution of the funds.

TIP

When income and principal are eventually distributed to a child at the age of distribution (18 or 21), there is no need to recalculate the tax on that income to account for the period of accumulation. With other types of trusts you might have to perform this complicated recalculation (known as the throwback rules).

The minor's trust you establish does have to comply with two major conditions:

- All the assets in the trust must be distributed to the beneficiary by the time he or she reaches age 21, and
- If the child dies before reaching age 21, the trust document must provide for the assets and accumulated income to be paid to his or her estate or be subject to the child's general power of appointment (i.e., the child must have the right to name the recipient of the balance in the trust in the event of his or her death).

CAUTION

You must evaluate whether a minor's trust is worth the trouble and expense. You are going to have to pay trustee and other fees including administrative fees to a bank or other institution that acts as trustee. (Bank fees typically range from 0.5 to two percent of the trust's principal.) You will probably benefit if you are able to put $10,000 a year or more in the trust.

EXAMPLE

You and your spouse together give your child $20,000 each year for three years, beginning with the child's first birthday. Assume that the trust funds earn income at a 6 percent annual rate and taxes are paid using the trust income tax rates for 1993 (discussed on the previous page).

By the time the child reaches 18 and the tuition bills begin to come due, the trust will have grown to $121,564. Had you simply saved the money and paid taxes at your normal 36 percent rate, the fund would have grown to only $109,696. You are $11,868 ahead by having set up the trust fund.

Remember to offset this amount by the administrative costs of the trust. These charges vary from institution to institution. Ask your bank or trust company about the charges it imposes.

CAUTION

If the income from the trust is used to support your child, it is taxable to you. The laws defining the parental obligation of child support vary from state to state.

CRUMMEY TRUST

Another type of trust can also be useful. It is called a Crummey Trust (named after the court decision that recognized it) and basically allows the distribution of principal and income at the trustee's discretion but does not require the mandatory termination of the trust when the child reaches 21. Instead, the trust document may allow distribution of the principal in stages.

However, the trustee must notify the beneficiary child annually of his or her right to withdraw over a reasonable period — usually 30 to 60 days — any gifts made to the trust each year.

Regardless of whether or not the child exercises their "Crummey power" and withdraws a portion of the annual gift from the trust, he or she will be taxed each year on a portion of the trust income that *could* have been withdrawn.

EXAMPLE

In 199A, you set up a Crummey trust for your daughter which gives her the right ("Crummey power") to withdraw the annual transfer to the trust within 60 days of its receipt. On January 1, 199J you transfer $20,000 to the trust bringing its total value to $200,000. During 199J, the trust earns $20,000 in income.

For 199J, your daughter will include a portion of the trust income on her 199J tax return. To determine the amount taxable to her you first multiply the income of the trust by 10 percent ($20,000/ $200,000 — which equals the ratio of the property subject to the Crummey power over the total value of the property in the trust) and then, multiply by a fraction (60 days divided by 365 days) which represents the portion of the year your daughter possessed the Crummey power.

Thus, for 199J your daughter's taxable income from the Crummey trust is $329.

CAUTION

Income that accumulates above this amount is subject to recalculation of income tax under the complex throwback rules.

Crummey Trusts are complicated, and because under some circumstances they may actually increase the overall tax liability of a child older than 14, consult your tax adviser before creating one.

BACCALAUREATE BONDS

An idea worth considering is purchasing baccalaureate bonds. These bonds are a special type of zero-coupon municipal bonds offered by some states.

These bonds are safer than many other types of municipal bonds because they are backed by the full faith and credit of your state.

In addition, income from these bonds is exempt from federal tax. They are also exempt from state and local taxes as long as you continue to live in the state that issued them. Also, baccalaureate bonds are less likely than other municipal bonds to be called early.

SAVINGS BONDS

The tax law gives you a break if you are twenty-four years of age or older, invest in Series EE bonds issued after December 31, 1989 and use the proceeds to pay for qualified education expenses for you, your spouse, your child or another dependent.

In this case, you don't need to pay taxes on the interest — as long as the interest and principal of the bonds you redeem in any year don't top your education expenses in such year.

If your interest plus principal adds up to more than your education expenses, the amount of interest you may exclude from taxation is capped.

To determine the amount of interest you may exclude, first calculate the amount of interest and principal on the bonds you're redeeming. Then add these two numbers together. Next, add up your qualified education expenses — tuition or other required fees that you pay a college or vocational school, excluding room and board.

Divide your qualified education expenses by the total amount of interest and principal on the bonds. Then multiply the result times your interest from the bonds to get the amount of interest you may exclude from your gross income. This calculation is performed on Form 8815, "Exclusion of Interest from Series EE U.S. Savings Bonds Issued after 1989."

EXAMPLE

You redeem savings bonds valued at $10,000 and use the proceeds to pay your qualified education expenses. Of that amount, $6,000 is principal and $4,000 is interest. Your qualified education expenses come to $8,000.

You divide your qualified education expenses — $8,000 — by the interest and principal from your bonds — $10,000. Now, you multiply the result — 0.80 — by your interest from the bonds — $4,000 — to get $3,200, the amount of interest that's not taxable to you.

You should know that in performing the above calculation, the tax law requires you to subtract from your qualified education expenses scholarships you receive that are not taxable to you as income.

You are responsible for keeping track of the serial numbers, issue dates, face values, and redemption dates of bonds you use to pay education expenses. You may want to use Form 8818, "Optional Form to Record Redemption of Series EE U.S. Savings Bonds Issued after 1989" for this purpose.

CAUTION

This exclusion is not available to married taxpayers filing separate tax returns.

You should also know that the IRS phases out the benefits of this exclusion for taxpayers within certain ranges of "modified adjusted gross income." These ranges are adjusted annually for inflation (check with your tax adviser for the amounts applicable for the current year).

Modified AGI is simply your regular AGI determined without regard to the interest exclusion and modified by adding back certain exclusions for income from foreign sources and certain U.S. possessions and Puerto Rico. You also take into account taxable social security benefits, your IRA deduction, and the passive-activity loss limitation.

TIP

Before you invest in these bonds, estimate your income for the year your child will enter college. If you won't be eligible for the exclusion, you may want to put your money elsewhere — municipal bonds or nondividend-paying growth stocks, for example.

STRATEGIES FOR THOSE 14 AND OLDER

Just because your child has reached age 14 does not mean it is too late to start saving for college expenses. Unfortunately, you will not have as much time to accumulate assets if you don't start until your child is this old.

On the other hand, it is only when the child reaches 14 that the IRS truly allows your child to become your partner in the savings effort. From this point on, the child's unearned income will be taxed at his or her rate, not yours.

Therefore, at this point you can begin to do some income-shifting — transferring income on which you would pay a high tax rate to your child who is in a lower tax bracket. This is usually accomplished through gifts.

Just give a child $10,000 or $20,000 with no strings attached? Not exactly. You will probably want to use the Uniform Gifts to Minors Act (UGMA) or the Uniform Transfers to Minors Act (UTMA), mentioned earlier in this chapter.

SHORT-TERM STRATEGIES

Your child is a high school senior and ready to choose a college. The time for long-range planning is over. Whether you have earmarked money for covering college expenses or not, now you have to come up with the money.

You have three options which you will probably want to use in some combination.

- You can tap your capital, including whatever assets if any you or your child have been accumulating,
- You or the prospective freshman can borrow money, or
- You can always apply for financial aid from the government or from the school.

Tapping Capital

If you have put aside some savings or assets specifically as college money, you will be well prepared to liquidate them when the bills come in.

Even if you have not had such foresight, you can nevertheless tap some of your assets and still get a bit of tax help from the IRS.

Assume you own stocks or bonds that have appreciated in value, you might think of selling some of them to raise college cash. But if you sell, you're probably going to be taxed on the gain that you realize at the top long-term capital gain tax rate.

A better strategy may be to give the stocks or bonds to your college-bound child. (Remember, you and your spouse each may make up to $10,000 worth of gifts annually tax free. If you give more, your gift tax liability will typically be covered by the unified gift and estate tax credit.)

Your child will have to pay the taxes on the appreciated value of the securities.

But he or she will probably pay taxes only at the 15 percent rate — as long as his or her gain plus other taxable income isn't great enough to trigger the 28 percent capital gains rate (see *The Price Waterhouse Personal Tax Adviser* for the income threshold at which the 28 percent rate first applies). By giving the stock to the child to sell, there is more after-tax money left to pay the college bills.

EXAMPLE

A stock you bought many years ago has appreciated in value by $15,000. If you sell it, you get the $15,000 appreciation minus $4,200 ($15,000 times 28 percent capital gains rate) in taxes. In other words, out of the $15,000 gain, you get to keep $10,800.

If you give the stock to your child who has very little other income, and he or she sells it, his or her tax bill will add up to just $2,250 ($15,000 times 15 percent). Your child gets to keep $12,750 of the $15,000 gain. By giving the stock to your child, he or she keeps $1,950 more to put toward tuition than you would.

CAUTION

Remember that your child does not have to sell the stock. Once you give it away, you have lost legal control over what your child does with it.

Borrowing Power

If you have to borrow to finance a child's education, probably the best way is through a home-equity loan. The interest is deductible if it satisfies certain conditions. (You may not write off the interest you pay on a student loan unless it is secured by your home and certain requirements are met.)

You may generally deduct interest on a home-equity loan of up to $100,000 no matter how you use the money. That fact makes home-equity loans very attractive for financing education costs.

CAUTION

Your children can always borrow some or all of the cash they need for college from you, provided you have it to lend. But use caution.

You must be careful to treat the transaction in a businesslike manner or the IRS might consider the loan a gift. So make sure to write up a promissory note that states the amount your child borrowed, the interest rate, and the repayment schedule.

CAUTION

Zero-interest loans are not looked favorably upon by the IRS. It will impute (meaning attribute) interest income to you and interest expense to the borrower.

Furthermore, whether it is a zero-interest loan or one made at fair market rates, you actually incur a tax disadvantage when you lend money to your children. These loans result in greater income to you, the higher-bracket taxpayer, and they do not result in a deduction to your child, the lower-bracket taxpayer, since the interest is personal interest, which is not deductible. So it probably isn't advisable from a tax point of view to lend money to your children.

Scholarships and Fellowships

Degree-seeking candidates who are awarded scholarships or fellowships may exclude from their income much of the money they receive. This is true whether they are in graduate or undergraduate school.

If your son, for instance, is in a degree-granting program, he may exclude from income amounts he uses for tuition and books, equipment, supplies, and other course fees. But amounts that are earmarked for room, board, or other living expenses are fully taxable.

Also, he must pay tax on wages he receives for research, teaching, or other services that the school may require as a condition of receiving the scholarship or fellowship.

CAUTION

The IRS has issued proposed regulations that strictly define related course expenses. To be considered related expenses, the fees, books, supplies, and equipment must be required of all students in the particular course of instruction.

Say your child uses part of his or her scholarship to buy a word processor because a professor suggested it might be useful. The professor, however, did not require that your child use the word processor as part of the course. In this case, the amount your child spends is not considered part of the tax-free scholarship. Instead, it is treated as taxable income.

TIP

If your child receives a scholarship or fellowship, keep records that prove that the money covered qualified expenses.

For example, he or she should hold onto copies of bills, receipts, canceled checks, or other documents that verify how scholarship proceeds were spent. In addition, the student should retain documents that list study aids — a calculator or personal computer, say — that are required for each course.

PREPAID TUITION PLANS

Prepaid tuition plans have developed over recent years as a cost-savings device. They come in two general types, each with some potential variations.

With the first type, you pay all four years of tuition when your child becomes a freshman. Since you pay at the first-year price, you are protected against future increases.

These plans may be a good idea under two conditions:

- You can afford the hefty up-front cost, and
- You are fairly certain your child will not want to transfer.

In any case, it makes sense to check whether your money is refundable if your son or daughter does switch schools.

The second type of prepaid plan established by some colleges and at least one state lets you pay four years' tuition at a steep discount when your son or daughter is a toddler. When your child is old enough to enter college, his or her tuition is already paid, presumably at a price far below current levels.

CAUTION

If your child decides against the college you have paid for, or should that institution close its doors, you may lose your money entirely. Alternatively, the college or state may refund only the amount you have paid in — with no allowance for many years' interest on your cash.

Some schools are forming umbrella plans that allow your scholar a choice of institutions. However, there is no guarantee that any of these colleges will appeal to your child.

These plans may have tax-related drawbacks. In one case, the IRS found that the plan created by the Michigan legislature triggered three tax liabilities:

- It triggered a gift tax to the parent when he or she purchased the contract. Furthermore, the IRS said the $10,000 annual gift tax exclusion did not apply in the case of prepaid education programs.

- The plan created a tax liability for the trust in which the funds were deposited on the amount of the trust's earnings.

- The prepaid plan also triggered a tax liability for the child when he or she began school. The amount taxed annually is the difference between the annual tuition cost and one quarter of the cost of the tuition contract (assuming that the contract covered four years of tuition). Income earned on the original purchase price of the contract is actually taxed twice — once when it is earned by the trust and then again when the child receives the education. (If you consider the fact that the original gift was probably made from after-tax dollars, the gift, in effect, has been subject to yet a third tax.)

The IRS ruling on the Michigan plan means that its only real savings (if any) to the individual who buys it is the difference between the future value of the current price paid and actual tuition charge when the child enters school. You will also want to determine whether the income earned by a prepayment trust in your state is subject to state as well as federal taxes. If it is, that is another reduction of savings overall.

But for many taxpayers these programs are one way to ensure that their children will not be denied college because of lack of funds.

TUITION GIFTS

Generous grandparents (or anyone else) may pay your child's educational expenses and still make other tax-free annual gifts of up to $10,000 each ($20,000 as a couple) per recipient.

The only qualification: They must pay the college or university directly. So make sure they write their check to the school — not to you or your daughter. Otherwise, the IRS will consider the amount of the payment as a gift to which the $10,000 annual exclusion will apply.

You may want to refer to *The Price Waterhouse Personal Tax Adviser* for other information you may need to know about financing children's education.

18

WHAT ELSE YOU
NEED TO KNOW

- How are investment clubs treated for tax purposes?
- What are the hobby loss rules and how might they apply to you?
- What is the tax impact of transactions with related parties?
- What are the at-risk rules and how might they limit your deductions?

There are a few other tax considerations which must be addressed when it comes to investments. This chapter discusses these matters starting with investment clubs.

INVESTMENT CLUBS

Many people get together with a group of friends or business associates, pool their money and make investments in the stock market. These groups are commonly referred to as investment clubs.

Regardless of how your club is organized, the law requires it to have its own employer identification number or EIN for short. If your club does not have one, obtain Form SS-4, "Application for Employer Identification Number." Upon completion of the form, you may then obtain an EIN by either contacting the IRS Tele-TIN telephone program for your state or mailing the form to the IRS office where your club would file its tax return. To use the Tele-TIN service, the individual placing the call must be authorized to sign Form SS-

4. To obtain the proper IRS telephone number or address, refer to the instructions for Form SS-4.

If the club makes investments in its name, it must give its EIN to any payor of dividends or interest. If the club makes investments in the name of one of its members, it must provide payers with the Social Security number of that person. That individual — as a "nominee" for the club — must file a Form 1099-DIV or 1099-INT listing the EIN of the club and showing that the dividends or interest belong to the club.

Most investment clubs are organized as partnerships and taxed as such. But a few are organized as trusts or corporations and are taxed accordingly.

If the club is organized as a partnership, the IRS requires it to file a Form 1065, "U.S. Partnership Return of Income," each year. It also must provide every partner with a Schedule K-1, "Partner's Share of Income, Credits, Deductions, Etc.," showing each partner's share of the club's income or loss and deductions for the year.

These amounts are then reported on each partner's Form 1040.

The IRS will allow an unincorporated investment club to choose *not* to be treated as a partnership for tax purposes, but only as long as the club isn't used for the active conduct of a business.

If the investment club elects not to be treated as a partnership, the members of the club report their share of income, deductions, and credits on Form 1040. Investment expenses are deducted as miscellaneous itemized deductions generally subject to the 2 percent floor limitation.

Tip

An investment club electing not to be treated as a partnership avoids a host of paperwork requirements, including the need to file an annual Form 1065.

To elect not to be treated as a partnership the club must file a Form 1065 for only its first year of operation by the due date, including extensions, of the return. Also, it must attach to this return a statement containing:

- the names, addresses, and identification numbers of all club members;
- a statement that the club is used solely for investment purposes and that the partnership has no income other than from its investments;
- information about where the terms of the agreement under which the club operates may be obtained (this agreement may be written or oral); and
- a statement that members have chosen unanimously for the club not to be treated as a partnership.

If the investment club is a corporation it must file a Form 1120, "U.S. Corporation Income Tax Return." All income, expenses, and gains or losses are reported by the corporation — not by the members personally — although the members will report any distributions they receive.

If the club is an association (that is, an unincorporated organization having certain corporate characteristics), the IRS may tax the club as a corporation if it is found to possess a majority of the following corporate-like characteristics: continuity of life, centralization of management, limited liability, and free transferability of interests.

In most cases, the IRS doesn't classify as an association an investment club that's organized as a general partnership in which each partner has a say in investment decisions and which restricts the rights of a partner to transfer his or her ownership interest.

CAUTION

If your club is organized as a limited partnership or trust. The IRS may, on examination, deem your club an association.

HOBBY LOSSES

The government doesn't mind, of course, if you dabble in a little business just for the fun of it. However, the IRS doesn't want to help subsidize your expenses if you're genuinely not interested in making a profit — hence, the rules governing hobby losses, or the rules affecting losses from what's known as "activities not engaged in for profit."

You may deduct hobby expenses up to the amount of your hobby income, but no more. Therefore, you're not allowed to use losses from your hobby to slash your overall tax bill.

A number of activities — horse breeding, farming, antique collecting, and coin collecting, to name a few — may not show an annual profit. In response, the IRS developed two tests to determine if your business is profit-oriented or a hobby.

IRS Tests

1) Objective test — you must have a profit for 3 of the last 5 years (2 of the last 7 years if the activity involves horse breeding or horse racing).

2) Subjective test(s):

- the manner in which you conduct your business.
- your finances and other sources of income.
- your expertise in the area.

- the time you devote to the business.
- the expectation that the assets used in your business will appreciate in value.
- your success in similar activities.
- your history of profits and losses.
- the element of recreation provided by the activity.

Let's discuss what they mean.

First, the IRS imposes an objective test. The law presumes that you're operating a for-profit business if you recognize a profit from your business in three out of the most recent five consecutive years.

The IRS carves out an exception for horse breeding and racing. If the sport of kings is your passion, you need to make a profit in only two out of seven consecutive years.

Second, there's a subjective "facts-and-circumstances" test. Under this test, the IRS weighs eight factors in determining whether you operate your business for profit. These factors — which apply to sole proprietorships, partnerships, and S corporations alike — are:

1. The manner in which you conduct your business. You should operate your business in a businesslike way. That includes maintaining a complete set of books.

2. Your finances and other sources of income. If you're a high-bracket taxpayer and claim large losses, the IRS may suspect that you're engaged in an activity solely to capture tax write-offs, especially if the activity is of a recreational nature.

3. Your expertise. If you know little about the activity in which you're engaged and don't seek outside counsel, the IRS may question your profit motive.

4. The time you devote to the business. The more hours you spend on your business, the easier it is to establish your profit motive.

5. The expectation that assets used in your business will appreciate in value. Example: You purchase a small apartment building. With interest and depreciation deductions, you report a loss for the year. But the property is appreciating a little each year. In this instance, you'd pass this test.

6. Your success in other similar activities. If you've made money in much the same kind of venture in the past, your business is more likely to be viewed as profit-making.

7. Your history of profits and losses. The IRS may question your profit motive if your business continues to operate in the red long past the time when similar businesses have turned a profit. This is not to say you should worry if your business is incurring losses during its initial phase — at least as far as

deducting the losses is concerned; such losses are expected. Further, if your business losses are due to circumstances beyond your control, such as drought, fire, theft, or depressed market conditions, the losses would not indicate that your business is not operated for profit.

8. The element of recreation involved. Beware if you devote your off-hours to the activity, and it's of a recreational nature such as fly-fishing.

EXAMPLE

You're an attorney and own a large sailboat that you use four months of the year. During the week and on holiday weekends you enjoy the boat with family and friends. On the remaining weekends, you lease your sailboat for chartered cruises.

You advertise your charter service in several local newspapers and magazines and fully expect to make a profit. You first started operating your sailboat charter service three years ago. Since that time, you've made a profit in two years and shown a loss in the other year.

You also anticipate a loss in the current year.

Under the law, you have to realize a profit next year to meet the objective statutory test. If you're unable to show a profit next year, you must then demonstrate that the charter operation wasn't a hobby under the subjective facts-and-circumstances test.

TIP

Some cash basis taxpayers may be able to legitimately manage the occurrence of a profit or loss for any particular year. Delaying paying bills from one year to the next could generate a profit in one of the periods, for example.

CAUTION

You are allowed hobby deductions only in the following order and only to the following extent:

1. Amounts such as real estate taxes or mortgage interest that are deductible regardless of whether the activity qualifies as a hobby or was engaged in for profit.

2. Amounts that are deductible if the activity has been engaged in

for profit, but only if the deduction doesn't result in an adjustment to the basis of property used in the activity. These amounts include utilities and maintenance. Such deductions are allowed only to the extent that the gross income of the activity exceeds the deductions under item 1.

3. Amounts such as depreciation that result in an adjustment to the basis of the property used in the activity are deductible only to the extent that income tops the deductions under items 1 and 2.

The deductions in items 1, 2, and 3 are subject to the total limitation placed on itemized deductions for adjusted gross income levels exceeding statutorily fixed levels. (See Chapter 1 for a discussion of this limitation).

In addition, the deductions in items 2 and 3 are classified as miscellaneous itemized deductions. You may claim miscellaneous itemized deductions only to the extent that their total exceeds 2 percent of your AGI.

Thus, while you must include the full amount of your hobby earnings in your taxable income, you must first reduce this income by expenses that would otherwise qualify as deductible expenses and your remaining hobby deductions may offset the remaining income only to the extent they are not reduced by the overall itemized deduction limitation and/or the miscellaneous itemized deduction floor. As a result, deductions relating to a hobby can be restricted to an amount less than your hobby income.

RELATED PARTIES

The IRS does not prohibit you from selling or exchanging property solely for the purpose of locking in a loss. But it won't allow you to claim this loss on your tax return if you sell the property to, or exchange it with, a related party.

A related party is anyone in your immediate family such as your spouse, grandparents, parents, brothers, sisters, or children. However, your immediate family, in this case, doesn't include uncles, aunts, nieces, nephews, cousins, or friends of the family.

Related parties also include corporations, partnerships, certain trusts, in which you or other related parties own more than a 50 percent interest, and corporations that are members of the same "controlled group," to use the language of the IRS. A controlled group is simply a group of corporations that have the same owners. A controlled group may also be groups of corporations that are subsidiaries of the same parent company.

At-Risk Rules

The IRS limits the losses you may write off on your return with what are known as at-risk rules. Congress adopted the at-risk rules to prevent people from deducting losses from investments where there was no economic risk of losing their money. In other words, the government wanted you to put your money where your mouth is — in order to get a tax deduction.

The at-risk rules generally apply to all investments financed by someone else — i.e., those purchased solely or partly with borrowed money. Under these rules, you may write off your losses only to the extent they don't exceed your total at-risk investment.

For purposes of these rules, the IRS defines your at-risk investment as the cash you've contributed plus any money you borrowed for the venture (but only those funds for which you're personally liable on the loan) plus your depreciated basis in any property or equipment you have contributed.

EXAMPLE

You're an investor in a video store. You contribute $5,000 of your own money, plus $20,000 that you borrowed on a nonrecourse note (one for which you're not personally liable). You also work every day in the store.

The losses you may claim from the store are limited for tax purposes. Under the at-risk rules, you may claim no more than $5,000 in losses on your return. That's because $5,000 is your total at-risk investment.

You'd be able to claim losses of up to $25,000 — your $5,000 investment plus the $20,000 you borrowed — if you borrowed the money on a recourse note (one for which you were personally liable).

CAUTION

Do not ignore the increased economic risk here. Economic considerations, not just tax considerations, must be seriously weighed when evaluating recourse financing.

Epilogue

We've discussed a mixed bag of tax topics in this chapter in an attempt to further define the role of taxes in your investment portfolio. However, no two investors are alike and there may be other topics relevant to you. Consult your tax adviser who can answer your questions with your particular investment needs as well as your past or present tax history fresh in his or her mind.

19

LOOKING AHEAD

■ How can your Form 1040 help you save taxes?
■ Why isn't a large tax refund the goal of tax planning?

Your Form 1040 can give you valuable clues to better tax and investment planning. How? By examining your return line by line you may uncover opportunities to maximize tax savings, thereby increasing your after-tax profits. Your return can effectively act as an important road map that gives you a good view of your recent financial history.

Note: In this chapter, we use references to lines on the 1992 version of Form 1040, "Individual Income Tax Return." Be careful to review the current year's Form 1040 to make sure the reference to the lines remains the same.

Line 7 — Wages, salaries, tips, etc.

Line 7 records your salary. How can you lower the amount that's subject to federal income tax?

Consider contributing some of your salary to a 401(k) plan. That way, you may collect three benefits at once:

- you cut your current taxes,

- you save for retirement and the earnings in the plan accumulate tax-free until withdrawn, and;

- in many cases, you pocket matching dollars from your employer.

The primary selling point of a 401(k) plan is that you contribute money on a pre-tax basis, and the earnings that accumulate grow tax deferred. That means your savings accumulate more rapidly than they would otherwise.

EXAMPLE

You've invested in two plans — one tax deferred and one not. With both plans, you invest in the same mutual fund each year for 20 years. The fund earns 10 percent a year, and you reinvest these earnings, less any taxes due, in the account. Your marginal tax rate is 31 percent.

In order to compare apples to apples, (or for those in Florida, oranges to oranges) assume you invest $8,994 from your salary (the maximum the law allowed for tax-deferred plans in 1993) in the taxable fund, minus the $2,788 you owe in taxes, or $6,206 each year.

How much will you have at the end of 20 years? This taxable fund will have grown to more than $355,000. A hefty sum, you say.

But the tax-deferred fund is much larger — it comes to $515,000 after taxes — and here's why. You've been able to invest a full $8,994 each year, since money earmarked for your 401(k) isn't taxed currently, and you've not had to pay federal income tax on the earnings as they accumulated.

Note: $8,994 per year is the maximum 401(k) contribution for 1993. This number is adjusted each year for inflation. Contact your tax adviser to determine the current year's maximum contribution.

Another advantage to a 401(k) is that your employer may match your contribution to the plan; for example, it may put in 50 cents for every $1 you deposit. If your employer matches contributions, and you don't participate in the plan, you're really losing a valuable fringe benefit.

Keep in mind, however, that tax deferred doesn't mean tax free. You pay taxes, usually at retirement, on the money you withdraw from your 401(k).

But the rules allow you to reduce these taxes using five-year averaging. With this tax-saving strategy, you calculate the tax due on a lump-sum withdrawal as if you received the money evenly over five years instead of all at once.

Some people worry that tax rates may be higher when they withdraw their money than rates are now, but they needn't be overly concerned, at least as long as five-year averaging remains law. Also, many people are in a lower tax bracket after they retire — a fact that could offset most tax rate increases.

Lines 8 and 9 — Interest income and dividend income

You record your interest and dividend income on Lines 8 and 9. Did most of your investment income come from a single source, such as stock in the company that employs you? If so, you're losing the protection that diversification can provide.

When you diversify, you reduce risk. Essentially, there are two ways to diversify. First, you can offset your risk by investing in a number of different areas such as cash equivalents, fixed-income instruments, equities, and hard assets.

The second way to diversify is to spread out your holdings in any one area. In other words, don't invest all the dollars you've allocated for equity investments in a single stock. Buy a number of stocks or invest in mutual funds, which give you instant diversification.

Also, check the average dividend yield on your stocks. If it's high — more than 6-8 percent, say — you probably own mostly conservative stocks.

In this case, you may want to divert some of your assets to a more aggressive investment — a growth fund, for example — if you won't need to cash out for five years or more. Over the long term, more aggressive investments should, in theory, achieve higher returns.

One more question you should ask if you're in the 28-percent or 31-percent tax bracket: Are you receiving any tax-exempt interest? If not, tax-free investments may make sense for you, especially if you live in a high-tax state, such as Massachusetts or New York.

EXAMPLE

You live in New York State and are taxed at a rate of 8 percent. You're also in the 31 percent federal tax bracket and itemize your deductions. That means your combined tax rate — 31 percent plus 8 percent — is 39 percent.

Although your combined tax rate is 39 percent, you deduct state income taxes on your federal return. So your net federal and state marginal tax rate is 36.5 percent, not 39 percent.

Your net marginal rate is the sum of your federal tax bracket — in your case, 31 percent — plus your true, or "effective," state tax rate, meaning your state tax rate after you calculate the benefit of deducting your state tax on your federal return.

Here's how you figure your true state tax rate. Multiply your actual state tax rate (8 percent in your case) times the sum of one minus your federal rate of 31 percent (0.69). The result — 5.5 percent — is your true state tax rate.

So a New York State municipal bond that pays 7 percent is the equivalent of an 11 percent taxable yield. Here's how we arrived at that figure. Divide the yield on the bond, 7 percent, by 0.635 — that is, 1 minus 0.365, your federal and state marginal tax rate.

TIP

What if you want to defer interest income until next year? Consider buying a certificate of deposit or Treasury bill that matures next year. Unless you receive interest during the current year, the IRS will tax your earnings when you receive them, that is when the CD becomes due.

But this strategy applies only to short-term certificates with a maturity of one year or less. The law requires you to pay taxes on interest from long-term CDs in the year the interest is earned, rather than in the year it's paid.

TIP

For more information on investment strategies, see the *Price Waterhouse Book of Personal Financial Planning*.

Line 13 — Capital gain or (loss)

You report your net capital gains or losses, which you determined by using Schedule D, on Line 13 of your Form 1040. Use this figure to calculate your return on your investments. Then compare the returns you received against the Standard & Poor's 500 index.

Also, examine the volume of trades and holding periods detailed on your Schedule D. If you've made frequent trades, you may want to consider holding securities for a longer period. Many savvy investors invest for longer-term performance.

Line 18 — Rents, royalties, partnerships, estates, trusts, etc.

You determined your net income (or loss) from rents, royalties, partnerships, estates, and trusts on Schedule E, then reported this amount on Line 18 of your Form 1040.

Before 1987, it made sense to invest with heavy emphasis on tax considerations, but no more — thanks to changes in the tax law. Now, it's smart to invest primarily on economic merits. In other words, you should steer clear of investments that make tax sense only.

But what if you still own investments that generate tax losses each year?

TIP

Consider investing in PIGs (passive income generators — not livestock — see Chapter 10) to offset these losses. But, again, make sure the investment is economically sound before you hand over your money.

Although the maximum tax rate is 39.6 percent, your *effective* marginal tax rate may be more because of the impact of the phaseout of personal exemptions and the 3 percent floor on itemized deductions. Therefore, reducing AGI becomes increasingly important. You calculate both the exemption phaseout and the floor on deductions based on your AGI. That means if you reduce your AGI, you can reduce the impact these new items might have on your tax bill. (See Chapter 1 for details.)

Line 34 — Itemized deductions

Check out your deductions, summarized on Line 34 and detailed on Schedule A. Are you paying interest no longer fully deductible? Is your interest expense from a loan with a very high interest rate?

The tax law does not allow a deduction for interest incurred on consumer loans. So you may want to restructure your debt. One path to take is to tap the equity in your home by applying for a home-equity loan.

The interest on a home-equity loan is 100 percent deductible, as long as the debt doesn't top the lesser of $100,000 ($50,000 if you're married and file separate returns) or the fair market value of your home minus the total acquisition debt.

Acquisition debt is a loan that's secured by your primary or second home and is incurred when you buy, build, or substantially improve your home.

Also, the law allows you to write off miscellaneous itemized deductions only to the extent that they exceed two percent of your adjusted gross income (AGI).

In order to get at least a partial write-off under the rules, you should attempt to bunch as many of these expenses as possible into a single year.

Toward the end of the year, take a hard look at your bills in these miscellaneous categories. If you see that by paying for, say, a continuing education course you took this year, you'll exceed the 2-percent floor, go ahead and write the check by December 31.

But if your calculations show that you'll fall below the floor, wait until January before paying these bills. You may beat the floor next year.

Similarly, your medical expenses must top 7.5 percent of your AGI before you may deduct any of them. So, if these expenses are already high, our advice is to pay as many of them as you can this year in order to exceed the deductibility floor.

Line 48 — Alternative minimum tax

Do you show an entry on Line 48 for the alternative minimum tax (AMT)? If so, consider new tax-planning strategies to avoid the AMT in the future. You may be able to save regular taxes this year as a result of paying AMT last year.

In most cases, you get the minimum tax credit, which, in effect, gives you credit for taxes that you prepaid under the AMT system in prior years. (For the details, see Chapter 8.)

If you know you're going to be subject to the AMT again this year, there are some strategies you should consider.

For example, you may want to accelerate income. It may be better to pay tax on that income at the AMT rate of 26 percent (28 percent for AMTI in excess of $175,00) than risk paying tax at a higher rate the following year. You may also want to defer deductions to the following year, when they may yield a higher tax benefit.

At a minimum, you should try to defer those expenses, such as state and local income and property taxes, that aren't deductible at all for AMT purposes. Because of the complexities of the AMT, check with your tax adviser before you adopt any game plan.

Line 62 — Amount of overpayment refunded to you

If you have an overpayment on Line 62, that means you've made an interest-free loan to the government. The idea of tax planning isn't to get a big tax refund from the IRS. You want to keep money in your own pocket — not the government's — for as long as possible. Then you can invest the cash or use it for purchases. In the future, you want to make sure you pay your taxes no sooner than is legally required, so that you, instead of the government, can earn that interest.

If you're a salaried employee, make sure when you fill out your W-4 or W-4A form that you take all the exemptions to which you're entitled. You may need to update your W-4 to reflect changed circumstances such as the birth of a child, a larger mortgage (and increased mortgage interest). You should know that the IRS will scrutinize your form W-4 if you take more than ten exemptions. But if you're entitled to them, go ahead and take them.

If you work for yourself, or have substantial income beyond your wages and salaries, plan your estimated taxes. But pay no more than is required.

If you underpay your estimated taxes you pay a penalty on the amount your payments fall short. The amount of the penalty varies; it rises or falls with current interest rates. As of the second quarter of 1993, it's 7 percent.

You can't deduct the amount you pay in penalties, and that's all the more reason to plan ahead. You can *generally* avoid the underpayment penalty for a given year, though, if your equal quarterly payments, along with your withholding, total 100 percent of your prior year tax liability or 90 percent of the current year's tax liability that will be shown on your current year return.

CAUTION

You generally will be required to base tax estimates on 90 percent of the current year's tax liability if:

(1) your AGI exceeds $75,000 ($37,500 for married couples filing separately);

(2) your AGI (adjusted for certain modifications) exceeds by $40,000 the prior year's AGI; **and**

(3) you made estimated tax payments in the previous three years (or have been assessed an underpayment penalty in any of those years).

For a discussion of these rules, see Chapter 26 of *The Price Waterhouse Personal Tax Adviser.*

If, as year-end approaches, you realize you've underpaid your tax, increase your payroll withholding to make up the shortfall. Simply file a new W-4, claim fewer allowances, and/or request that additional amounts be withheld.

INDEX

237

As We Went to Press . . .

The ink has dried on sweeping tax legislation intended to help cut the federal budget deficit by nearly $500 billion over five years. The Omnibus Budget Reconciliation Act of 1993, signed into law August 10 by President Clinton, increases the top income tax rates for higher-income individuals and large corporations — effective beginning January 1, 1993 — and makes numerous other changes that call for careful tax planning.

The 1993 Tax Act makes the most significant changes to the tax law since the Tax Reform Act of 1986. The 1993 Tax Act includes nearly $277 billion in tax increases and $36 billion in tax incentives, producing a net tax increase of about $241 billion over fiscal years 1994-98. The following are among the key provisions affecting individuals:

- New top regular individual income tax rates of 36 percent and 39.6 percent, and higher alternative minimum tax rates of 26 percent and 28 percent.
- Repeal of the prior-law cap on the amount of wages and self-employment income subject to the Medicare payroll tax.
- An increase in the amount of Social Security benefits subject to income tax.
- A 4.3 cents per gallon tax on transportation fuels.
- Repeal of the luxury excise taxes on boats, planes, jewelry and furs, and indexing of the threshold for automobiles.
- New estimated tax payment requirements.
- Limits on business deductions for meals and entertainment, club dues, lobbying, executive compensation and spousal travel, and on moving expense deductions.
- Retroactive reinstatement of a number of tax provisions that had expired June 30, 1992, including several tax credits, the exclusion for employer-provided education assistance, and the partial deduction of health insurance costs of the self-employed.
- New incentives for investment in emerging businesses.
- New and enhanced incentives relating to real estate.
- Expansion of the earned-income tax credit for lower-income families and individuals.

- Tighter substantiation and disclosure requirements for charitable contributions.

- Higher top estate and gift tax rates, and higher income tax rates for trusts and estates.

Guidance to be issued by the IRS on these and other provisions of the Act could affect your tax planning this year and in the future.

In the wake of the lengthy debate over the 1993 Tax Act, the Clinton Administration and Congress generally have shifted their attention to reform of the nation's health care system and other issues. However, tax policy issues will remain on the Congressional agenda.

A variety of tax increases are being eyed as means of financing the costs of extending health care coverage to all Americans under a health reform plan. These include higher excise taxes on tobacco, and possibly a limit on business deductions for health care coverage provided to employees or on the exclusion for employer-provided health coverage, among other possible proposals.

Also, House and Senate tax-writers are examining a number of targeted changes to the Tax Code. For example, a proposal to modify the rules for paying Social Security taxes on household employees may be considered.

The House Ways and Means Committee is examining more than 100 miscellaneous tax proposals — including revenue raisers and revenue losers affecting individuals, businesses, and nonprofit taxpayers — suggested by committee members. The Ways and Means Committee later this year may package some of these proposals with legislation that would aim to simplify various areas of the tax law and make technical corrections to recent tax legislation, including corrections to the 1993 Act.

You should consult with your tax adviser to determine how the 1993 Tax Act and other tax proposals — if enacted into law — may affect you.

How Price Waterhouse Can Help You And Your Business Succeed

Today's executives and employees continually face demands in both their personal and professional lives to make financial decisions with often unexpected, but potentially far-reaching tax ramifications.

On the home front, savings for your children's education, evaluating executive compensation or retirement plans, or determining the right asset allocation for investments can be confusing and time-consuming. Price Waterhouse professionals can help you resolve these and other issues in an effective manner, enabling you to attain your personal financial goals while minimizing taxes.

As for your professional life, many decisions you make may affect your company's tax bill and minimizing taxes obviously enhances the profitability of your business. Price Waterhouse advisers can keep you informed of legislative and regulatory developments that affect your company's taxes and help identify advantageous tax strategies.

To respond to the wide-ranging tax needs of businesses, Price Waterhouse has developed specialized tax expertise. Some of those capabilities include:

- **Employee Benefits Services** (EBS) — EBS helps companies design and implement compensation and benefits programs that are both cost- and tax-effective and competitive so businesses can attract, motivate and retain valued personnel.

- **International Assignment Tax Services** (IATS) — IATS helps companies address the complex tax and administrative issues encountered as they move employees around the world.

- **International Tax Services** (ITS) — ITS helps multinational companies and others meet the changing corporate tax challenges of their international operations.

- **Multistate Tax Consulting** (MTC) — MTC helps businesses minimize state and local taxes and develop efficient administrative systems for doing business in multiple jurisdictions.

- **Personal Financial Services** (PFS) — PFS helps companies meet objectives of corporate restructuring, employee benefits and financial planning programs — whether designed for top executives, middle management or rank and file employees — by helping employees understand and accept the company's initiatives. PFS also helps individuals with a wide range of tax and financial planning and compliance issues.

- **Tax Technology Group** (TTG) — TTG helps corporate tax departments get the most from technology by offering a full range of advanced products and services designed to assist with many tax compliance and planning issues.

- **Valuation Services** (VS) — VS helps companies and individuals make objective determinations of the current value of assets, stock and business interests that are crucial to effective tax and business planning.

- **Washington National Tax Service** (WNTS) — WNTS, under the direction of former Congressional tax officials and senior IRS personnel, monitors tax developments at the international, federal, state and local levels and assists both growing enterprises and multinational corporations in complying with new tax laws and developing appropriate tax strategies.

This list highlights only some of the tax services offered. Price Waterhouse tax professionals provide comprehensive tax planning advice to reduce federal, state, local and foreign taxes. They assist with administrative procedures involving the Treasury or IRS such as obtaining private letter rulings and reviewing technical and policy issues that cannot be satisfactorily resolved at the audit or appeals level. They prepare economic studies of the impact of proposed legislation on businesses, industries and federal and state governments. In addition, Price Waterhouse tax professionals consult on a wide variety of tax issues including acquisitions, mergers, closely-held businesses, trusts and estates, and the selection of tax accounting methods.

Further, Price Waterhouse, as a leading business advisery services firm, offers a wide range of professional services provided by accountants, auditors and management consulting professionals. To learn about these other services or any of the tax services, please contact the Price Waterhouse office nearest you. For your convenience, we have provided a listing of Price Waterhouse offices in the United States, along with telephone numbers.

Price Waterhouse US Offices

For additional information, contact a Price Waterhouse office convenient to you.

NATIONAL-NEW YORK
New York, NY 10020
1251 Avenue of the Americas
(212) 819-5000

OFFICE OF GOVERNMENT SERVICES
Washington, DC 20006
1801 K Street, N.W.
(202) 296-0800

ARIZONA
Phoenix, AZ 85004-4563
1850 North Central Avenue
Suite 700
(602) 379-5500

CALIFORNIA
Century City, CA 90067
(West Los Angeles)
1800 Century Park East
(310) 553-6030

Costa Mesa, CA 92628-5041
(Orange County)
575 Anton Boulevard
Suite 1100
P.O. Box 5041
(714) 435-8600

Long Beach, CA 90802
Arco Center
200 Oceangate
Suite 600
(310) 491-0440

Los Angeles, CA 90071-2889
400 South Hope Street
(213) 236-3000

Menlo Park, CA 94025
68 Willow Road
(415) 322-0606

Palo Alto, CA 94301
525 University Avenue
Suite 200
(415) 853-8380

Riverside, CA 92501
3403 Tenth Street
Suite 800
(714) 684-9411

Sacramento, CA 95814
455 Capitol Mall
Suite 500
(916) 441-2370

San Diego, CA 92101
750 "B" Street
Suite 2400
(619) 231-1200

San Francisco, CA 94104
555 California Street
(415) 393-8500

San Jose, CA 95113-2007
(Silicon Valley/San Jose)
150 Almaden Boulevard
P.O. Box 2-C, Zip 95109*
(408) 282-1200

Santa Monica, CA 90405
Price Waterhouse Technologies
2800 28th Street
Suite 306
(310) 396-3844

Woodland Hills, CA 91367
Warner Center
5950 Canoga Avenue, Suite 100
(818) 704-1117

COLORADO
Denver, CO 80202-2872
950 17th Street
Suite 2600
(303) 893-8100

CONNECTICUT
Glastonbury, CT 06033
Insurance Industry Services
Corporate Center II
628 Hebron Avenue
(203) 657-7300

Hartford, CT 06103
One Financial Plaza
(203) 240-2000

Stamford, CT 06901
300 Atlantic Street
P.O. Box 9316, Zip 06904-9316*
(203) 358-0001

DISTRICT OF COLUMBIA
Washington, DC 20006
1801 K Street, N.W.
Suite 1000
(202) 833-7932

Bethesda, MD 20817
6500 Rock Spring Drive
(301) 897-5900

Falls Church, VA 22042
3110 Fairview Park Drive
(703) 538-7982

Washington, DC 20006
Washington National Tax Services
1801 K Street, N.W.
Suite 700
(202) 296-0800

FLORIDA
Fort Lauderdale, FL 33301
One East Broward Boulevard
Suite 1700
P.O. Box 6368, Zip 33310*
(305) 463-6280

Miami, FL 33131-2330
First Union Financial Center
200 So. Biscayne Blvd.
Suite 3000
(305) 381-9400

Orlando, FL 32801
Barnett Bank Center
390 N. Orange Ave.
Suite 1900
(407) 236-0550

Tampa, FL 33602
400 North Ashley Street
Suite 2800
P.O. Box 2640, Zip 33601-9975*
(813) 223-7577

Tampa, FL 33607
Applied Technology Center
1410 North Westshore Blvd.
P.O. Box 30004, Zip 33630*
(813) 287-9200

West Palm Beach, FL 33401
222 Lakeview Avenue
Suite 1100
(407) 820-0800

GEORGIA
Atlanta, GA
50 Hurt Plaza
Suite 1700
Atlanta, GA 30303
(404) 658-1800

Atlanta North
Marietta, GA 30067
3200 Windy Hill Road
Suite 900 West
(404) 933-9191

Savannah, GA 31401
2 East Bryan Street
P.O. Box 9088, Zip 31412*
(912) 232-0123

HAWAII
Honolulu, HI 96813
841 Bishop Street
Suite 1700
(808) 521-0391

ILLINOIS
Chicago, IL 60601
200 East Randolph Drive
(312) 565-1500

Chicago, IL 60603
Tax Technology Group
55 E. Monroe Street
30th Floor
(312) 419-1565

Oak Brook, IL 60521
Drake Oak Brook Plaza
2215 York Road
(708) 571-7250

Peoria, IL 61602
411 Hamilton Blvd.
Suite 2000
(309) 676-8945

INDIANA
Indianapolis, IN 46204
300 North Meridian Street
Suite 1700
(317) 632-8361

South Bend, IN 46601
202 South Michigan Street
P.O. Box 47, Zip 46624*
(219) 233-8261

KENTUCKY
Florence, KY 41042
250 Turfway Ridge Office Park
7300 Turfway Road
(606) 283-1901

Lexington, KY 40503
771 Corporate Drive
Suite 505
(606) 224-3337

LOUISIANA
New Orleans, LA 70112
909 Poydras Street
Suite 1500
(504) 529-2000

MARYLAND
Baltimore, MD 21202
7 St. Paul Street
Suite 1700
(410) 685-0542

Bethesda, MD
See District of Columbia.

Columbia, MD 21044
10420 Little Patuxent Parkway
20 Corporate Center
Suite 300
(410) 992-6700

MASSACHUSETTS
Boston, MA 02110
160 Federal Street
(617) 439-4390

*Mailing address

DIVISIONS OF PRICE WATERHOUSE

Employment Economics
New York
See 1177 Avenue of the Americas

Management Horizons
See Columbus, Ohio

Price Waterhouse Technologies
See Santa Monica, California

CAMBRIDGE, MA 02139
ONE KENDALL SQUARE
BUILDING 200
(617) 439-4390

MICHIGAN

BATTLE CREEK, MI 49017
67 WEST MICHIGAN AVENUE
SUITE 600
P.O. BOX 1637, ZIP 49016*
(616) 965-1351

DETROIT, MI 48243
200 RENAISSANCE CENTER
SUITE 3900
(313) 259-0500

TROY, MI 48084
DETROIT NORTH
SOMERSET PLACE
2301 WEST BIG BEAVER RD.
SUITE 700
(313) 259-0500

MINNESOTA

MINNEAPOLIS, MN 55402
3100 MULTIFOODS TOWER
33 SOUTH SIXTH STREET
(612) 332-7000

MISSOURI

KANSAS CITY, MO 64105
1055 BROADWAY
10TH FLOOR
(816) 474-6590

ST. LOUIS, MO 63101
ONE BOATMEN'S PLAZA
P.O. BOX 1097, ZIP 63188*
(314) 425-0500

NEBRASKA

OMAHA, NE 68102
2800 WOODMEN TOWER
(402) 346-8560

NEW JERSEY

HACKENSACK, NJ 07601
(BERGEN COUNTY)
411 HACKENSACK AVENUE
(201) 646-1550

MORRISTOWN, NJ 07962-1965
4 HEADQUARTERS PLAZA NORTH
P.O. BOX 1965
(201) 540-8980

PRINCETON, NJ 08543
214 CARNEGIE CENTER
P.O. BOX 7133
(609) 987-9444

NEW YORK

BUFFALO, NY 14203
3600 MARINE MIDLAND CENTER
(716) 856-4650

LONG ISLAND
JERICHO, NY 11753
100 JERICHO QUADRANGLE
(516) 681-7114

NEW YORK, NY 10036
1177 AVENUE OF THE AMERICAS
(212) 596-7000

NY-INTERNATIONAL
ASSIGNMENT TAX SERVICES &
EMPLOYMENT ECONOMICS DIVISION
1177 AVENUE OF THE AMERICAS
NEW YORK, NY 10036
(212) 596-7000

1221 AVENUE OF THE AMERICAS
(212) 302-4850

ROCHESTER, NY 14604
1900 LINCOLN FIRST TOWER
(716) 232-4000

SYRACUSE, NY 13202
ONE MONY PLAZA
(315) 474-6571

NORTH CAROLINA

CHARLOTTE, NC 28280
NATIONS BANK PLAZA
SUITE 3200
(704) 372-9020

DURHAM, NC 27705
2200 WEST MAIN STREET
SUITE 300
(919) 286-9423

RALEIGH, NC 27604
3100 SMOKETREE COURT
SUITE 900
P.O. BOX 95115, ZIP 27625*
(919) 878-5700

WINSTON-SALEM, NC 27101
ONE TRIAD PARK
200 WEST SECOND STREET
SUITE 1800
(919) 725-0691

OHIO

CINCINNATI, OH 45202
2200 CHEMED CENTER
255 E. FIFTH STREET
(513) 621-1900

CINCINNATI NORTH
SPRINGDALE, OH 45246
EXECUTIVE PLAZA I
144 MERCHANT STREET
SUITE 100
(513) 772-7117

CLEVELAND, OH 44114-2301
BP AMERICA BUILDING
200 PUBLIC SQUARE, 27TH FLOOR
(216) 781-3700

COLUMBUS, OH 43215
THE HUNTINGTON CENTER
41 SOUTH HIGH STREET
(614) 221-8500

COLUMBUS, OH 43215
MANAGEMENT HORIZONS DIVISION
THE HUNTINGTON CENTER
41 SOUTH HIGH STREET
(614) 365-9555

DAYTON, OH 45402
350 NATIONAL CITY CENTER
6 NORTH MAIN STREET
(513) 222-2100

TOLEDO, OH 43604
ONE SEAGATE
SUITE 1800
(419) 247-1800

OKLAHOMA

OKLAHOMA CITY, OK 73102-5410
COLCORD BUILDING
15 NORTH ROBINSON
SUITE 400
(405) 272-9251

OREGON

PORTLAND, OR 97204
121 S.W. MORRISON
SUITE 1800
(503) 224-9040

PENNSYLVANIA

PHILADELPHIA, PA 19103
30 SOUTH SEVENTEENTH STREET
(215) 575-5000

PITTSBURGH, PA 15219
600 GRANT STREET
SUITE 4500
(412) 355-6000

PUERTO RICO

SAN JUAN, PR 00936
THE CHASE MANHATTAN
   BANK BUILDING
MUNOZ RIVERA AVENUE
SUITE 900
HATO REY, P.R. 00936
G.P.O. BOX 363566, ZIP 00936-3566*
(809) 754-9090

RHODE ISLAND

PROVIDENCE, RI 02903
50 KENNEDY PLAZA
SUITE 800
(401) 421-0501

SOUTH CAROLINA

COLUMBIA, SC 29201
1441 MAIN STREET
SUITE 1200
(803) 779-0930

TENNESSEE

JOHNSON CITY, TN 37604
207 MOCKINGBIRD LANE
SUITE 402
(615) 929-9121

MEMPHIS, TN 38103
ONE COMMERCE SQUARE
SUITE 2600
(901) 523-8000

NASHVILLE, TN 37205
4400 HARDING ROAD
SUITE 300
(615) 292-5000

TEXAS

AUSTIN, TX 78701
ONE AMERICAN CENTER
600 CONGRESS AVENUE
SUITE 2000
(512) 476-6700

DALLAS, TX 75201-4698
1700 PACIFIC AVENUE
SUITE 1400
(214) 922-8040

DALLAS COLONNADE
DALLAS, TX 75248
15301 DALLAS PARKWAY
SUITE 300, LB 24
(214) 386-9922

FORT WORTH, TX 76102
1700 CITY CENTER TOWER II
301 COMMERCE STREET
(817) 870-5500

HOUSTON, TX 77002-5678
1201 LOUISIANA
SUITE 2900
(713) 654-4100

SAN ANTONIO, TX 78205
ONE RIVERWALK PLACE
SUITE 900
(210) 226-7700

UTAH

SALT LAKE CITY, UT 84111
175 EAST 400 SOUTH, SUITE 700
(801) 328-2300

VERMONT

BURLINGTON
BURLINGTON, VT 05401
INSURANCE SERVICES
95 ST. PAUL STREET
(802) 864-1600

VIRGINIA

FALLS CHURCH, VA
See District of Columbia.

HAMPTON ROADS
NORFOLK, VA 23510
700 WORLD TRADE CENTER
(804) 622-5005

WASHINGTON

SEATTLE, WA 98154
1001 FOURTH AVENUE PLAZA
SUITE 4200
(206) 622-1505

WISCONSIN

MILWAUKEE, WI 53202
100 EAST WISCONSIN AVENUE
SUITE 1500
(414) 276-9500